Dedicated to

DR. & MRS. ROLF K. McPHERSON

THE FOUR-SQUARE GOSPEL

Aimee Semple McPherson

compiled by Dr. Raymond L. Cox

published by the Heritage Committee, California

PREFACE

"The Foursquare Gospel" represents an endeavor to make available both to the constituency of the movement and to interested inquirers of other fellowships a panorama of Foursquare faith and practice imbued with the spirit and enthusiasm which motivated the founder, Aimee Semple McPherson, and her co-workers during the period the movement was launched and spread speedily around the world. The three parts of this volume deal with backgrounds, fundamentals, and practices, though some overlapping of subject matter from section to section is inevitable. The plan of the book is to alternate explanatory chapters authored by the compiler with sermons on the same subjects by Aimee Semple McPherson. Some of these messages by the Founder have never before been published. Thus the fourteen sermons contained herein come from the pen of Sister McPherson while the ten chapters were prepared by the present writer.

In acknowledging assistance in the compiling of this volume I desire to mention especially the invaluable help provided by Dr. Rolf K. McPherson, President of the International Church of the Foursquare Gospel, and the Rev. Charles Duarte, Executive Secretary and Chairman of the Heritage Committee.

This volume is sent forward with the hope and prayer that it will contribute to a re-emphasis upon Foursquare fundamentals and experiences and a revival of enthusiasm in projecting our message of Jesus the Saviour, Baptizer, Healer, and Coming King.

Raymond L. Cox, Th.D., F. R. G. S.
Salem, Oregon
November 20, 1969

TABLE OF CONTENTS

Preface

PART ONE–FOURSQUARE BACKGROUNDS

Chapter I–What Is the Foursquare Gospel? 3
Sermon: Lost and Restored 13

Chapter II–The Bible Basis of the Foursquare Gospel 39
Sermon: The March of the Bible 53

PART TWO–THE CARDINAL DOCTRINES

Chapter I–Jesus Christ the Saviour 69
Sermon: The Scarlet Thread 81

Chapter II–Jesus Christ the Baptizer 93
Sermons: The Baptism of the Holy Ghost 114
The Gifts of the Holy Spirit 122
What about Manifestations? 133

Chapter III–Jesus Christ the Healer 145
Sermon: The Healing Cup 157

Chapter IV–Jesus Christ the Coming King 166
Sermon: The Wedding in the Air 180

PART THREE–THE PRACTICE OF THE FOURSQUARE FAITH

Chapter I–Devotional Expression 197
Sermon: Praising the Lord 204

Chapter II–Sacramental Participation 212
Sermons: Initiation Ceremonies 217
The Lord's Supper 221

Chapter III—Practical Dedication 226
Sermons: Soul Winning 230
The Greatest Robber in Town 241

Chapter IV—Projecting the Foursquare Gospel . . . 246
Sermon: The Lighthouse Foursquare 252

APPENDIX

Foursquare Gospel Battle Songs 257
Creedal Statements 269
Declaration of Faith 271

PART ONE FOURSQUARE BACKGROUNDS

chapter one

WHAT IS THE FOURSQUARE GOSPEL?

Sermon: Lost and Restored

chapter two

THE BIBLE BASIS OF THE FOURSQUARE GOSPEL

Sermon: The March of the Bible

Chapter I WHAT IS THE FOURSQUARE GOSPEL?

"What is the Foursquare Gospel?"

Some might suppose it strange that such a question could persist in view of the widespread diffusion of this gospel throughout the world. For many years it has been true that the sun never sets on the Foursquare flag. On every continent of earth the Foursquare message now goes forth. In several lands Foursquare Churches boast the largest Protestant congregations in the country. For decades this movement, through its ambitious home and foreign missions outreach, has endeavored faithfully and fearlessly to perform its part in consummating Christ's great commission, "Go ye into all the world, and preach the gospel to every creature" (Mark 16:15).

In spite of noteworthy growth, however, the question persists, "What is the Foursquare Gospel?" Sometimes people ask, "What do you mean by 'Foursquare'?"

Rather than react with surprise or disappointment that many remain uninformed or even misinformed about the facts of this faith, the Foursquare believer ought to stand ready to give an explanation and a reason for that faith, both Biblically and historically.

The International Church of the Foursquare Gospel developed out of the evangelistic ministry of Aimee Semple McPherson. But while she became the founder of the movement, she would have been the first to repudiate the idea that she originated the Foursquare message. Though the Foursquare movement, like all other Pentecostal and Full Gospel organizations, commenced in the twentieth century, the Foursquare message began in Bible days!

The movement exists to promote proclamation, experience, and practice of the message. The aim or goal is nothing less than to recover for the present day church all the benefits and blessings which crowned with glory the apostolic church. The sermon, "Lost and Restored," which follows this chapter, outlines, we might say, church history according to Joel and powerfully insists that the church of Jesus Christ need not climax with less power than she manifested when she commenced! Every Foursquare auditorium reflects this confidence by its display of Hebrews 13:8 as the denominational motto: "Jesus Christ the same yesterday and today and forever."

ORIGIN OF THE EXPRESSION "FOURSQUARE GOSPEL"

It was in the uplifting of Jesus Christ as the answer to every human need that the very expression "Foursquare Gospel" originated. Sister McPherson had proclaimed the Foursquare message for about fourteen years before she suddenly grasped the term "Foursquare" to describe that gospel!

The inspiration came in Oakland, California, in late July 1922 during her final revival campaign in the United States prior to the opening of Angelus Temple in Los Angeles the following New Year's Day. (The intervening months were spent evangelizing in Australia.)

An overflow congregation had crowded the great tent. On the platform sat the sponsoring pastors representing Episcopal, Presbyterian, Baptist, Congregational, Methodist, Nazarene, Salvation Army, Christian Missionary Alliance, and Pentecostal churches. Perhaps the evangelist never addressed a more attentive audience. Her subject was "The Vision of Ezekiel." Here is how Sister McPherson recalled the occasion:

> "My soul was awed. My heart athrill. The blazing glory of that heavenly vision seemed to fill and permeate not only the tabernacle but the whole earth.
>
> "In the clouds of heaven—which folded and unfolded in fiery glory—Ezekiel had beheld that Being, whose glory no mortal can describe. As he gazed

upon that marvelous revelation of the Omnipotent One he perceived four faces. The faces—those of a man, a lion, an ox, and an eagle. These four faces we likened unto the four phases of the gospel of Jesus Christ.

"In the face of the Man we beheld that of the Man of Sorrows and acquainted with grief, dying on the tree.

"In the face of the Lion we beheld that of the mighty Baptizer with the Holy Ghost and fire.

"The face of the Ox typified the Great Burden-bearer, who Himself took our infirmities and carried our sicknesses, who in His boundless love and divine provision had met our every need.

"In the face of the Eagle we saw reflected soul-enrapturing visions of the Coming King, whose pinions soon would cleave the shining heavens, whose silvery voice would set the Milky Way to echoing as He came to catch His waiting bride away.

"A perfect gospel. A complete gospel for body, for soul, for spirit, and for eternity. A gospel that faces squarely in every direction.

"As the wonder, the power, the majesty of it cascaded over the battlements of glory, filling, flooding, enveloping my very being, the fingers of the Spirit swept the aeolian harp strings of my heart and evoked a grand and wondrous melody like the sound of a great Amen. It was as if the lost chord was found again! In my soul was born a harmony that was struck and sustained upon four, full, quivering strings, and from it were plucked the words that sprang and leaped into being—the Foursquare Gospel.

"The whole tent was enveloped, was aquiver! 'Twas as though every soul was brought into harmony with celestial music. I stood there still and listened, gripping my pulpit, shaking with wonder and with joy, then I exclaimed, 'Why—why it's the F-o-u-r-s-q-u-a-r-e G-o-s-p-e-l.' The words burst from the white heat of my heart.

"Instantly the Spirit bore witness! Waves, billows,

oceans of praises rocked the audience. Borne aloft upon the rushing winds of a Holy Ghost revival, the melody evoked that day has been carried round the world. The term 'Foursquare Gospel' which the Lord gave to me that day, as vividly and fittingly distinguishing the message which He had given me to preach, has become a household word throughout the earth!"

THE WORD "FOURSQUARE" IN THE GOSPEL

When this phrase "Foursquare Gospel" was born, Sister McPherson was unaware how prominently the word "foursquare" appeared in the Scriptures. Subsequent study showed that the expression begins Biblically with the description of the foursquare altar in the book of Exodus in the Old Testament and ends with the surveying of the foursquare city in the book of Revelation in the New Testament.

While the word looms but ten times in Sacred Writ, the significance of its associations prove almost overwhelming, for this term is applied exclusively to elements representing sinful men's approach to, acceptance by, and adoration of Almighty God! Moreover, the first three times the word appears in the Bible it is articulated by the voice of Jehovah! The Lord commanded from Mount Sinai concerning the tabernacle's altar of sacrifice and altar of incense and concerning the high priest's breastplate that they all be foursquare.

The next three occasions where this word appears relate how workmen obeyed the divine direction and made both of those altars and the breastplate foursquare. The references follow.

Exodus 27:1 quotes God's instruction regarding the brazen altar of sacrifice which would stand at the entrance to the tabernacle court: "And thou shalt make an altar of shittim wood, five cubits long, and five cubits broad; the altar shall be foursquare: and the height thereof shall be three cubits."

Exodus 28:16 conveyed to Moses the divine direction concerning the breastplate the high priest would wear:

"Foursquare it shall be being doubled; a span shall be the length thereof, and a span shall be the breadth thereof."

Exodus 30:1-2 gives God's orders about the golden altar of incense which would stand before the veil inside the tabernacle's holy place to curtain off the holy of holies: "And thou shalt make an altar to burn incense upon: of shittim wood shalt thou make it. A cubit shall be the length thereof, and a cubit the breadth thereof; foursquare shall it be: and two cubits shall be the height thereof: the horns thereof shall be of the same."

Now the Lord appointed and anointed a man named Bezaleel to oversee the construction of the tabernacle and its appointments. How faithfully Bezaleel and his workmen carried out God's commands concerning the shape of the altars and breastplate is documented in the following passages.

Exodus 38:1 relates concerning the altar of sacrifice: "And he made the altar of burnt offering of shittim wood: five cubits was the length thereof, and five cubits the breadth thereof; it was foursquare; and three cubits the height thereof."

Exodus 39:9 describes the breastplate: "It was foursquare; they made the breastplate double: a span was the length thereof, and a span the breadth thereof, being doubled."

Exodus 37:25 records how Bezaleel "made the incense altar of shittim wood: the length of it was a cubit, and the breadth of it a cubit; it was foursquare; and two cubits was the height of it; the horns thereof were of the same."

Thus the first three times *foursquare* appears in the Bible this word was spoken by the voice of God, and the next three times it appears Moses relates how workmen obeyed God's directions and made the altars and breastplate foursquare. The brazen altar symbolized in the Old Testament that final altar, Christ's cross, where Jesus offered the one sacrifice for sin forever. The golden altar of incense and the high priest's breastplate are connected with intercession by which man approaches God. And now since the veil of the Temple was rent in twain from top to bottom as a result of Calvary, every believer—and not just a hereditary priesthood—is invited, "Let us therefore come boldly unto the throne of grace, that we may obtain mercy, and find grace to help in time of need" (Hebrews 4:16).

Is not the use of the term foursquare in connection with these Old Testament symbols significant, especially in the light of their New Testament fulfillments?

This word appears four more times in the Bible. First Kings 7:31 describes a detail of Solomon's Temple as "foursquare, not round." That temple, of course, replaced the tabernacle as the center of Israel's worship.

To be sure, Solomon's Temple perished, as did the tabernacle before it. Its successors, erected by Zerubabel and Herod the Great, also perished. Many premillenial Bible scholars believe that the closing chapters of the book of Ezekiel provide blueprints for a coming Jewish Temple on Mount Moriah, the millenial temple. A study of these specifications suggests that almost everything of importance in this temple seems to be foursquare. However, specifically the Scripture states that the court of this shrine will be such: "So he measured the court, an hundred cubits long, and an hundred cubits broad, foursquare; and the altar that was before the house" (Ezekiel 40:47). Moreover, the holy oblation to be offered in this temple is said to be the same: "All the oblation shall be five and twenty thousand by five and twenty thousand: ye shall offer the holy oblation foursquare, with the possession of the city" (Ezekiel 48:20).

The final occurrence of this word is found on the next to the last page of most Bibles. Regarding the New Jerusalem John declares, "And the city lieth foursquare, and the length is as large as the breadth: and he measured the city with the reed, twelve thousand furlongs. The length and the breadth and the height of it are equal" (Revelation 21:16). Here we have the antitype of the holy of holies of both tabernacle and temples which likewise had been foursquare, with length, breadth, and height equal.

So in each of the ten Biblical references containing the word foursquare this term is applied to elements representing man's redemption by, worship of, and acceptance with God. What a fitting term to describe the full gospel of Jesus the only saviour, baptizer, and healer, Jesus the coming king!

THE FOURSQUARE MESSAGE

Perhaps the simplest Scriptural summary possible of Foursquare faith and experience would be the testimony, "Jesus saves us according to John 3:16. He baptizes us with the Holy Spirit according to Acts 2:4. He heals our bodies according to James 5:14-15. And Jesus Christ is coming again to receive us unto Himself according to I Thessalonians 4:16-17."

While this gospel received the name "Foursquare" in 1922, and while it had been proclaimed by the denominational founder for about fourteen years before the descriptive phrase was coined, the message itself, as was insisted earlier, is by no means modern, by no means new, by no means novel. Foursquaredom strives to propagate the identical message, ministry, emphasis, and experiences which formed the norm of the early apostolic church as described in the book of Acts and the New Testament epistles.

Moreover, the roots of this message reach back into Old Testament times. You might hesitate to call Isaiah a Foursquare preacher, but the prophet certainly was a proclaimer of the Foursquare *gospel*. Isaiah prophesied concerning Jesus Christ as Saviour and Healer: "But he was wounded for our transgressions, he was bruised for our iniquities: the chastisement of our peace was upon him; and with his stripes we are healed" (Isaiah 53:5). The New Testament applies this very prophecy to Jesus as Saviour and Healer (cf. I Peter 2:24). Isaiah also foretold the phenomena of Acts 2:4 and the baptism of the

Holy Spirit: "For with stammering lips and another tongue will he speak to this people" (Isaiah 28:11). St. Paul's application of this prophecy to speaking in tongues demolishes the objection sometimes presented that Isaiah 28:11 is not pertinent to the Pentecostal gifts (cf. I Corinthians 14:21).

Isaiah further foretold the Coming King: "Behold, the Lord God will come with strong hand, and his arm shall rule for him: behold, his reward is with him, and his work before him" (Isaiah 40:10). How similar is that promise to the very words of Jesus, "Behold, I come quickly; and my reward is with me" (Revelation 22:12)!

The message of Jesus the Saviour, Baptizer, Healer, and Coming King stands firmly rooted in Old Testament prophecy. But it is when we turn to New Testament fulfillment that this gospel blazes in its brightest brilliance.

First and foremost, the Lord Jesus Christ Himself preached this gospel. He proclaimed Himself the Saviour: "For the Son of man is come to seek and to save that which was lost" (Luke 19:10). Jesus further promised to fulfill John the Baptist's presentation of Him as the Baptizer with the Holy Ghost: "And, behold, I send the promise of my Father upon you: but tarry ye in the city of Jerusalem, until ye be endued with power from on high" (Luke 24:49). Christ moreover proved Himself to be the great physician, of bodies as well as of souls, by healing the sick, "That it might be fulfilled which was spoken by Esaias [Isaiah] the prophet, saying, Himself took our infirmities, and bare our sicknesses" (Matthew 8:17). And He commissioned believers to lay hands on the sick in His name (cf. Mark 16:18). Of course, He personally promised His Second Coming in passages like John 14:2-3: "I go to prepare a place for you. And if I go and prepare a place for you, I will come again, and receive you unto myself; that where I am, there ye may be also."

Peter was the first of Christ's apostles receiving the opportunity to proclaim the Foursquare message. In his very first sermon, on the day of Pentecost, he used an Old Testament text to identify Jesus Christ as the incarnate divine Saviour. Peter proclaimed, "And it shall come to pass, that whosoever shall call on the name of the Lord shall be saved" (Acts 2:21). The apostle made it clear that by the Lord he meant the Lord Jesus!

In the same sermon Peter championed Christ as the Baptizer with the Holy Spirit, promising, ". . . ye shall receive the gift of the Holy Ghost. For the promise is unto you, and to your children, and to all that are afar off, even as many as the Lord our God shall call" (Acts 2:38b-39).

Peter proclaimed Christ as healer in his first epistle: "by whose stripes ye were healed" (I Peter 2:24). Of course, this apostle witnessed many marvelous miracles, beginning with the healing of the lame man at the gate Beautiful in Acts 3. Peter explained the miracle by attributing it to Jesus: "And his name, through faith in his name hath made this man strong, whom ye see and know: yea, the faith which is by him hath given him this perfect soundness in the presence of you all" (Acts 3:16).

Peter also espoused Jesus as Coming King. He warned his hearers to prepare for the times of refreshing coming from the presence of the Lord when "he shall send Jesus Christ, which before was preached unto you" (Acts 3:20). And he denounced scoffers who would challenge in the last days, "Where is the promise of his coming?" (II Peter 3:3-4).

James the Lord's brother—son of Mary and Joseph (not to be confused with James the apostle, son of Zebedee)—also promulgated the Foursquare message. James apparently became the leader of the church in Jerusalem. He wrote the general epistle which bears his name. Therein he exhorted, "Receive with meekness the engrafted word, which is able to save your souls" (1:21). His words, "For as the body without the spirit is dead" (2:26), enforce the necessity of being filled with the Holy Spirit as they do the natural body's need for the indwelling soul in order to enjoy life. James phrased that classic text about healing, "Is any sick among you? let him call for the elders of the church; and let them pray over him, anointing him with oil in the name of the Lord: And the prayer of faith shall save the sick, and the Lord shall raise him up" (5:14-15). And James also encouraged, "Be ye also patient; stablish your hearts: for the coming of the Lord draweth nigh" (5:8).

Paul perhaps outstripped all the other apostles in championing Jesus Christ as Saviour, Baptizer, Healer, and Coming King. In the book of Acts and in his epistles he proclaimed and promoted these truths and experiences. "Believe on the Lord Jesus Christ, and thou shalt be saved," he challenged the Philippian jailer (Acts 16:31). Sensing an emptiness in the experience of the believers he met at Ephesus he questioned, "Have ye received the Holy Ghost since ye believed?" (Acts 19:2). They had not. But "when Paul had laid his hands upon them, the Holy Ghost came on them; and they spake with tongues and prophesied" (Acts 19:6). The Apostle to the Gentiles moreover exercised a spectacular healing ministry and included "gifts of healings" in his list of the operations of the Holy Spirit which congregations ought to covet earnestly (cf. I Corinthians 12:9). And it was, of course, Paul who gave us the classic text about the rapture, "For the Lord himself shall descend from heaven with a shout, with the voice of the archangel, and with the trump of God: and the dead in Christ shall rise first: Then we which are alive and remain shall be caught up together with them in the clouds, to meet the Lord in the air: and so shall we ever be with the Lord" (I Thessalonians 4:16-17).

So the Foursquare message surely is not modern, new, or novel. The Foursquare organization is hardly half a century old at this writing. But echoing across the centuries from the days of Isaiah reverberate prophetic anticipations of Jesus as Saviour, Baptizer, Healer, and Coming King. Christ Himself proclaimed the same message, as did all of His apostles and ministering disciples in the apostolic age, and not just Peter and James and Paul who have been mentioned. "Peter and Barnabus and Paul might find themselves more at home," wrote Dr. Henry P. Van Dusen, then President of New York's Union Theological Seminary, "at a Pentecostal revival than in the formalized and sophisticated worship of other churches, Catholic or Protestant" (LIFE Magazine, June 9, 1958, p. 122). Those apostles would certainly be at home with the Foursquare message, for that is the very gospel which they preached, though they could not call it by that name!

What is the Foursquare gospel? The name was born in the white heat of Pentecostal revival in Oakland, California, in 1922. The movement sprouted from the mighty move of God at Angelus Temple by which the Lord stirred the whole southland. But the message is milleniums older than either the name or the organization. The message is identical to that of Jesus and His apostles in the New Testament.

Sermon

LOST AND RESTORED

Introduction

On the day of Pentecost Peter in explaining the working of the supernatural power of the Holy Spirit seen upon those filled with the Spirit quotes from the prophet Joel saying, "It shall come to pass in the last days, saith God, I will pour out of my Spirit upon all flesh, and your sons and your daughters shall prophesy." It was as a direct result of this outpouring of God's Spirit that this message was given in vision and prophecy under the power of the Holy Spirit.

In the year 1908 the Lord found me a thoughtless little country girl of seventeen. He not only convicted me of sin, saved and baptized me with the Holy Spirit according to Acts 2:4, but He also called me to leave father and mother, houses and lands, school, and future dreams of earthly popularity, and bade me go into all the world and preach the message of salvation, the baptism of the Holy Spirit, and the soon coming of the Lord.

Thus it was that before the age of eighteen I found myself preaching the Gospel, weak in myself, but strong in Him. Never having attended any earthly Bible school, I clung to the promise that I was to take no thought for what I would say, but that He would teach me in the needed hour, also that out of my innermost being should flow rivers of living water, knowing that "This spake he of the Spirit" who had come to dwell within me.

Time and space will not here permit me to relate the numerous times and ways the Lord took this poor, ignorant tongue of mine and spoke through me words I had never learned; without any thought on my part they came rolling out. Vital, forceful, eloquent words poured through my lips, not from my head but from my innermost being. While speaking thus with closed eyes and uplifted hands, the tears would stream down my face, and many precious souls would flock to the altar seeking salvation and the baptism of the Holy Spirit, and to Jesus belongs the glory, for He did it all. Hallelujah!

While in London, England, waiting with my husband Robert Semple for the boat in which to embark for China, I was asked by Mr. Polehil, a wealthy Christian who was our host in the city, to speak to a congregation of people that night. Inquiring of the Lord I felt it was His will and told the man that I would go. On the way in his beautiful limousine with liveried attendants I prayed, "O Lord, do help me to do Thy will tonight." I wondered whether the meeting would be held in a cottage or in a mission hall, and as I gazed with wonder upon the beautiful streets and buildings, the car stopped in front of the most imposing and spacious edifice in sight. Thinking that perhaps a small room in this immense building was used for a mission hall, I was hurried up the steps and into the side door of the place.

I was led through the door and on to the platform before I had time to realize that this whole building, one big city block square, was packed with people and I was to speak to them at once. I remember vaguely my attendant whispering into my ear that we were late, and then I heard the voice of a man on the platform saying: "Now our sister will speak to us and bring the message." Before I realized it, I was standing dazed and confused before the largest audience I had ever spoken to. The gallery, the balcony, the pit and the rostrum were all filled; there was no seat for me to sit in; and to add to my confusion the footlights flashed into brilliancy all around me, and there I stood, a slip of a girl with my Bible in my trembling hands. I had never prepared a sermon in my life before, nor did I know then how to go about it. And not a thought came to me. I just lifted my heart to God and silently prayed: "O God, if You ever helped me in my life, help me now!"

Just then something happened! The power of God went surging through my body. Waves of glory and praise swept through my soul, until I forgot the throng of eager faces that had a moment before seemed to swim before me. I forgot the footlights, forgot that I was only a child of eighteen, and that many there with their grey hair knew more in a moment than I in the natural could know in a lifetime, and I was in the Spirit!

All this takes a long time to relate, but it happened in a moment, for those who put their trust in God shall never be put to shame. My mouth opened. The Lord took control of my tongue, my lips and vocal organs, and began to speak through me, not in tongues but in English. The Spirit spoke in prophecy, and as He spoke through me I did not know what the next word would be. Certainly the rivers did flow, not from my head but from the innermost depths of my being, without my having aught to do with it.

As I spoke thus for one hour and a quarter, there did not seem to be a stir in all the vast audience. And as I spoke I saw a vision of a great circle, composed of ten smaller circles. The big circle seemed so large that its top reached the sky. It represented the dispensation of the Holy Spirit, from its opening on the day of Pentecost, to its closing at the coming of the Lord Jesus. Before starting to speak, I opened my Bible with closed eyes, trusting God for my text, and my finger was guided to a certain verse. When I opened my eyes and read it, this was the verse the Lord had given me: "That which the palmerworm hath left hath the locust eaten; and that which the locust hath left hath the cankerworm eaten; and that which the cankerworm hath left hath the caterpiller eaten" (Joel 1:4).

Just so when I came to the bottom of the circle, and the dark ages were pictured in their horror, my hand automatically turned the page over to the second chapter and placed my finger upon the following verse: "I will restore to you the years that the locust hath eaten, and the cankerworm, and the caterpiller, and the palmerworm, my great army which I sent among you" (Joel 2:25).

I have in the following pages written the message as it was given to the best of my memory. As you read forget the poor earthen vessel, forget the present writer, and give the glory to the Lord, for it is He, and not I, who is worthy of praise forever.

I am yours, the least of all saints,

Aimee Semple McPherson

THE THREE DISPENSATIONS

Just as there are three persons in the Godhead, Father, Son, and Holy Spirit, so there have been three separate and distinct dispensations or periods of time.

First came the dispensation of the Father as recorded in God's Word throughout the Old Testament from Genesis to Malachi. Throughout the dispensation of the Father, He promised that at the close of that dispensation He would bestow a great gift, even Jesus His only begotten Son, upon the earth, as our redeemer and the propitiation for our sins. At the close of that period of time God the Father kept His word, and true to His promise gave Jesus, as His great love gift to the sinner.

Second came the dispensation of the Son, as recorded in the four gospels, Matthew, Mark, Luke, and John. Now just as the Father had a gift to bestow upon the world, even so Jesus, who is our salvation, tells us over and over again that He longs to bestow a gift upon all those who believe on Him, even the gift of the Holy Spirit. All throughout His ministry upon this earth, with ever increasing emphasis, Jesus depicted to His followers the importance of their receiving this gift which He was to bestow upon them when He went away.

Jesus seemed to a certain degree to be limited in the scope of His ministry. He was sent only to the lost sheep of the house of Israel. He was able to be in only one place at a time. And He declared in John 16:7, "It is expedient for you that I go away: for if I go not away, the Comforter will not come unto you; but if I depart, I will send him unto you." Plainly Jesus thought it more important for us to receive the Holy Spirit than for Himself to stay upon this earth. Thus just as the Father kept His promise and sent Jesus as His love gift to the sinner, so now in turn Jesus kept His word and prayed the Father to send the Holy Spirit, His gift to the believer.

Third came the dispensation of the Holy Spirit which opened on the day of Pentecost. This dispensation we are still living in and will be living in it until Jesus comes for His waiting Bride.

The days of Jesus' tender ministry upon earth were over. He had eaten the Last Supper. He had been tried in the sinner's stead and had died in the sinner's place. He had been laid in the lonely tomb, resurrected in power and triumph, had walked forty days upon earth after His resurrection. He had promised for the last time that He would not leave His little ones comfortless, but that He would pray the Father that He would send another Comforter, even the Holy Spirit, who when He was come would take of the things of Jesus and reveal it unto them (John 16:13), lead them into all truth (John 16:13), show them things to come (John 16:13), glorify Jesus (John 16:14), reprove of sin, of righteousness, and of judgment (John 16:8), teach them all things (John 14:26), testify of Jesus (John 15:26), endue them with power from on high (Luke 24:49), and pray through them with groanings that could not be uttered.

The last words of Jesus before His ascension, before the clouds received Him out of their sight, as recorded in Luke 24:49 and Acts 1:8, were concerning the importance of receiving the Comforter whom He would send.

TARRYING FOR THE COMING OF THE HOLY SPIRIT

With glowing hearts and the Master's command, "Tarry until ye be endued with power from on high," still ringing in their ears, the little flock of about 120 went their way to the upper room in Jerusalem, to await there the advent of the Holy Spirit, the opening of this great new dispensation of the Spirit sent from heaven. For ten days they waited. They "continued with one accord in prayer and supplication." One accord: O what unbroken harmony is depicted in these simple words. Thomas was not saying to Peter, "Peter, what are you doing here? You denied the Lord thrice. You cursed and swore. The Lord will never baptize you with the Spirit." Peter was not saying to Thomas, "Well, Thomas, what are you doing here? You always were an old doubter anyway. I don't think you will receive anything from the Lord." Ah no! They were with *one accord* in one place in prayer and supplication.

THE COMING OF THE HOLY SPIRIT

"And when the day of Pentecost was fully come, they were all with one accord in one place. And suddenly there came a sound from heaven" (Acts 2:1-2). (Bless God, there has been a sound ever since when the Spirit falls and comes in.) "From heaven"—yes, thank God, in spite of what man may say, undoubtedly this sound is from heaven! ". . . as of a rushing mighty wind, and it filled all the house where they were sitting. And there appeared unto them cloven tongues like as of fire, and it sat upon each of them. And they were all filled with the Holy Ghost, and began to speak with other tongues, as the Spirit gave them utterance" (Acts 2:2-4).

I have often tried to picture the sudden consternation and excitement which surged through the streets of Jerusalem when the 120 men and women were filled with the Holy Spirit and burst out talking in other tongues, so filled that they acted like drunken people (Acts 2:13). I can seem to see the crowds running up this street and that, windows flying open, heads thrust out, doors opening, everybody running, devout men gathering up their long ministerial robes and forgetting their dignity, running with the rest to swell the one great question, "What meaneth this?"

"Now when this was noised abroad, the multitude came together" (Beloved, if the Holy Spirit is falling in your midst you will not need oyster suppers or box socials to bring the multitude. Your only trouble will be to find seats for the people), "and were confounded," just as you have been perhaps, "because that every man heard them speak in his own language." They were amazed, they marveled, they were in doubt. Soberminded folk asked the question, "What meaneth this?" Mockers declared, "These men are full of new wine." Oh what an uproar! What excitement! You dear people who dislike confusion and demand things to be done decently and in order would have been scandalized!

But Peter, a new Peter, no longer afraid of the opinions of people, "standing up," (the Holy Spirit when He endues you with power puts a real stand-up for Jesus Spirit within you and takes the cowardice out) said, "For these are not drunken, as ye suppose. . . . But this is that which was spoken by the prophet Joel: And it shall come to pass in the last days, saith God, I will pour out of my Spirit upon all flesh." Then as Peter preached that mighty sermon under the power of the Holy Spirit, he told, among other things, his vast audience to "Repent and be baptized every one . . . in the name of Jesus Christ for the remission of sins," and they too would "receive the gift of the Holy Spirit." Furthermore, just as though he looked away ahead through the coming years and saw the doubts in some of your minds, Peter declared that the promise is not only unto you but also "unto your children, and unto all that are afar off," and that means you, brother, sister, for Peter goes on to say, "even as many as the Lord our God shall call." Now, if God has called you, the promise is unto you. How glad I am that the Spirit through Peter drove these nails and clinched them on the other side till there is not the shadow of a loophole for you to thrust the wedge of doubt into.

CIRCLE I
The Ushering In of the Dispensation of the Holy Spirit Accompanied by Mighty Signs and Wonders

On the day of Pentecost some 3000 souls were saved. Then we see Peter and John going up to the temple to pray, pass a lame man at the gate Beautiful who asks alms of them. Peter answers, "Silver and gold have I none," (I do not think the Pentecostal people ever were or ever will be overly blessed with silver or gold) "but such as I have I give unto thee; in the name of Jesus Christ rise up and walk." The lame man was healed instantaneously, and whether the priests in the temple believed in manifestations or not I know not, but at any rate the man went into that temple walking, leaping, and praising God.

In Acts 5:16 we see the multitudes out of the cities round about Jerusalem bringing sick folks and those who were vexed with unclean spirits, and they were healed

every one. Sick were brought forth into the streets, and laid on beds and couches that at least the shadow of Peter passing by might overshadow some of them. Signs and wonders were wrought everywhere by the hands of the apostles, true to the word of Him who had said, "Greater works than these shall ye do because I go to My Father."

While the tree seen in Circle I stood in its perfection the Church stood blazing with the full Pentecostal power and glory of the Holy Spirit. Jesus' words were fulfilled, and in deed and truth they were endued with power from on high. Timid Peter, who had feared a little girl who asked him if he knew Jesus, was timid no longer. Illiterate men and women were turned into flashing evangels.

The outpouring of the Holy Spirit was not unto the Jews alone but also unto the Gentiles. In Acts 10 we see Peter answering the voice of the Lord who spoke to him through a vision, going down to preach Jesus unto the Gentiles. "While Peter yet spoke the Word the Holy Ghost fell on all that heard." The Jews who came with Peter were astonished that on the Gentiles also were poured out the gifts of the Holy Ghost, "For they heard them speak with tongues and magnify God."

Again in these wonderful days of the former rain outpouring of the Holy Spirit, we see Saul, on his way to Damascus to persecute the Christians, blinded and prostrated in the road by the power of the Spirit, hearing the voice of Jesus saying, "Saul, Saul, why persecutest thou me?" Later we find Paul not only converted and baptized with the Holy Spirit with the Bible evidence of speaking with other tongues (I Corinthians 14:18), but himself preaching salvation and the baptism of the Holy Spirit. In Acts 19 Paul, finding certain disciples at Ephesus, asks them whether they have received the Holy Ghost since they believed. They tell him, "No." They have not even heard whether there was any Holy Ghost. "And when Paul had laid his hands upon them, the Holy Ghost came on them; and they spake with tongues, and prophesied." This marvelous manifestation of speaking in other tongues accompanied the infilling of believers with the Holy Spirit everywhere. Simon the Sorcerer offered money for the power to bestow that which he saw and heard at Samaria.

THE TREE WITH ITS PERFECT FRUIT

Every gift and fruit of the Spirit was manifested in the church till the nine gifts and the nine fruit of the Spirit hung as eighteen perfect apples upon the perfect tree. "For to one was given by the Spirit the word of wisdom, to another the word of knowledge by the same Spirit, to another faith by the same Spirit, to another gifts of healing by the same Spirit, to another the working of miracles, to another prophecy, to another discerning of spirits, to another divers kinds of tongues, to another the interpretation of tongues." The sick were healed, miracles wrought, and when messages were given in other tongues in the assembly, some one gave the interpretation (I Corinthians 14:27). Each of the nine fruit of the Spirit was also in the church: love, joy, peace, gentleness, goodness, faith, meekness, temperance, and long-suffering. So we have the perfect picture visualized in the first circle of the chart. Thus ends the first chapter of the early church's history, leaving the tree rooted and grounded in the faith of Jesus Christ, with every limb, branch, leaf, and fruit in perfect power and strength.

CIRCLE II
The Palmerworm at Work

O glorious days of harmonious love and unity, days when none called aught that he had his own, days when the children of the Lord had all things in common, days when they were beaten and imprisoned, days when prison bonds were broken, signs and wonders were wrought! How we have often wished they might have continued.

These puny minds of ours only feebly grasp events of the past and are utterly unable to probe the depths of mystery shrouding the future. Unlike us, however, the great mind and eye of the Almighty God beholds the future as clearly as the past. Before His burning eyes of fire and the glory of His presence darkness turns to day, and the deepest mists are rolled away. Looking thus ahead with clear, unerring eye, God saw, and moreover prophesied through Joel, that the church would not always retain this glorious state of power, saw that the palmerworm, the locust, the cankerworm, and the caterpillar were going to rob and strip and mutilate and destroy this perfect tree with its gifts and fruit. He saw that the church, or tree, was going to lose gradually more and more, till it would be left desolate, barren and despairing. The falling away and destruction of the perfect tree did not occur in one day. It was a gradual deterioration accomplished day by day, and stage by stage.

One day the palmerworm appeared, eating and destroying as it went, until as years went by the gifts and fruit of the Spirit began to disappear from view. Not so many sick were healed as of yore, not so many miracles were performed. Faith was on the wane. When someone in the assembly had a message in tongues there was no one who had the gift of interpretation. Messages in prophecy were not so frequent as of yore. The fruit of unselfish love and joy and peace were also attacked by the palmerworm who grew bolder and bolder day by day. Gradually the apples began to disappear from the staunch and upright tree which had stood so gloriously heavy-laden for many years after the day of Pentecost.

This state of fruitlessness was indeed a condition worthy of lamentation, but the pity of it all is that the devastation did not stop with the havoc wrought by the palmerworm. Other years and other worms took up the work of destruction where the palmerworm had left off, and "that which the palmerworm hath left hath the locust eaten."

CIRCLE III
The Locust at Work

The work of the locust is of course wrought upon the leaves. Sweeping over vast territories of country, it strips and lays barren all that it touches. Thus not only were the gifts and fruit of the Spirit lost sight of by the vast majority of believers, but the personal incoming and indwelling of the Holy Spirit accompanied by speaking in other tongues was also in a great measure lost sight of. The old-time seekers' meetings, the earnest prayer-and-praise meetings were disappearing. Formality and sectarianism were taking their places.

As humility, godliness, and the manifestations of the Holy Spirit vanished, persecution and reproach vanished also. As meetings of the older order were changed into dignified services with more liturgical form, the Holy Spirit as a gentle dove was quenched and grieved and stifled till He silently withdrew His wonder-working manifestations, and joy and gladness were withheld from the sons of men.

Because it meant too great a sacrifice, too much emptying out and humbling in the dust before God, too much seeking and waiting, the baptism of the Holy Spirit was not received as of old. Then came men who professed to have the Holy Spirit in a new way, without the Bible sign or evidence of speaking with other tongues as the Spirit gives utterance. This simplified matters greatly, and the professor no longer needed to be a possessor. Thus the baptism of the Holy Spirit was lost sight of by many, though there always was a remnant of a faithful few Spirit-filled saints through whom God manifested Himself in a real and supernatural way.

It was a sad day when the leaves were thus stripped from the tree and the locust had done its work, but days that were still more sad were to follow, for we read, "That which the locust hath left hath the cankerworm eaten."

CIRCLE IV
The Work of the Cankerworm

After the fruit and the leaves had been destroyed, the cankerworm immediately made its appearance and began its work upon the branches and tender shoots of the tree, making cankerous and unsound that God-fearing walk of holiness above the world and sin, so long enjoyed by the children of the Lord. As the sap, the life of the tree, was consumed and the branches became more and more cankerous, and unsound things that used to seem sinful appeared sinful no longer, the world that used to be barred outside the doors of the church now leaned back in contented languor in the cushioned pews, or sang in the choir.

Christians let down more and more in the high standard of holiness unto the Lord which they had been holding aloft and now it trailed bedraggled and unnoticed in the dust. Quickly upon the trail of the cankerworm followed the caterpillar, and we read: "That which the cankerworm hath left hath the caterpiller eaten."

CIRCLE V
The Work of the Caterpillar

We are now nearing the bottom of the large circle. The perfect tree is perfect no longer. Stripped of her fruit, denuded of her leaves, her branches made white, laid clean bare, it was not long till the trunk and the roots began to decay and the caterpillar made his nest in the decayed and rotted hollows of the tree.

No tree can eke out an existence without leaves through which to breathe, or branches and limbs through which the sap and life courses through its veins. For a believer to live without the Holy Spirit, the breath of life, or the holy life of Jesus as revealed by the Spirit coursing through his veins, is to eke out a meager, barren existence nowhere recorded in the Word of God. And now in Circle V we see the tree in the most lamentable condition yet described, with fruit gone, leaves gone, branches bare, trunk decayed and rotten, a nest for the caterpillar. In other words, the gifts and fruit of the Spirit gone, the baptism of the Holy Spirit gone, separation and holiness gone, justification by faith gone. Well might the angels lean over the battlements of heaven and weep—the noble church, the perfect tree which had once stood clad with power and glory of the Holy Ghost—there remained now naught but a name, not even a remnant of her former splendor, as she entered into the dark ages.

CIRCLE VI
The Dark Ages

No wonder it is called the Dark Ages. Ah! dark indeed is the night without Jesus. He is the Light of the world, and when the church lost sight of justification by faith, lost sight of the atonement, the blood of Jesus, there was a total eclipse and the face of the Sun of righteousness was obscured, and the succeeding years are known as the Dark Ages.

Men and women groping in this gross darkness tried to win their way to heaven by doing penance, by locking themselves up in dungeons, walking over red hot plowshares in their bare feet, and inflicting unnameable tortures upon themselves and upon one another, blindly trying by some work or deed to pay the debt that had already been paid on Calvary's rugged cross. They had lost sight utterly of the fact that

"Jesus paid it all,
All to him we owe,
Sin had left a crimson stain,
He washed it white as snow."

The great arrow you see in the chart had been steadily going down and down and down, pitilessly and relentlessly going down as I saw the vision, till it seemed as though it would never reach the bottom. And now it had struck the bottom, the church had lost all, the tree was dead.

Angels might have wept, mortals might have wrung their hands, and their souls have failed within them in utter despair, but *God*, Hallelujah, looking on ahead into the future still, had spoken through the prophet Joel (2:25) saying, "I will restore to you the years that the locust hath eaten, the cankerworm, the caterpiller, and the palmerworm, my great army which I sent among you." O beloved, do you see it? Then shout aloud and praise Him! That was all, ALL, think of it! All that has been lost was to be restored. Hallelujah! What is impossible with man is possible with God.

Now the church had not lost this all at one time. The restoration came as "meat in due season," as line upon line, precept upon precept, here a little and there a little, till *today* we are nearing the completion of this restoration, and Jesus is coming soon to take His perfect church, His bride, His fruit-laden tree unto Himself, where transplanted from earth to heaven the tree will bloom and yield her fruit by the great river of life forever.

No, God did not restore to the church all at once what she had lost. He was willing to do so to be sure, but they did not have the light at that time. Therefore the last thing that had been lost was the first to be restored. They had had a name that they did live but were dead and therefore must needs repent and do their first works over again before taking any higher step.

CIRCLE VII
The Years of the Caterpillar Restored

Just before the arrow began to ascend, and the work of restoration began, we see the scene of ruin depicted by Joel in all its awfulness (chapter 1): the meat offering and the drink offering cut off, the field wasted, the corn wasted, the new wine dried up, garner laid desolate, barns broken down, the beasts groaning, the herds of cattle perplexed, the sheep made desolate, the rivers of water dried up, and the fire devouring the pastures of the wilderness. Then one day amidst all this desolation God began to move, the treading of His footsteps was heard, and in Circle VII we see the roots of the tree again sinking deep into the earth and justification by faith restored. This is the way it all came about.

Martin Luther one day was walking up the steps of the cathedral on his hands and knees, over broken glass, endeavoring to do penance, thereby seeking to atone for his sins. As he was toiling painfully and laboriously up the steps in this manner, blood trickling from his hands and knees, cut by the broken glass, he heard a voice from heaven saying, "The just shall live by faith."

At those words a great light fell from heaven. It banished the darkness and doubts. It illuminated the soul of Martin Luther and revealed the finished work of Calvary and the blood that alone can atone for sin.

"For nothing good have I
Whereby Thy grace to claim,
I'll wash my garments white
In the blood of Calvary's Lamb."

The days that followed were eventful days, epoch-making days, fraught with self-sacrificing and suffering. The Lord had spoken, and promised that all the years that had been eaten should be restored. Out of the seas of travail and suffering that followed the preaching of justification by faith there was born a little body of blood-washed, fire-tried pilgrims, willing to suffer persecution for His name's sake.

You have read perhaps how Martin Luther and his followers were turned out of the churches, spoken against falsely, and accused of all manner of evil. As Luther, Calvin, Knox, Fletcher, and many other blessed children of the Lord stood firm for the truths of salvation and a sinless life, they suffered all manner of persecution. God's Word says, "They that will live godly shall suffer persecution." (If you or your church profess to live godly and yet never suffer persecution, if you have become popular and the shame and reproach of the cross is gone, there is something radically wrong somewhere, for those who live godly still suffer persecution.)

As the noble tree again put down her roots of justification into the fertile soil of faith, as life again began to surge through the trunk and the limbs of the tree, every demon in hell seemed to be raging and howling against those who saw and accepted the light of salvation. Martyrs were burned at the stake, stoned to death, swung from public scaffolds; suffered the tortures of the Inquisition, their eyes were put out with hot irons, they were beaten till great gashes were cut in their backs, salt was rubbed into the wounds and they were cast into the dark dungeons still true and unflinching for Jesus. They were tortured in unspeakable ways, beheaded, sent to the guillotine, the Covenanters were driven from hill to hill and often had to hide themselves in caves in order to pray or sing the praises of the Lord, hunted and harassed at every turn.

But God had said, "I will restore the years that have been eaten," and in spite of the burning stake, in spite of the blood and fire and the deep waters of tribulation, in spite of the raging of the demons of hell, the great arrow that had so long been going down had at last started upward and was never to stop till it reached the top and the tree was again restored to its perfection.

Persecutions cannot stop God. Floods cannot stay His step. Fire cannot delay His progress. So line upon line, precept upon precept, here a little and there a little, the work of restoration has been going on. Not only did the Lord restore the years the caterpillar had eaten but also those devoured by the cankerworm.

CIRCLE VIII
The Years of the Cankerworm Restored

An entire consecration and holiness unto the Lord were preached; God called out a still more separated people with a deeper realization of what it meant to live a life wholly given up and consecrated to the Lord. The people a step lower always seem to fight the people a step higher. Nevertheless as the work of sifting and separation went on, God led His people to higher heights.

As one church grew cold, lost its first love, or fought

higher truths, it lost out spiritually. As soon as one creed would refuse to walk in the light as given by the Lord or begin to organize and set up man rule, the Lord simply stepped over their walls and left them to their forms and ceremonies and took with Him the little "called out, out of a called out" flock. In many instances the recording angel had to write upon the door of fashionable churches, "Thou hast a name that thou livest, and art dead," or "You have a form of godliness, but deny the power thereof."

But the work was not stopped; somewhere people were praying. Somewhere hungry hearts were meeting in little cottage prayer meetings or on the street corners, and the tender shoots and branches were being thrust forth on the tree. Consecration and holiness were being preached and the years of the cankerworm were being restored.

John Wesley was a man with a message. He too suffered persecution. Preaching on the street corners in those days, faithful followers were stoned and rotten-egged. They were fought but not defeated. The power of God was manifested in the dear old Methodist Church, and later also in Charles Finney's meetings in a wonderful manner. Men and women were slain under the power of God. At times the floors were strewn with the slain of the Lord. Signs and wonders accompanied those who preached the "meat in due season."

While these churches lived godly, prayerful, mighty lives in Jesus, they suffered persecution. But when they too began to drift into the same cold, formal state as the others before them, the power and manifestation of the Spirit began to lift from their presence. When supper rooms took the place of upper rooms, and concerts took the place of prayer meetings, the Spirit was grieved. As each body began to organize and throw up walls of difference, God simply stepped over them again and called out another separated people, willing to suffer and sacrifice for Him.

Then came the day when William Booth was called upon to decide whether he would compromise or would follow the greater light God gave him. As he hesitated a moment his wife called from the balcony of that thronged church, "Say *No!* William."

And William Booth said "No!" And refusing to compromise he went forth preaching the message that had been given him. In the early days of the Salvation Army they were unpopular, suffered persecution, were a peculiar people, just as the others before mentioned had been in the beginning. They too were stoned and imprisoned. Some were even martyred, but neither the devil nor his agents could stop God and His work of restoration. In those early days of the Army it was nothing uncommon to see men and women slain under the power of God. Some of their number received the Holy Spirit and spake with other tongues. All night prayer meetings, dancing before the Lord, and mighty power were manifested in their midst. True to prophecy, while they lived their separated holy lives they were persecuted and unpopular with the world. Then came the Holiness churches wonderfully blessed of God, and the Lord moved in their midst in a mighty manner.

These dear people, many of them, thought that the Lord had now restored all He was going to restore to the Church, and believed that they had all the Lord had for them. But not so! God had said, "I will restore the years that the locust, the cankerworm, the caterpillar, and the palmerworm hath eaten." This necessarily meant A-L-L. Now so far only the years eaten by the caterpillar and the cankerworm had been restored. What about the years eaten by the locust and the palmerworm? When God says "all" does He mean all or only half? Why, He means *all* to be sure. Therefore next comes restoration of what the locust had eaten.

CIRCLE IX
The Years of the Locust Are Restored

Although in previous years many saints had received the Holy Spirit and spoken in tongues as in Bible days, yet upon the church at large the years which the locust had eaten in Circle III, the baptism of the Holy Spirit in other words, had not been restored in any great measure. Therefore this was the next to be restored. Peter in quoting from the prophet Joel said, "In the last days, saith God, I will pour out my Spirit upon all flesh." Joel says that He who gave us the former rain moderately will cause to come down for us the rain, both the former and the latter rain, in the first month!

It was just a few years ago that this latter rain began to fall. Perhaps you recollect the great Welsh revival where under the preaching of Evan Roberts the fire fell. Many were saved and baptized with the Holy Spirit. Those who received spoke with other tongues.

Over in Muki, India, a missionary, Pandita Ramaba, was praying with a band of Hindu girls. They had spent days and nights in prayer, when suddenly the Spirit was poured out in their midst as He had been on the day of Pentecost. Visible fire is said to have been seen upon one girl's bed and when the other girls went for water to extinguish the fire, it was discovered that this was the fire of the Holy Spirit, such as Moses saw in the burning bush that was not consumed. These dear Hindu girls who received the Holy Spirit spake with other tongues as the Spirit gave them utterance. One girl spoke in the English language (which she had never learned) and this is the message which was spoken through her: "Jesus is coming soon, get ready to meet Him."

The great revival spread on and on. Almost simultaneously the Spirit was pouring out in the United States of America, in England, in Canada, in Africa, upon missionaries in China and in the islands of the sea. Never was such worldwide revival known to spread so quickly and simultaneously. The Spirit was poured out upon praying bands in numberless places, people who had never heard before of the incoming of the Holy Spirit. In every instance, without exception, those who received the Holy Spirit spake in other tongues exactly as those who had received in Bible days had done. The latter rain was falling on the earth.

In order to receive the Holy Spirit one had to be empty and humble. Poor and rich, black or white, the mistress and the maid alike received the Holy Spirit when they humbled themselves and sought with all their hearts. Those who received praised the Lord and magnified His name, as no one but Spirit-filled saints can do. Waves of glory, floods of praise swept over assemblies who had received the Holy Spirit. There was no way of stopping the great revival, it seemed.

Just as demons and men had fought the restoration of the years eaten by the caterpillar and cankerworm, so now they fought with renewed vigor the restoration of the years that had been eaten by the locust. Again history repeated itself and the saints a step lower, unwilling to humble themselves, fought those who had gone a step higher, and many refused to walk in the light. They failed to realize that God really meant what He said when He promised to restore *all* that had been lost. They lost sight of the fact that the Lord was coming for a perfect church clad with all power and glory of the Spirit. Some even declared that the baptism of the Holy Spirit was not for these days and did not understand that we are still living in the dispensation of the Holy Spirit and will be till Jesus comes.

Preachers jumped to their pulpits and began to condemn those who had received the Holy Spirit in the Bible way. They cried, "Wildfire! Excitement! Hypnotism! False Teaching." All sorts of names were flung at them, and Oh, the blindness of these dear persecutors' eyes! They who themselves had been persecuted for former light of a few years previous were now themselves persecuting those who were moving on into greater light. Papers were printed to condemn the outpouring of the

Spirit. Great preachers mounted their platforms and denounced it, but they could no more stop God from restoring the baptism of the Holy Spirit and pouring out the latter rain than the former persecutors had been able to stop the restoration of salvation and holiness unto the Lord.

Those who fought the Holy Spirit, barred their doors or put up umbrellas of unbelief, began to dry up spiritually immediately. Assemblies and churches that once were on fire for God and preaching holiness without which no man shall see the Lord, the moment they rejected the Holy Spirit, began to lose their power. Oh why could they not see that this latter rain outpouring of the Spirit was just what they needed and had been pining for? Why could they not just have humbled themselves and let the Spirit who had been with them, now come in them, making them the temple of the Holy Ghost? All the fighting and persecution, however, were unable to quench the outpouring of the Spirit upon those who sought earnestly with pure and humble hearts.

To fight the outpouring of the Holy Spirit was just like a man with a broom in his hand endeavoring to sweep back the tidal waves of the Atlantic Ocean. While he is sweeping it back in one place it rolls in in countless others. Moreover, if he remains long where the full tides are rolling in and does not withdraw, the waves will soon flow over him and he will become "one of them."

A broom cannot stop the tide of the ocean, neither can fighting stay the falling of the latter rain, for God has spoken it, "In the last days I will pour out my Spirit upon all flesh." Oh, stop fighting God and open up your hearts to receive and welcome His gift, the Holy Spirit.

Since God restored Pentecost to the church on a large scale in the early years of the twentieth century, tens of millions of hungry seekers have received the baptism of the Holy Spirit.

Thus in Circle IX on the chart, I saw in my vision, the leaves which had been eaten by the locust were again restored to the tree. Just as many in Circles VII and VIII had believed that when the Lord had restored full salvation and holiness they had all there was for them, so now many who have received the baptism of the Spirit believed that they had all the Lord had for them. They conscientiously believed that once they had been filled with the Spirit and had spoken with other tongues, they really had all the Lord had for them, and they stopped seeking for more.

This, however, had not been all the church had lost, and was therefore not all that was to be restored.

CIRCLE X
The Years of the Palmerworm Restored

Just as the Father bestowed the gift of His only Son Jesus to the world and just as Jesus bestows the gift of the Holy Spirit, the promise of the Father upon the believer, so now in turn, the Holy Spirit has gifts to bestow upon those who receive Him. The nine gifts and fruit of the Spirit seen in Circle I are again being restored to the tree. Many blessed children of the Lord stop short at salvation and consecration and fail to receive the Holy Spirit. Also many who have received the Holy Spirit stop short and fail to covet earnestly the best gifts.

In seeking more of God's will to be wrought in our lives after having received the Holy Spirit's baptism, do not ask for more of the Holy Spirit, because if you have received Him you have received all of Him. He is not divisible. Either you have or have not received the Holy Spirit. Therefore if He has filled you and spoken through you with other tongues, as in Acts 2:4, pray that you may be more yielded to the Spirit who dwells within.

Someone says, "Oh, do not seek the gifts, seek the Giver." But beloved, if you have received the Spirit you have received the Giver, and Paul says, "Covet earnestly the best gifts. Seek that you may excel to the edifying of the church. Let him who speaketh in an unknown tongue pray that he may interpret, that the church may be edified. Covet to prophesy." There is a real, genuine gift of prophecy even though the enemy has tried to imitate it. Discerning of spirits is needed. Gifts of healing, and the other operations of the Spirit, should be in our midst.

In Circle X we see the fruit not yet fully mature, perhaps, but as we pray and yield ourselves to the Spirit, He will divide to each man severally as He will and cause the gifts and fruit of the Spirit to be visible in our midst.

Jesus is coming soon, coming for a perfect church, clad in power, in glory, for the perfect tree with every gift and fruit hanging in luscious mellow, developed perfection upon her branches. O let us wake up and press on to perfection! The winter is over and gone, the spring with its former rain has passed, the summer is passing and the latter rain has long been falling. The harvest is at hand and the Master is searching for ripened, developed fruit. Praise God for the roots and trunk of salvation. Praise God for the firm strong limbs and branches of holiness and consecration! Praise God for the green leaves, for the Holy Spirit, but the Master demands fruit from His tree these last days before His coming. Not green, immature fruit, but perfect fruit. He is whispering just now, "I will restore all the years that have been eaten."

Dear ones, there is land ahead to be possessed. Let the fruit of love be wrought in your life, with joy, peace, long-suffering, gentleness, goodness, faith, meekness, and temperance. Let us get back to Pentecost and go on to the fullness of Pentecostal power and glory recorded in God's Word, for Jesus is coming soon, very soon, for His perfect, waiting church, His bride, unspotted with the world, His tree with its unblemished and perfect fruit. Soon He will lift us up and transplant us to the heavenly garden where our leaves shall not wither, neither shall the fruit decay.

The arrow is almost to the top now; the hour when Jesus will burst the starry floor of heaven and descend, for His beloved is at hand. The great clock of time has almost reached the appointed hour. Let nothing hinder the work of preparation in your life. Let us beware that we quench not the Spirit.

Watch that we do not fall into the same snare which other people formerly used of God have fallen into: snares of formality, of coldness and organization, building walls about ourselves and failing to recognize the other members of our body (for by one Spirit are we all baptized into one body). If ever we put up walls and fall into these snares of formality, God will step over our walls and choose another people as surely as He did in days of yore. He will not give His glory to another, but will take the foolish to confound the mighty, the weak to confound the strong.

Press on therefore to perfection. Do not stop short of God's best. If you lay down your crown, another will take it up, the number will be complete, none will be missing, only those who have pressed on all the way to His standard will be caught up. If you have been doubting God, doubt no longer. He is waiting to restore all the years that have been eaten, and cause you to stand forth in that glorious perfect tree company, ready and waiting for Jesus.

Chapter II THE BIBLE BASIS OF THE FOURSQUARE GOSPEL

"Where do you get your doctrines? Upon what authority do you base your teachings?"

Foursquare people need never be nervous about how to phrase proper replies to such questions. From the beginning of the movement the Bible has occupied unchallenged preeminence as the one supreme rule of faith and practice. "Preach the *Word!*" has ever been the battle-cry of our witness.

ABSOLUTE AUTHORITY OF THE HOLY SCRIPTURES

This movement stands foursquare for the absolute authority of the Holy Scriptures as the inspired, inerrant, infallible Word of God. We resist wholeheartedly every effort to dilute this insistence with compromise formulas like, for example, the profession, "The Bible contains the Word of God!" We confess instead, "The Bible *is* the Word of God!" The Bible is the Word of God in its entirety.

Why can we not tolerate the idea expressed in the statement, "The Bible *contains* the Word of God"?

That proposition may sound innocent enough until you confront its application. To say the Bible contains the Word of God implies that it also contains portions which are *not* the Word of God. If you say the Bible merely contains inspired words of God, you suggest that it also contains parts which God did not inspire!

Now how could we decide authoritatively what parts of the Bible actually are God's Word and what parts are not—if the Bible did merely *contain* the Word of God? You might select a passage as inspired which another person would reject, and every man could become a law unto himself in accepting or rejecting any portion of the Scripture, if the Bible only contained the Word of God!

The book of Jonah is one of the portions of Scripture which many would like to dismiss as not inspired by God. The Foursquare attitude, however, reflects the position credited to Martin Luther. "The story of Jonah and the whale is so unbelievable," the reformer reportedly remarked, "that if it were not written in the Bible, I would probably not believe it. But since it is in the Bible I do believe it. And if the Bible said that Jonah swallowed the whale, I would believe that too!" Of course, the Lord Jesus Christ vindicated the historicity of the account of Jonah when He declared, "For as [Jonah] was three days and three nights in the whale's belly; so shall the Son of man be three days and three nights in the heart of the earth" (Matthew 12:40). Jesus evidently understood and interpreted the book of Jonah literally.

The Foursquare Gospel interprets the Bible literally throughout its pages, except in those passages which obviously communicate figurative significance. Where the plain sense of Scripture makes common sense, we need seek no other sense.

Moreover, since we embrace the Bible as God's infallible Word from cover to cover, we reject the growing modern tendency to treat the early chapters of Genesis, particularly the first ten or eleven, as mythology.

There are no myths in the Bible! There are no myths, though indeed there are parables and occasional allegories. But the context of the particular passages will indicate when a figurative meaning prevails.

So Foursquare makes no apology for its profession that the Bible *is* the Word of God. Accepting the Scriptures as inerrantly inspired from cover to cover, the Foursquare Gospel repudiates the various and constantly changing theories of evolution and proclaims our belief that God created the universe by His Word, that He created all vegetable and animal life to reproduce after their kinds, and that He made man in His own image and likeness, forming his body from the dust of the ground and inbreathing his living, immortal soul.

The name of the first man, thus, was not *Zinjanthropus* or *Gigantopithecus erectus* or any of the other polysyllabic scientific jaw-breakers coined by evolutionists. The name of the first man was Adam. God installed Adam within the Garden of Eden and provided him with a helpmate, Eve. In that inimitable environment humanity succumbed to Satanic temptation and fell. The fall of man there in Eden represented the greatest calamity ever to engulf our race.

Many deny the fall of man in the beginning, but how can anyone in our time who witnesses men fall again and again in everyday temptations and situations dispute the fact that man fell at the first, as the Bible relates?

There might never have been a Bible had sin not infiltrated Eden. God apparently communicated directly with man before the fall. However, transgression ruptured that relationship. While God occasionally revealed Himself more or less directly to men thereafter, His most usual method of communication after the fall was through appointed spokesmen—prophets, priests, and even kings, many of whom committed God's Word to writings which comprise our Old Testament. Then God inspired evangelists and apostles to produce the New Testament. About forty different authors penned the Holy Scriptures over a period covering approximately fifteen hundred years.

CHRIST THE PARAMOUNT THEME OF THE BIBLE

In spite of the variety of subjects broached in the Bible over the centuries of its divinely-directed compilation, one tremendous theme pervades the whole compass of the Scriptures. Jesus Christ is the paramount subject of the whole written Word of God! Remove Him from the Scriptures and very little of the Bible would be left. The Bible without Jesus would be like the Tower of London without the Crown Jewels or like the Louvre in Paris stripped of its Mona Lisa and all other celebrated treasures. If Christ could be taken out of the Scriptures, there would be better books than the Bible. But Christ cannot be removed from the Scriptures. He permeates its contents from cover to cover. In promise and prophecy, in type and shadow, in antitype and fulfillment, Jesus saturates the Scriptures completely.

His presence pervades the Pentateuch. In Genesis He is the seed of the woman who would in the fullness of times crush the serpent's head. In Exodus He is our Passover lamb. In Leviticus He is the great high priest. In Numbers He stands as the pillar of cloud by day and the pillar of fire by night. Deuteronomy anticipates Jesus as the prophet like unto Moses.

Christ proves preeminent also in the historical books. In Joshua He is the captain of our salvation. In Judges He is our lawgiver and judge. In Ruth He appears as our kinsman-redeemer. In Samuel He is our trusted prophet. In the books of Kings and Chronicles He is our reigning ruler. In Ezra and Nehemiah He is the rebuilder of the tumbled walls of human life. In Esther He is our Mordecai.

Jesus permeates the poetic books as well. In Job He is our ever living redeemer who inspires the confession, "For I know that my redeemer liveth, and that he shall stand at the latter day upon the earth" (Job 19:25). In Psalms He is the Lord our shepherd. In Proverbs and Ecclesiastes He is our wisdom. In the Song of Solomon He is our bridegroom. In Isaiah, He is the wonderful counselor and prince of peace, for Christ pervades the prophetic books besides. In Jeremiah He is our Righteous Branch, while in Lamentations He is our weeping prophet. In Ezekiel He is the wonderful four-faced man, the inspiration of one of our Foursquare emblems. In Daniel He is the stone cut out without hands who will smite to smithereens the world order of the last day and go on to become a great mountain and fill the whole earth in what we might call the "coming stone age" (cf. Daniel 2:34-35).

Minor prophets as well as the major prophets focus on Jesus. In Hosea He is the faithful husband forever married to the backslider. In Joel He is the dispenser of the former and latter rain. In Amos He is humanity's burden-bearer. In Obadiah He is the mighty to save. In Jonah He is the great foreign missionary. In Micah He is the messenger with the beautiful feet. In Nahum He is the avenger of God's elect. In Habakkuk He is God's prophet crying, "O Lord, revive thy work in the midst of the years" (3:2). In Zephaniah He is the Lord in the midst of His people. In Haggai He is the restorer of God's lost heritage. In Zechariah He is the fountain opened in the house of David for sin and uncleanness. And in Malachi He rises as the Sun of righteousness with healing in his wings.

Christians sometimes permit their preference for the New Testament to rob them of understanding the rich truths concerning Jesus' place in the Old Testament. But the Foursquare Gospel has never proclaimed a Christ more or less confined to the New Testament. From the ministry of the Founder to this day Foursquaredom has thrilled to the revelation of the Redeemer as enfolded in the Old Testament. This emphasis, moreover, actually echoes the claims of Christ Himself.

Jesus personally emphasized His own prominence in the Old Testament, a fact which contradicts any complaint that the recitation of Christ's place there is far-fetched. Christ conscripted the extremities of the Hebrew Bible as testimonials to His career. When He talked with travelers on the Emmaus road, Luke 24:27 reports, "And beginning at Moses and all the prophets, he expounded unto them in all the scriptures the things concerning himself." "Beginning at Moses"—Moses wrote Genesis. "And all the prophets"—the prophets concluded the Hebrew canon. "He expounded unto them in all the scriptures the things concerning himself." And some hours later He told His disciples, " . . . all things must be fulfilled, which were written in the law of Moses, and in the prophets, and in the psalms, concerning me" (Luke 24:44).

You cannot understand the Old Testament without recognizing its testimony to Christ. As T. DeWitt Talmadge put it pictorially:

> "Here is a long lane, overshadowed by fine trees, leading up to a mansion. What is the use of the lane if there were no mansion at the end? There is no use in the Old Testament except as a grand avenue to lead us up to the gospel dispensation. You may go early to a concert. Before the curtain is hoisted, you hear the musicians tuning up the violins, and getting ready all the instruments. After a while the curtain is hoisted, and the concert begins. All the statements, parables, orations, and miracles of the Old Testament were merely *preparatory,* and when all was ready, in the time of Christ, the curtain hoists, and there pours forth the Oratorio of the Messiah—all nations joining in the Hallelujah Chorus!
>
> "Moses, in his account of the creation, shows the platform on which Christ was to act. Prophets and apostles took subordinate parts in the tragedy. The first act was a manger and a babe; the last a cross and its victim. The Bethlehem star in the first scenery shifted for the crimson upholstery of the crucifixion. Angels applauding in the galleries; devils hissing in the pit.
>
> —"Christ is the Beginning and the End of the Bible" (Sermon, "The A and the Z," *Foursquare Magazine,* Dec. 1948, p. 8).

Of course, the New Testament far outdoes the Old in projecting the Lord Jesus Christ. His appearance in its every book is altogether obvious. In Matthew Jesus is the Messiah, the son of David and Abraham. In Mark

He is God's miracle man of action. In Luke He is the son of man and in John He is the Son of God. In Acts He is the baptizer with the Holy Ghost. In Romans He is the justifier. In the two Corinthian epistles He is our sanctifier. In Galatians Christ redeems us from the curse of the law. In Ephesians He shares with us His manifold wisdom and unsearchable riches. In Philippians He is the source from which God supplies all our needs. In Colossians He is the fullness of the Godhead bodily. In the Thessalonian letters He is our soon-coming king. In Timothy He is the one mediator between God and man. In Titus He is our faithful pastor. In Philemon He is our friend who sticketh closer than a brother. In Hebrews He is the blood of the everlasting covenant. In James He is our great physician, "And the prayer of faith shall save the sick, and the Lord [the Lord *Jesus*] shall raise him up" (5:15). In Peter's epistles He is our chief shepherd. In John's letters He is Love. In Jude He is the Lord coming with ten thousands of saints. And in Revelation He is the Lamb of God in the midst of the throne of heaven.

Thus the Lord Jesus Christ is the preeminent subject and theme of the whole written Word of God. But He is also in Himself personally the *living* Word of God.

CHRIST THE LIVING WORD

The term, "the Word of God," has two profound meanings. As expressive of the inspired, infallible written revelation, the phrase means a book—the Bible, the Book of books. As descriptive, however, of God's self-expression in the generation and revelation of His only-begotten Son, this term, "the Word of God," means a person—the second person of the eternal Godhead, of whom John wrote in the first verse of his Gospel, "In the beginning was the Word, and the Word was with God, and the Word was God." In some following verses the evangelist unveiled unmistakably the identity of the being he designated as the divine Word. The Word who existed in the beginning, who was with God and was Himself divine, is the person known to history as Jesus Christ (cf. John 1:17). Jesus Christ is "God only-begotten," as the original Greek text of John 1:18 has it, who reveals to men the nature of God which they cannot see in the flesh.

So Jesus is not only the paramount subject of the written Word of God, He is also in His own person the eternal living Word of God incarnate in human flesh. His existence did not begin with His birth at Bethlehem. Christ could truthfully claim, "Before Abraham was, I am" (John 8:58). He could recall in the days of His flesh the glory which He had shared with the Father in His preexistent state "before the world was" (John 17:5).

No system of faith can remain sound if it strays at all from the Scripturally revealed truth concerning the person of Christ. Here heresy first reared its ugly head to torment and threaten the early church, and here truth conquered in the historic church's confessions. At the very heart of the Foursquare Gospel is the Christ of the Bible.

The Bible presents Jesus Christ as the God-man. Theologians have split hairs defining positions, doctrines, and interpretations, but until recent undermining of the historic Christian faith by modernism, liberalism, and so-called neo-orthodoxy, the whole church—Protestant, Catholic, and Orthodox—the whole church has stood virtually unanimous in her understanding of the person of Christ. Jesus Christ is very God. And Jesus Christ is very man. These two complete and perfect natures unite in His one person.

Basically, most heresy concerning the person of Christ arises from either denial of or overemphasis or neglect of one or the other of the two natures of Christ, His perfect humanity and His inherent deity.

Martin Luther's comment concerning John 1:1 was most intriguing: " 'The Word was with God' is against

Sabellius," Luther declared, "And 'the Word was God' is against Arius."

Arianism and Sabellianism were names given to schismatic teachings concerning the person of Christ which in the early centuries threatened the orthodoxy of the mainstream of Christendom. Both these heresies survive to this day under different guises.

This is not the place for a detailed analysis or a polemical refutation of either error. Foursquaredom has always outrightly rejected both positions.

Arianism, which persists to this day in a debased form (Arius would be ashamed to be identified with the present posture of his theological position) in the "reduced Christ" of the modern liberal theology, overemphasized the humanity of Jesus to the neglect and ultimate denial of His unique Godhead. Quests for a "historical Jesus," as Schweitzer initiated, or for a "more believable Christ," as took Bishop Pike to the desert of Judaea, represent the survival in a debased form of this ancient heresy condemned by the church in the Council of Nicaea in 325 A.D.

Foursquaredom champions no reduced Christ, stripped of His miracles and "trappings of deity." Rather we recognize the real "historical Jesus" in the virgin-born, miracle-working, atoning and resurrected Saviour presented on the pages of the four Gospels of the New Testament. He is the wholly believable Christ whose message shook the world, as chronicled in the book of Acts.

No one can be sincerely Foursquare who denies or even faintly doubts the fundamentals pertaining to the person of Christ, His eternal deity, virgin birth, true humanity, sinless life, incontrovertible miracles, sacrificial death, bodily resurrection, or literal second coming. Bible-believers can confidently attend services at any Foursquare church in the world with the full assurance that not only will these facts be never questioned or doubted but also that they will be faithfully proclaimed and emphasized. There is not a single modernist or theological liberal holding credentials or pastorate or appointment with the International Church of the Foursquare Gospel.

Thus the doctrinal odyssey experienced by Earl Douglass in one of America's leading Protestant denominations could not conceivably happen in the Foursquare ranks. I mention Mr. Douglass by name because he subsequently confessed his error and repudiated his unbelief (cf. "Our Lord's Virgin Birth" by Earl L. Douglass in *Christianity Today,* Dec. 9, 1957, p. 7-8).

Douglass, as a theological student in 1917, faced with some misgivings an ordination board meeting of his denomination before which he was scheduled to appear. He hoped he would be able to evade affirming faith which he did not hold in the virgin birth of Christ. He rehearsed four reasons which he would plead before the presbytery as justifying his dissent. "I was quite sure, in my youthful confidence," he reports, "that once I had presented these four reasons to any group of competently trained men, they would see the inescapable logic of the situation and all further discussion of this controversial issue would probably cease and for all time."

Douglass had four arguments, but he managed to declare only one—the argument from silence, that is, from the silence of all New Testament authors except Matthew and Luke. "If the event were as important to Christian faith as many claim it to be, certainly all four evangelists would have mentioned it and without doubt other New Testament writers also," Douglass pleaded. Since none but Matthew and Luke alluded to the event, Douglass expected to be excused from accepting it.

But then an elderly minister arose and remarked, "The candidate admits, does he not, that these accounts appear in two Gospels?" "Yes, I do," Douglass conceded respectfully.

"Then in a voice which I am sure was plainly heard out on the street, and probably a block away," remembers Earl Douglass, "he thundered out, 'Mr. Moderator, how often does the Holy Spirit have to speak to this young man before he hears?' "

Nevertheless, Earl Douglass, despite his deviations from his denomination's doctrinal position, eventually obtained ordination. About fifteen years later his doubts fled and he declared, "I now believe not only that the virgin birth is true, but that it is an essential doctrine." However, candidates receive ordination in all America's historic denominations now despite reservations about or outright denial of essential doctrines like the virgin birth and deity and resurrection of Christ. And most of these clergymen stop far short of ever returning to the faith of their fathers. However, in Foursquaredom no minister may receive license or ordination who expresses the slightest reservation about any fundamental of faith. And this movement will always spurn any temptation to compromise our emphasis on the deity of Jesus Christ.

Arianism has never represented much of a threat to the orthodoxy of Pentecostal churches. The story is different so far as Sabellianism goes. In the early years of the Pentecostal renewal in this century that ancient heresy, now more familiarly known as "Jesus-only" or "Oneness" doctrine, almost swept some Full Gospel movements from their moorings. Nothing short of the providence of God in supernatural intervention stemmed the tide which seemed irresistible.

As Luther commented, "The Word was God" contradicted Arius, by vindicating Jesus' absolute deity. And "the Word was with God" contradicted Sabellius who denied the Trinity and declared that the terms Father, Son, and Holy Spirit merely represent different modes of divine manifestation. Sabellius refused to recognize three persons in the Godhead and admitted only one. Thus Jesus was His own Father, and the doctrine on that account was sometimes called *Patripassianism*, a word which means that God the Father was crucified at Calvary. In subsequent development Sabellianism came to teach that Jesus is all there is to God, hence the term, "Jesus-only."

It is understandable why this teaching assumed such attractiveness to Pentecostal pioneers in the first two decades of this century. The Holy Spirit who baptized believers glorified Jesus, and Pentecostal Christians welcomed any opportunity to express their devotion to Him. Sabellianism at the time seemed to ascribe to Christ all the worship which some believers mistakenly imagined had otherwise to be shared with the Father and Holy Spirit also, according to the Trinitarian formula. "Why not give all the glory to Jesus?" some enthusiastically proposed. And the Pentecostal movement came within a whisker of swallowing Sabellianism.

This was about the time Aimee Semple McPherson was just commencing her climb to prominence as America's leading Full Gospel evangelist. She was trying to steer clear of controversial doctrines which might jeopardize the appeal to the masses with her pure and simple gospel message. However, on this subject she could not remain silent. Thus she inserted the following notice on page 10 of the "Bridal Call" for July, 1918:

CONCERNING OUR TEACHING

> Several inquiries have come to us in our correspondence asking us as to the stand we take regarding the new teaching which advocates water baptism in Jesus' Name and denies the tri-personality of the Godhead.
>
> Now while we have always endeavored to keep away from controversy and doctrinal issues, yet we feel at this time that in justice to ourselves and to our readers we should make it very plain that after two years of prayerful study we still believe more firmly than ever in the Father, and in His Son Jesus Christ, and in the Holy Spirit as three persons, and

in water baptism according to our Lord's commission: Matthew 28:19.

Aimee S. McPherson

"The Word was with God" means that the Son is divine, that Jesus Christ is God, but that He is not all there is of God. Foursquaredom hails "God in three persons, blessed Trinity," Father, Son, and Holy Ghost.

So preeminent is the Lord Jesus Christ in the Foursquare faith that Dr. Howard P. Courtney could declare during an International Convention at Angelus Temple, "When you say 'Foursquare,' you say, 'Jesus'!" Now this speaker could not and did *not* declare that when one says "Jesus" he says "Foursquare." Such a claim would constitute the most outlandish bigotry. No movement has a monopoly on Jesus. No denomination or church has a corner on Christ. Or as the General Supervisor has sometimes put it, "We're not the only duck in the puddle, but bless God we're in the puddle!" What Dr. Courtney was emphasizing was the fact that one name is sufficient to describe the Foursquare faith and emphasis, and that name is Jesus! Said Courtney, "When you say 'Foursquare,' you say 'Jesus'! *He* is our message. Our message is Jesus, the Son of God, and if you tell the story correctly and dynamically, every illustration you give of what we believe within a sentence brings you to Jesus Christ."

Sometimes you hear the Foursquare Gospel capsulized as "Salvation, the Baptism with the Holy Spirit, Divine Healing, and the Second Coming," but that is not really the Foursquare emphasis. We emphasize not simply salvation but *Jesus* the Saviour, not merely the baptism with the Holy Spirit but *Jesus* the Baptizer, not divine healing but *Jesus* the Healer, and not the second coming but *Jesus* the Coming King. Our gospel is Jesus. Our message is Jesus. Our emphasis is Jesus.

Aimee Semple McPherson manifested many noteworthy talents but perhaps her greatest gift was her ability to exalt and glorify Jesus Christ and to make Him remarkably real to her audiences. Even those who opposed her often recognized this aspect of her ministry.

As a student at L. I. F. E., young Howard Courtney worked secularly in an establishment side by side with a notorious French atheist. The infidel delighted in tormenting his young colleague, and when he learned that Courtney attended Angelus Temple, the discovery brought out the very worst in the man. "You mean you go to that church and hear Aimee McPherson preach?" he exploded angrily.

"Indeed, I do," the young student replied, "And I like it there!"

The infidel waxed increasingly indignant. When his arguments failed to shake the student's faith, his face turned livid. His eyes blazed. His fists clenched. His lips went white, and he raved in rage, "All that I hear, and all anyone hears at that church is"—and he spat the next words in venom-tinged tones—"Jesus, Jesus, Jesus, Jesus, Jesus!"

Unconsciously that atheist may have articulated the most significant compliment ever paid to a preacher. Every Foursquare member and minister ought to aspire to a reputation as one whose words and life reflect Jesus!

The Bible is the basis of the Foursquare Gospel. Jesus Christ is the one supreme subject of the written Word of God. And He is Himself personally the living Word of God incarnate in human flesh. The Jesus we worship and proclaim is the Christ of Holy Scripture. The Bible must always be Foursquaredom's supreme rule of faith and practice. Nor does this dependence on the Bible represent a limitation. Rather it communicates enormous freedom!

Dr. Harold W. Jefferies listened to a critic complain, "Is it true that Foursquare preachers are restricted in their preaching to the Bible?" Dr. Jefferies replied, "Are fish limited to the seas? Are birds limited to the skies?" What would happen to a fish if it tried to swim up in the air? What would happen to a bird if it tried to fly under the water? A fish conceivably has the whole sea and a bird the whole sky. We have the whole Bible, and so long as we preach the Word and witness the Word and live the Word, emphasizing Christ's supremacy therein, that long will the Foursquare Gospel make an impact for God in the world.

Sermon

THE MARCH OF THE BIBLE

Upward! Onward! Yet ever outward—

Down through the years has marched the Bible. It is as a light that bringeth gladness, peace and blessing. It is like a lion in battle. It is like a judge upon a bench—its judgments are supreme and they are just.

It is like a king upon a throne with a scepter outheld to all who will believe and touch; like a mighty two-edged sword in conquest, bringing triumph and blessing. It is like a captain in battle, leading forth the hosts to certain victory; yet it is like a mother with her babe, giving strength, support and love. It is the living water, the bread of life, the honey in the comb—sweet to the taste. It is the document of the King concerning our pardon and is sealed with the crimson seal of the Court of Heaven.

The Bible—you have one, haven't you? Perhaps it's in the bottom of your trunk or on the top of the dresser; perhaps you have it on the parlor table where everyone will see it, especially the preacher when he comes to call; but you don't use it quite as much as you should. Mayhap you have the marriages, births, and deaths written in it, but it remains rather startlingly new and has no little round spots on it where your tears have fallen or where your lips were pressed in praise upon its sacred pages.

How wonderful is this Book of books—the Word of the Living God! Sometimes we scarcely appreciate it when we pick it up, put it under our arm and carry it along to church, go home and throw it down again. Yet, it is so precious thousands have died for it.

To some of us it is merely a book of two Testaments—the old and the new. We know that the Old Testament was under the law, and the New Testament was under grace; that in the Old Testament Christ is enfolded and in the New Testament Christ is unfolded; that Christ is in the old contained and by the new explained; but we really know very little of how it came to us.

Yet we have an awe and reverence for it, for we have seen the three great outstanding sentinels that guard the Bible, just as stern, grim and straight as any sentinel that ever guarded the palace of a king, or the crown jewels of any monarch. These three sentinels stand, one at the beginning, one in the middle, and one at the close of the dear old Bible. If we come near with the scissors of higher criticism, of modernism, of atheism, or anything that would destroy the Bible or cut away one part of it, they instantly lift up warning voices and sternly command,

"HANDS OFF! HANDS OFF!"

The first of these sentinels is Moses, who said:

"Thou shalt not add unto the Word, I command you, neither shalt thou diminish it."

The second sentinel who stands in the middle is Solomon, who cries:

"Add not to these words nor take therefrom."

The last sentinel is John, the Beloved, who speaks to us in Revelation 22:18-19, declaring that if we take from the Word of God there will be taken from us the right to that celestial City; and if we add thereto, there shall be added to us all the plagues contained in the Bible.

Wonderful Book! It has come down to us through the writings of some forty penmen who gave to us from God this message of life. It was penned on the mountain top, in the valley, in the shepherd's tent, upon the throne of kings. It was written under God's instruction by the rich and the poor, the poet, and the captain of armies, by legislators, philosophers, emperors, sages, judges and rulers. The high and the lowly helped to pen this wonderful Book in various places and circumstances from the brilliantly lighted palace to the deep, dark dungeon where was only the flickering of a candle in the midnight watches.

God had originally intended, you know, to talk face-to-face with man. When Adam was in the Garden of Eden God was wont to come in the cool of the day and walk with him, and talk to him as a man talked to his friend. But when sin came there was fixed a great gulf 'twixt God and man. As sin increased the breach grew wider and wider. Then it was that God decided to send a letter—a letter from the King to His subjects, from the Father to His children, from the Saviour of men to poor, lost sinners.

One day God spoke to Moses and bade him come to Mount Sinai that through him He might speak to the people.

In that trysting place, on the mountain, hidden in the cleft of the rock, Moses met his Maker. God was to come and bring with Him the first part of His Word, written on tables of stone. As Moses waited, listening, methinks he heard the tramp, tramp, tramp! of God's feet coming over the mountains, stepping from peak to summit and from mountain spiral to smoking hilltop. The whole mountain was covered, as it were, with smoke and there were thunders and lightnings. None of the thousands standing below dared stretch their fingers out to touch the mountainside as God communed here with Moses and gave him His first Word on the great tables of stone.

Down below at the foot of the mountain stood the people, waiting for the first division of God's wonderful letter to mankind.

Moses came down. The people listened for the sound of his footsteps. There they were—tramp, tramp, tramp! the marching of God's Word.

Receiving it gladly, the people began to pore over it

and to think and meditate upon it. They carried it with them wherever they went. The Ark of the Covenant was builded at God's command, and within it was placed God's Holy Word.

So it was that the Bible began its march around the world. Wherever the children of Israel journeyed, they took the Ark of the Covenant with them. Wherever the Word of God was borne, enemies fell back before them. Whenever God's Word rested, the angels hovered over the Mercy Seat, there the Shekinah glory did abide.

They carried it under Joshua's command, and stood one day at the edge of the flowing banks of the Jordan, bearing with them the Ark of the Covenant containing the precious Word upon those tables of stone.

"O rivers, part! O waters, be divided! Hither we bring God's Word!"

Tramp! Tramp! Tramp! The march of the Bible! No sooner were the feet of the priests touching the edge of the waters than they parted asunder and the Bible marched through triumphant.

Tramp! Tramp! Tramp! The people followed after, victorious, ever pressing onward.

As they journeyed, the walled city of Jericho arose before them, but in their hands they carried the precious Ark. The city defied them because its walls were mighty—so mighty that houses were builded upon the top of them.

"You will never capture our city," the people jeered. "You are defenseless. You have no weapons."

"Ah, but we have a weapon. We bring with us the Word of God!" they replied.

God's Word swept onward! They marched round the city seven times, and the walls fell flat.

How they treasured it! God opened the heavens and spake to holy men and they did write as they were inspired by Jehovah, word by word as He gave it to them. Added to the tables of stone was the Pentateuch, the books of Moses. Thus on through the centuries came the march of the Bible!

There was Eli, who kept the lamp burning night after night that there should never be darkness where the Word of God was kept. There was little Samuel, who helped him care for the light.

Then came the heart-breaking day when the Ark of the Covenant was stolen and with the Word of God contained in it, was carried away into the enemy's camp. When Eli received word of this he fell, his neck brake and he lay dead. He loved it so he could not bear the thought of God's Word falling into the hands of the enemy.

O Eli! Eli! Little did you realize that was only the beginning of it; that the dear Word of God, added to by the prophets, by the teachings of our Lord Jesus Himself and by the apostles through the years, should many times fall into the hands of the enemy, should be sunk into the deepest sea, should be burned in blazing furnaces, should be torn page from page and scattered to the winds.

Poor Eli! He thought he must defend the Bible and die if it fell into the enemy's hands; but this is the Book that cannot be destroyed. Glory to God! When it was taken into the enemy's camp and the Ark put before the great god of stone called Dagan, methinks the Shekinah glory of the Lord shone round about the Ark and Dagan fell and lay prostrate upon his face; for before the God of the Bible every mountain and rock shall some day bow and every tongue shall confess that He is the Lord indeed.

They picked up old Dagan and the next night he fell again and this time his old head broke and fell off and rolled over to lay by the side of the Ark of the Covenant that contained the precious Word of God.

"We can't keep this thing here," they said. "It will kill all of us. This is too mighty for us to keep in the camp of the unbeliever. Take it out of here."

So onward went the Bible until it came to rest at a certain threshing floor. The blessing and the glory of the Lord was upon that place.

David heard of it and said, "We must bring it and restore it to its rightful place in the tabernacle."

So with singing, music, dancing, choirs, auxiliary choirs, officers, rulers, and captains they went out, picked up the Ark, bore it upon their shoulders, and again came the triumphal march! march! of God's Word. David went before, leading the whole procession and he danced, leaped, skipped and sang and the glory of the Lord filled the Temple.

Came those wonderful days when David wrote the Psalms, embreathed with the praise of God and of the Holy Scriptures. I can see him, the sweet singer of Israel, poring over the Word of God, hiding it in his heart, and then turning it into song, setting it to music and sweetening the whole land with its glorious melody.

Then came Isaiah, Jeremiah, Ezekiel, Daniel, Obadiah, Micah, Nahum, Habakkuk, Zephaniah, Haggai, Zechariah, Malachi. One after another, writing as God commanded and the Word was increasing in volume, still marching on.

It was not all accomplished with ease. Jeremiah was buried to his armpits in the pit of slime, but he arose with shining face and again wrote at God's command.

Then, after four hundred terrible years of silence, came the New Testament, the coming of Jesus Christ, His wonderful teachings, the Sermon on the Mount, and the thrill of His glorious Beatitudes and of His saving and healing power.

Following immediately upon the heels of the four Gospels came the Acts of the Apostles, written by Luke. Then came the pennings of Paul, John, Peter and others, writing oftimes in dungeon, sometimes in the prison: but the Word went marching on. God was revealing His Holy Word to one and to another, adding a third, a fourth, a fifth, a thirty-sixth and a fortieth chapter until the Word of God was at last completed and compiled, every bit of the writing corresponding one with another, not one contradiction any place whatsoever.

Then the Bible, completed, was to begin its trip around

the world. Up to that time men could not walk into a store as we can today, and purchase a Bible. If they wanted God's Word they must either hire somebody to copy it for them, or at least a page of it, or a special chapter, or they must themselves go and, in their hieroglyphics and with the papyrus they had at hand, start to copy laboriously. If you have ever tried to write even one book of the Bible through, you know a little of what it means to copy it, poring over it day and night, much of the work being accomplished in caves and dungeons for fear of those who would destroy them if they were found with the Word of God.

Oh, Wonderful Book! It had come now into its present state, being gathered together from the ends of the earth. The different penmen and writers were like so many carpenters who had each formed on a blueprint, as God had commanded, a certain part of a board or a beam; and when everything was brought together that which Moses had written and that which Isaiah, David, Solomon, Malachi and Matthew had written fitted together exactly and made a wonderful, living boat that could go sailing out like a great beautiful ship, white sails aglow, out upon the bosom of the waters, bearing each one who trusted in it safely to the ocean of God's deep and eternal love.

It met all kinds of opposition and persecution. No sooner was it compiled than the devil knew if that Bible, God's Word, was let to live and circulate through the country it would turn everything upside down for God as soon as the people should read and comprehend it.

So the devil sent forth his emissaries and those who marched with the Bible were seized, thousands of them were slain, some were crucified like their Lord, others were cast to the lions which, with great gaping jaws, sprang upon them, tore their flesh from their bodies and their bones one from another. Some were made torches —dipped in pitch and then lighted and burned through the night while the merrymakers danced, sang and played at Nero's garden parties.

Undaunted by adverse winds, by the persecution and fury of the devil, down through the years and through the centuries it could not be destroyed and the march of the Bible went on.

It came down to the Dark Ages, when it seemed that surely it would be destroyed and lost in the gross darkness that covered the world and enslaved the minds of the people. Men were still copying away with pencil and pen, but the progress was agonizingly slow.

Tyndale had it in his heart that some way must be provided whereby the Living Word should be brought forth at a smaller cost so that common people could afford to possess it for at that time they were paying as high as $876.00 for a copy of the Bible. Oh, that a way might be made for the people to have this precious Book instead of having to go into the catacombs, out into the deserts and into the caves and among the rocks to hear someone read a few verses while someone else stood guard lest the soldiers find them! If they could only have it in their own chambers and all read it for themselves, how marvelous it would be! I wonder if, today, we appreciate our Bibles as much as they who had to go through such hardships in order to hear its sacred pages read?

A brighter day dawned. The printing press came into being—one of the greatest discoveries in the world for Christ's people; and the first book to come off the press was the Bible.

Someone discovered what Tyndale was doing and he fled to Germany. There, in a cellar, he went to work. He and his helpers set up the type, all of which had to be hand-carved from wood. Page after page, chapter after chapter—patiently and anxiously they worked, scarcely pausing to eat or sleep excepting when their weary bodies demanded.

But it was learned that someone was preparing to print the Bible, and the soldiers were sent to scour the country until they should find and destroy the work and the workmen. Someone was untrue. The soldiers made Tyndale's guards drunken and they told the secret of the underground printing plant. This emergency, however, had been anticipated and a hidden tunnel made for a hurried escape should it become necessary. As the feet of the soldiers approached the door, Tyndale caught up the sheets that were printed, still wet from the press, fled out through the tunnel and to Martin Luther's home where, in privacy and seclusion, he was enabled to complete his wonderful work.

Then the great problem of distributing the Bibles presented itself. The Old and the New Testament were printed separately, the New Testament being made very small so that it could be easily concealed. Never mind how small and difficult was the print to read. If only the people could read it and conceal it long enough to get it into their hearts, the great work would be accomplished. Bibles were hidden in bales of cotton, crates of tea and other merchandise, smuggled into England and into the hands of hundreds of believers.

The Bible began to appear all through the country, here, there and yonder. The kings were enraged and the rulers gnashed their teeth and sent their soldiers through the country to search houses and whole villages and collect all the Bibles. These were piled in huge stacks and burned.

But listen! Through the crackling of the flames I hear it!

Tramp! Tramp! Tramp! It was the march of the Bible! God's Word was moving on. "Surely it was defeated with such great odds against it," you say.

No! Never! Have you ever seen a large stack of paper burn? Have you noticed how the pages go up and up, are caught by the wind and carried far away to fall into some distant spot?

That is exactly what happened to the burning Bibles. Lifted high by the winds of opposition they were carried far—only to drop on some printing press. Soon the whir and hum of the press was heard, and more Bibles were going out to the world.

October 6th, 1536, was the great bonfire when the Bibles were burned: but their pages were going flutter, flutter, to fall here and there, only to be caught, read, kissed and pressed to the heart. If His Word goes forth, it will surely come again, bearing precious seed.

It became an offense to possess a Bible or be found reading one. People were cast into prison, burned at the stake or worse if they refused to give up their faith and love for the Word of God. Others were torn limb from limb or tortured in unspeakable ways. Little children, ten and twelve years of age, laid down their lives gladly rather than fall out of the procession as God's Word went marching on.

Oh, I love it! When, in these times of peace, I see men dare to become higher critics and begin to doubt and blue-pencil this, red-pencil that or take parts out of the Bible, it almost makes my blood boil. I believe that Bible from cover to cover! Our fathers died for it! Let us live for it and let us preach it–the dear Word of the Living God.

On through the years there had been one series of martyrdoms. Then, in 1555, Ridley and Latimer sealed their faith by their blood and with their lives. These two had worked to send out the Bible. They had surreptitiously taken it to people's homes. They had passed it into hands as people stood in the stores, and those people had hurried away to their homes and read, while another guarded that they might not be discovered with the sacred page.

When Ridley and Latimer were to be led out to die, it seemed that the Bible was doomed. It seemed every demon in hell and all the rulers of the world had banded themselves together against it. But as those two stood by the burning stake, the flames already licking their helpless bodies, there came those wonderful words:

"Play the man, Ridley; for today we shall kindle a light in England that shall never be put out!"

Tyndale had been strangled and burned at the stake, but his last words had been, "Let there be light!"

Events moved rapidly then. Just one year to the day from the burning of Ridley and Latimer the Bible became an authorized open book in England. Throughout Great Britain people were free to print it, read it and tell the story everywhere. It always makes me happy to know that the man who was the means of putting to death those wonderful men of God who died so bravely, was the first man whom the king made to take a Bible, sit down and read the entire Book without stopping until it was finished.

"March! March! March!"

But the Bible must not stop in England, or yet must it stop in France. Though in France came the guillotine and a time of woe, yet the Bible never ceased its marching.

Seeking greater religious freedom, our forefathers came to America, this land of the glorious free, bringing with them on the Mayflower their precious Bibles. The Indians gathered around the campfire in front of their wigwams and listened to the story of Christ of Galilee who died that we might live. The red man laid aside his tomahawk, his scalps, and said:

"Tell me the story of the Man acquainted with sorrow and with grief, the Light of the World, the Prince of Peace."

Missionaries packed the Bible, translated into many languages, in their kits as they traveled across the ocean and carried it to the far-off lands.

The Bible knows no bounds of white, black or yellow–rich or poor. It is to be found in the hovel and in the mansion. In his igloo of ice and snow the Eskimo pores over its glistening pages by the light of his tallow lamp. The black man in his African hut laid aside his weapons of murder and cannibalism; and his oiled face shone the brighter as he heard the story of the God who lives and the Saviour who loves him. In China and in Japan the yellow man heard the story. It was carried to Turkey and to Afghanistan, Norway, Sweden, Denmark and round about the world.

The sun never sets on its gleaming pages! Thank God! Wherever it marched and wherever it was planted that Book became a torch that flamed and blazed and cast its light o'er the darkened land. Wonderful Bible! Gift of God and Lamp of Light!

"We will stop the march of the Bible!" infidels and atheists have cried. Tom Payne, Ingersoll, Darwin and others have said that it could not live. Some infidels have said that it was dying—that men were too intelligent to read the Bible and that within a hundred years it would be in the morgue. The men who said that are in the grave now themselves, but the Bible goes on. Hallelujah! It shall never die!

Now Bibles are being printed wholesale. As you read this the Bible is being circulated. The printing presses are whirring and humming, turning out more Bibles for circulation.

The American Bible Society alone, from 1816 to the present day, has not only printed but has distributed 158 million copies of the Bible in 152 languages.

It has been burned, torn, buried, but it has been resurrected. You and I must be living epistles for this dear Word of God. We must hide it in our hearts.

Dear old Bible! It is an all-man's Book. What its march through the ages has meant to all mankind! It is the Book that the poor and ignorant may read and understand. It is the rich man's Book, telling him how to be converted and how impossible it is for him to enter through the narrow gate unless he is born again.

It is the Book for the learned. In it they will find astronomy, chemistry, civics, information on international questions, art, architecture and working in metals. Though so simple that a child may understand and fool need not err therein.

O wonderful Book! Infallible Book! Courageous Book! Indomitable Book! Sink it in the bottom of the sea and it will come up encrusted with pearls. Crush it and, like a diamond broken with a hammer, each little particle will sparkle, gleam and glow in myriad pieces where before it was but one. Tear it apart, scatter its pages to the winds—immediately it will take unto itself wings of a dove or the pinions of a mighty gull, and sweep on across the ocean to drift into the hearts of men and women everywhere with its message of hope, light, life and comfort.

The Bible is a mighty white ship sailing down the Amazon with spotless sails flying. At every bend of the stream little boys with gaily-painted cheeks, bows and arrows in hand, come out and cry:

"Great ship, go back! We will shoot you through with our little arrows!"

But the ship goes calmly by, answering never a word. The little arrows strike its glistening sides and fall, shattered into a thousand pieces, into the river, while the stately vessel sails on.

It stands as a man riddled with a thousand bullets, yet unscathed. It is a man who has been poisoned a thousand ways, but has never been contaminated or hurt thereby—he stands sweet, pure and noble—yea, stronger than ever before.

In my hand I hold a Book—rather a worn Book in a leather binding, that I can bend—a Book that is slim and beautiful with gilt-edged pages—a Book that is the greatest treasure in this world, given by God to man.

Many a time, without realizing my actions, I have caught it to my heart and pressed it just a little closer. In the night when I lay me down to sleep my Bible is never far from me—either under my pillow, the counterpane or on a table within arm's reach, that I may touch it in the night and draw it close to me when the day comes.

This Book is my partner, my counselor, guide, comfort, stay, my food and light. It is the Word of God—given to me, to you.

Will you love it, too? Will you prize it more? Will you hide it in your heart? American men and women, will you vote it back into the public schools? Will you take my hand and join hands with the one next to you, and will you pledge yourself before God to join the march! march! march! of the Bible, carry it with you and let it be an open Book?

Hark! Hear the tramp! tramp! tramp! It is going on and on, and when we go home to Heaven, when we go through the gates, hearts washed in the Blood of the Lamb, white-robed, radiant-faced, victory-crowned, we will still hear it leading us—Tramp! Tramp! Tramp! We will be marching with it, its vanguard. It will go to the Throne, and then we will make a wonderful discovery—that the Lamb Himself has enbreathed it and lives in it, walks in it, speaks from it—it is the very Word of God.

Hallelujah! It lives in my heart! I wish I knew it better. I wish I could memorize it from cover to cover. I wish I could read it through once a day. You won't find many pages in my Bible but have marks or tear stains upon them. I love it. It is God's Word.

Thank God for you, dear old Bible! Thank God for what you mean! May we who live in the twentieth century, who can pick You up without fear of being thrust through with a spear or burned at stake, never forget how You came to us and how You were purchased at such a price. May we ever hear ringing and reiterating in our ears the tramp! tramp! tramp! of your feet down through the centuries. You came through blood, You came through floods, You came through torrent, through flame and through conquest; but You came to us intact, with every word there!

We love You, dear old Bible!

PART TWO THE CARDINAL DOCTRINES

chapter one

JESUS CHRIST THE SAVIOUR
SERMON: THE SCARLET THREAD

chapter two

JESUS CHRIST THE BAPTIZER
SERMONS: THE BAPTISM OF THE HOLY GHOST
THE GIFTS OF THE HOLY SPIRIT
WHAT ABOUT THESE MANIFESTATIONS?

chapter three

JESUS CHRIST THE HEALER
SERMON: THE HEALING CUP

chapter four

JESUS CHRIST THE COMING KING
SERMON: THE WEDDING IN THE AIR

Chapter I JESUS CHRIST THE SAVIOUR

A guide in London's Westminster Abbey frowned with annoyance. The elderly woman he was conducting through the celebrated precincts seemed manifestly unimpressed. He pointed out the architectural glories of the edifice. He rhapsodized about its striking appointments. He waxed eloquent in lauding the stained-glass windows. Any other tourist would have drooled at his descriptions, but this particular American seemed strangely indifferent to the lecture. This prompted the guide to redouble his efforts to praise the place, but it was all to no avail. Eventually the woman interrupted his enthusiastic remarks with the observation, "That is all very well, but has anybody been saved here lately?"

Foursquaredom boasts beautiful buildings, though none may be so splendid as Westminster Abbey. The glory of our movement, however, is not in real estate and architecture, but rather in the temples of the Holy Ghost which God has erected in the lives of men, women and children who have exercised faith in our gospel and received the Lord Jesus as their own personal Saviour. The conversion of sinners to Christ accomplishes the purpose of Christian preaching and witness as enunciated by none other than Jesus Himself in the Great Commission: "Go ye into all the world, and preach the gospel to every creature. He that believeth and is baptized shall be saved; but he that believeth not shall be damned" (Mark 16:15-16).

The first and foremost phase, therefore, of the Foursquare Gospel is Jesus Christ the Saviour, the *only* Saviour offering any genuine hope to lost mankind. "Neither is there salvation in any other," proclaimed the apostle Peter, "for there is none other name under heaven given among men, whereby we must be saved" (Acts

4:12). Christ Himself enunciated the identical exclusive claim when He announced, "I am the way, the truth, and the life: no man cometh unto the Father, but by me" (John 14:6). A few days earlier He had said, "I am the door of the sheep" (John 10:7). "I am the door: by me if any man enter in, he shall be saved" (John 10:9). "He that entereth not by the door into the sheepfold, but climbeth up some other way, the same is a thief and a robber" (John 10:1).

Jesus Christ is the only Saviour, and salvation represents the greatest project God ever initiated.

SALVATION–GOD'S GREATEST UNDERTAKING

Contrast the divine exertion expended for creation and redemption! To create God had only to speak. "By the word of the Lord were the heavens made; and all the host of them by the breath of his mouth" (Psalm 33:6). "Through faith we understand that the worlds were framed by the word of God, so that things which are seen were not made of things which do appear" (Hebrews 11:3). When God commanded, "Let there be light," there was light (Genesis 1:3). When God commanded the earth to bring forth plants, vegetation appeared. To create the star-studded reaches of measureless space, the whirling galaxies and island universes which spangle the skies even far beyond the reach of our most powerful telescopes, to create this earth and all that is therein, God had only to speak! But to redeem He had to suffer!

God could create this world with a word, but He could not save the world with a word. He could make man a living soul by His breath, but He had to save him by His blood! God suffered no sacrifice in creating. Compared to salvation, creation was a simple project! The greatest thing God ever did was to give His only begotten Son as an expression of His love for the world with the effect that whosoever believes on Jesus shall not perish but have everlasting life (John 3:16). Even in the eternity future God will delight to glory in this provision of a Saviour, for St. Paul exults that God saves sinners in order "That in the ages to come he might shew the exceeding riches of his grace in his kindness toward us through Christ Jesus" (Ephesians 2:7).

The sending of a Saviour occupies the mind of God from eternity to eternity, in the eternity past as well as in the eternity future. John the Revelator beheld "the Lamb slain from the foundation of the world" (Revelation 13:8), while St. Peter extolled Jesus as a "lamb without blemish and without spot: Who verily was foreordained before the foundation of the world, but was manifest in these last times for you" (I Peter 1:19-20). The first promise God gave man in time, moreover, anticipated the coming of Christ to redeem! David may well have overheard, as A. E. Mitchell suggested in "The Philosophy of the Cross" (volume 2, page 23), the conversation between God the Father and God the Son when the preincarnate Christ accepted the commission to become the world's Saviour, for the psalmist quotes Him as saying, "Lo, I come: in the volume of the book it is written of me, I delight to do thy will, O my God" (Psalm 40:7-8; cf. Hebrews 10:7).

The need for a Saviour was occasioned, of course, by Adam's fall in the Garden of Eden. The sin of mankind's pristine parents involved not only themselves in iniquity beyond human repair but infected all their descendants as well. "By one man sin entered into the world, and death by sin; and so death passed upon all men, for that all have sinned" (Romans 5:12). Every man born on earth of normal generation not only becomes a sinner by practice but is brought forth also as a sinner by nature. What David confessed of himself is true of us all: "Behold, I was shapen in iniquity; and in sin did my mother conceive me" (Psalm 51:5). The natural man is born "dead in trespasses and sins" (Ephesians 2:1) and finds himself by nature a child of wrath (cf. Ephesians 2:3).

This sinful nature, transmitted universally to all by birth, erupts into universal sinful practice. No one in his right mind would contradict Solomon's observation, "there is no man that sinneth not" (I Kings 8:46). Everyone must agree with the apostle Paul that "all have sinned, and come short of the glory of God" (Romans 3:23). Any who entertain doubts about this issue stand in disagreement with Almighty God Himself, for the psalmist reports, "The Lord looked down from heaven upon the children of men, to see if there were any that did understand, and seek God" (Psalm 14:2). What were the results of this divine investigation? Here is God's verdict: "They are all gone aside, they are all together become filthy: there is none that doeth good, no, not one" (Psalm 14:3).

The sense of sin pervades human thought even where the gospel has never penetrated. Savages propitiate rude fetishes hoping to escape the consequences of acknowledged guilt. Missionaries rarely encounter difficulty convincing natives of their sinfulness, though they may experience resistance to the remedy for sin they proclaim.

In all Jacob Chamberlain's years in India, this missionary only once met a man who denied his sinful state. One evening as Chamberlain declared to his audience the universal sinfulness of mankind, a Brahman, a member of Hinduism's highest caste, interrupted him. "I deny your premise," the Brahman shouted. "*I* am not a sinner!" Chamberlain hardly knew how to react to the disturbance. He feared lest the interruption dissuade some penitents from confessing Christ as Saviour at the close of the meeting. He breathed a silent prayer for help. Almost unconsciously there escaped from his lips the question, directed toward the Hindu, "But what do your neighbors say?"

Some of the man's neighbors were present. They did not hesitate to bear witness concerning the Brahman's character. "He cheated me at trading horses!" blurted one neighbor indignantly. Another stabbed a forefinger in the direction of the high-caste Hindu and accused, "He defrauded a widow of her inheritance!" As additional charges were aired, the professedly sinless Brahman rose and stormed out of the meeting, never to return again to the mission.

"That," remarked Jacob Chamberlain, "was the only time I ever heard a man in India deny that he was a sinner." Surely that incident vindicates I John 1:8: "If we say that we have no sin, we deceive ourselves, and the truth is not in us." The man who says he is not a sinner deceives himself. He does not deceive others. And most assuredly he cannot deceive God. Isaiah confessed for us all when he acknowledged, "But we are all as an unclean thing, and all our righteousnesses are as filthy rags; and we all do fade as a leaf; and our iniquities, like the wind, have taken us away" (Isaiah 64:6).

Sin is not simply a nuisance on the circumference of human life. It is not an insignificant trifle. Sin reaches to the very heart of man's nature. The heart—using the term in the spiritual sense the Bible attributes to it—is the center of the trouble. "The heart is deceitful above all things, and desperately wicked," God Himself complains in Jeremiah 17:9, "who can know it?" Men may not recognize it, but God knows. He continues, "I the Lord search the heart, I try the reins, even to give every man according to his ways, and according to the fruit of his doings" (Jeremiah 17:10). St. Paul expressed the same warning in Romans 6:23: "For the wages of sin is death."

Jesus also emphasized that the source of sinfulness is within man. When Pharisees suggested He defiled Himself by eating without ritually washing His hands, Christ proclaimed that defilement results not from what a man puts in his mouth but from what comes forth from his heart: "That which cometh out of the man, that defileth the man. For from within, out of the heart of men, proceed evil thoughts, adulteries, fornications, murders, Thefts, covetousness, wickedness, deceit, lasciviousness, an evil eye, blasphemy, pride, foolishness: All these evil things come from within, and defile the man" (Mark 7:20-23).

There is nothing—absolutely nothing—man can do in

and for himself to rid himself of this deep-dyed guilt. Man by his own efforts cannot even stop sinning, let alone atone for past transgressions. No cleansing agent of human invention can remove the stains of sin which God sees as "scarlet" and "red like crimson" (cf. Isaiah 1:18). God dismisses as utterly ineffectual every attempt to expiate sin. "For though thou wash thee with nitre, and take thee much soap, yet thine iniquity is marked before me, saith the Lord God" (Jeremiah 2:22). Moffatt translates the word rendered nitre in the Authorized Version as lye. Man is helpless to escape his sin and guilt. He desperately needs a Saviour, but no man can qualify to save himself, let alone others. We must have a Saviour who can do for us what we cannot do for ourselves and what we cannot do without! And only a Saviour will suffice!

The human race, to overcome the consequences of its sin, did not need a better teacher or a better example than it had. The world has never lived up to either its best teachings or best examples. The world required not a saviour who would merely say something or be something. Humanity's crying need was for a Saviour who would do something–do something effective about ridding sinners of their sin.

GOD PROVIDES THE SAVIOUR

God Himself proposed to provide just such a Saviour! No sooner had He pronounced the curse on creation in consequence of the fall of man than He articulated the first promise of the coming redeemer: "And I will put enmity between thee [the serpent] and the woman, and between thy seed and her seed; it shall bruise thy head, and thou shalt bruise his heel" (Genesis 3:15). If John 3:16 is the Golden Text of the Bible, as it is often called, may we not consider Genesis 3:15 as the Golden Text of the Old Testament? Here we have the first proclamation on the pages of Sacred Writ of the coming Lamb of God who would take away the sin of the world.

In the ensuing centuries God unveiled little by little His plan of redemption in promise and prophecy and in types and shadows, as graphically described in Sister McPherson's sermon, "The Scarlet Thread," which follows this chapter.

When Isaac wondered, as he climbed Mount Moriah with his father Abraham, where the victim of the sacrifice would be found, Abraham replied, "God will provide himself a lamb" (Genesis 22:8). God did, in the fullness of times, provide Himself as the Lamb for Calvary's sacrifice. He could not send an angel. He could not accept indefinitely the substitute preliminary sacrifices of sheep, bulls and goats. Only the death of His incarnate sinless only-begotten Son could satisfy the divine justice offended by human sin.

God as the offended party had the right to establish the terms of salvation, and a divine decree as old as human sin proclaimed, "without shedding of blood [there] is no remission" (Hebrews 9:22).

On the cross of Calvary the Saviour spilled His blood, thereby laying out a welcome mat on which sinful man might approach the holy God, for Christ made peace by the blood of His cross, and we are made nigh by that precious blood, made nigh to God! As Secker said, "We do not sail to glory in the salt sea of our tears, but in the red sea of our Redeemer's blood. We owe the life of our souls to the death of our Saviour. It was His going into the furnace which keeps us from the flames. Man lives by death. His natural life is preserved by the death of the creature; and his spiritual life by the death of the Redeemer."

At Golgotha Jesus Christ offered the one sacrifice for sin forever. In one effective antitype He consummated the redemptive purposes of God which had hitherto required constant sacrifices and offerings from the morning of time. Abel's lamb outside the gates of Eden atoned for only one man. The Passover lamb atoned for one family. The lamb on the Day of Atonement atoned for one nation. But Jesus Christ the Lamb of God atoned for the sins of a whole world!

Ken Chapman put it graphically when he said, "All the sin of the world can be taken and piled up until like a mighty mountain it rears its ugly head into the sky. It can be piled up until it reaches the throne of God. It can be painted with the midnight blackness of hell. It can be striped with the crimson of scarlet iniquity. But I can give you one sentence which will wipe it all completely away forever: 'The blood of Jesus Christ his Son cleanseth us from all sin' (I John 1:7)."

The blood of no ordinary man could have accomplished this salvation. George Bennard was not exercising poetic license when he cherished "The Old Rugged Cross stained by blood so divine." A saviour less than divine would have been like a bridge broken at the far end. But Jesus Christ was not a saviour less than divine. Titus 2:13 hails Him as "our great God and Saviour, Jesus Christ" (*Twentieth Century New Testament*, and other versions). St. Paul speaks of the "church of God, which he hath purchased with his own blood" (Acts 20:28). If words mean anything, the blood of Jesus is described by the apostle as God's own blood! Jesus is the Saviour from sin, then, not because of His teaching or example but because of His sacrificial bloodshed at the cross! Here God offered the most tremendous manifestation of love the universe will ever witness: "But God commendeth his love toward us, in that, while we were yet sinners, Christ died for us" (Romans 5:8). God provided Himself as the Lamb! God provided the atonement at His own cost!

John Newton of "Amazing Grace" fame was not the only man to hear an acquaintance object, "I cannot see the doctrine of the atonement in the Scriptures." But Newton perhaps gave the best reply, "I tried to light my candle the other evening with the extinguisher on it." A person reading the Bible but not observing therein the atonement must have on his mind an extinguisher of false doctrine or prejudice. As A. C. Dixon expressed it, "The atonement is the sun in the heavens of revealed truth. The types of the Old Testament, the ordinances of the New, and the teachings of prophet and apostle join with John the Baptist in saying, 'Behold the Lamb of God.' As the scarlet thread runs through all the cordage of the British Navy, so the atonement of Christ runs through all the teaching of the Bible." Foursquaredom can never neglect the truth of Christ's atonement, for the very first phase of our gospel is Jesus Christ the Saviour.

But how does a sinner appropriate salvation? Or are all men automatically saved as a result of Christ's sacrifice and atonement?

Universalism—the teaching that all men of all time are to be saved—is again fastening its octopus-like tentacles upon large segments of the professing church. The mission of evangelism, say some, is not to influence people to become Christians but to tell them that they already are Christians, so they should start acting like Christians!

One statement of Jesus Christ is sufficient to expose the falsehood of this idea: ". . . he that believeth not shall be damned" (Mark 16:16). If any man could be saved apart from appropriating the atonement of Christ's cross, then that cross was an extravagance on God's part. If God could save any man any other way, Calvary was a waste! But God cannot save any man any other way. "How shall we escape, if we neglect so great salvation"? (Hebrews 2:3). No one can escape if he rejects or neglects Jesus as Saviour! Dixon did not exaggerate when he exclaimed, "God's throne would fall if a sinner who refuses atonement should be saved!"

Only those who appropriate the salvation of Jesus Christ will ever find welcome in heaven. But how does a sinner appropriate salvation? How does Jesus Christ become one's personal Saviour?

SALVATION BY FAITH IN JESUS

John the Beloved put it this way: "But as many as received him, to them gave he power to become the sons of God" (John 1:12). How does anyone receive Jesus? The evangelist explained in the same verse, "even to them that believe on his name." The sinner receives Christ by believing on Christ. "Whosoever believeth in him should not perish, but have everlasting life" (John 3:16). "For by grace are ye saved through faith; and that not of yourselves: it is the gift of God: Not of works, lest any man should boast" (Ephesians 2:8-9).

Salvation by faith is not a mental attitude but a heart experience. Billy Graham warns that many people will miss heaven by eighteen inches, the distance between their heads and their hearts! Since sin infects the heart of human nature, salvation must disinfect, as it were, that center! Thus salvation is an experience, not an experiment, and not a theory.

William Jennings Bryan, the Christian statesman who three times was the candidate of the Democratic Party for the presidency of the United States—a man who more than once preached from the pulpit of Angelus Temple, grew impatient with those who tried to amputate experience from Christianity. Bryan waxed especially unhappy when a critic denounced all conversions as "religious spasms." Bryan commented, "He understands how one can have a spasm of anger and become a murderer, or a spasm of passion and ruin a life, or a spasm of dishonesty and rob a bank, but he cannot understand how one can be convicted of sin, and in a spasm of repentance be born again" (p. 45, "In His Image," New York, 1922).

Nicodemus couldn't understand that at first either. When Jesus told him he must be born again or he would never see or enter the kingdom of God, his mind could not immediately comprehend either the necessity or the nature of the miracle. But Jesus explained, and subsequent references indicate Nicodemus experienced the new birth. He accepted Jesus Christ as his Saviour. He received regeneration and justification.

The new birth represents the manward side of salvation, while justification involves the Godward side. In regeneration believers become new creatures in Christ. In justification God declares us righteous, imputing our sins to Christ and His righteousness to us. And once a sinner is saved, his new nature and standing with God should express itself in holiness of life. As Dr. Walter Mussen declared, "Jesus did not come to save us in our sins but from our sins. Christ did not break into the devil's corral and put His brand on certain sheep and leave them there." No, God has "delivered us from the power of darkness, and hath translated us into the kingdom of his dear Son: In whom we have redemption through his blood, even the forgiveness of sins" (Colossians 1:13-14). We are to walk as children of light. Thus Paul exhorts, "Wherefore, my beloved, as ye have always obeyed, not as in my presence only, but now much more in my absence, work out your own salvation with fear and trembling. For it is God which worketh in you both to will and to do of his good pleasure" (Philippians 2:12-13). A professing believer who is not working out (notice Paul did not say, "Work *for*" but to "Work *out*") fruit meet for repentance may have good reason to question whether God is actually working within him! Jesus declared, "Ye shall know them by their fruits" (Matthew 7:16). Jesus Christ as Saviour includes His work as Jesus Christ the sanctifier!

How highly heaven hails the salvation of a sinner is revealed by Christ's statement that an ovation of joy convulses the celestial citizens when even just one sinner repents! Salvation eclipses creation as the greatest act of God! No wonder God the Father ascribes to the Saviour Jesus Christ the "name which is above every name: That at the name of Jesus every knee should bow, of things in heaven, and things in earth, and things under the earth; And that every tongue should confess that Jesus Christ is Lord, to the glory of God the Father"

(Philippians 2:9-11)! And in heaven the saints will ever hail the Saviour, singing, "Thou art worthy . . . : for thou wast slain, and hast redeemed us to God by thy blood out of every kindred, and tongue, and people, and nation" (Revelation 5:9).

Years ago, in a foreign land, two brothers were caught stealing sheep. In accordance with the unusual justice prevailing in the area, instead of imprisonment the judge sentenced them to have the initials of their crime branded upon their foreheads. Painfully the brothers submitted to the iron. They were etched for life with the letters S T—signifying "sheep thief." One brother fled in disgrace, but everywhere he roamed he carried his shame. People would inquire the meaning of the brand. The other brother remained in his village. He heard the gospel and accepted Jesus as Saviour. He tried to redeem his reputation. In time he was accepted in the community as a worthy citizen. People forgot about his crime, and the practice of branding felon's foreheads passed out of fashion.

Decades later, when this citizen was an elderly man, a stranger happened into the remote village and noticed the brand S T on the former sheep thief's brow. "What do those letters mean?" the stranger accosted a villager.

"It all happened many years ago, and I have forgotten the exact details," came back the reply. "But I think those letters are an abbreviation for *saint*!"

Jesus Christ the Saviour certainly transforms sinners into saints, and even God Himself forgets their past misdeeds. Because of the certainty of Calvary God could promise, even in Old Testament times, "I, even I, am he that blotteth out thy transgressions for mine own sake, and will not remember thy sins" (Isaiah 43:25). The Foursquare Gospel glories in exalting the Lord Jesus Christ, who bore our sins in His own body to the tree, as Saviour. He is the only Saviour, but one Saviour is enough if He is able, as the Scripture assures us He is, "to save them to the uttermost that come unto God by him" (Hebrews 7:25).

Sermon

THE SCARLET THREAD

This was considered by some to have been the most impressive of all Sister McPherson's sermons. As it was given in Angelus Temple, great streamers of crimson were brought to the pulpit by white-clad Crusaders. Upon the completion of each point, those pertaining to the Old Testament were fastened to an altar on the platform and those connected with the New Testament were clustered together atop a glistening white cross. Hundreds of converts confessed Christ as Saviour at the close of the message and scores of them eventually entered the ministry.

From the first verse of Genesis to the closing words of Revelation there runs a Scarlet Thread. It is the Blood line of the Lamb, slain from the foundation of the world. What a beautiful, glorious theme! Surely every evangelist and minister in the world must enjoy telling this story, and what a privilege is ours in being able to witness of it.

Did you ever read the fairy story about the little boy and girl who got lost in the woods? This little boy and girl were going through a large forest where tall trees rose far heavenward, and they had to wind their way about. Fearing they would be lost, they took the bread which their mother had given them for lunch and scattered crumbs all along the way so that they might have something to guide them back. In the meantime, the birds came and ate up the crumbs and the children were lost. They would never have reached home if it were not for a kind friend, who rescued them and took them back.

The next time they went into the forest, they said, "We will have to take something that the birds won't eat." So they took paper, cut it into bits and scattered it along the trail. Surely the birds would not eat them. No—but when they came to find their way back, the winds had blown the bits of paper away. Again they were rescued and brought home by the efforts of a kind friend.

Once again as they were about to journey into the forest, they went to their mother's sewing machine drawer, took out a spool of red thread, and, after bidding good-bye to their mother, tied one end of the thread to the gatepost. As they went along, they wrapped it around first a tree, then a stump, and another tree. Then when it was time to come home, the birds hadn't eaten the thread, neither had the winds blown it away. Even though the sun was rapidly sinking over the western hills, they didn't tremble or become frightened, for they could see the scarlet thread guiding them from tree to tree and stump to stump through the gathering gloom. At last, under their searching fingers, the scarlet thread led them safely to the old gatepost and the next moment they heard their mother's voice and her welcome smile shone upon them.

We of the world are children lost in the mighty mountain passes of Life. The shadows are deep and dark. We have tried to find our way home by many paths but we have failed and become tangled and lost. Thank God! There is a Scarlet Thread which is attached to the throne of God in the Homeland far away.

This Scarlet Thread goes out through all the world. In the mighty forests of the earth, through the dark corridors of time, through the gloom and the shadows, even the sinner and the veriest unbelievers can reach out their hands and beside them they will find the Scarlet Thread. Grasping it firmly in their hands they may follow it home where the light is burning in the window; where the angels are singing at their returning and the Father's smile awaits. Hallelujah!

"What is the Scarlet Thread?" you ask. It is the story of redemption, of the Saviour who shed His blood for you and for me. If you take your red crayon and mark the references of it in your Bible you will find that you have a complete Scarlet Thread from the beginning to the end, and that it will lead you home.

We find men and women every day who are saying, "Be born again? What is that? I don't mean to be ignorant. In fact, I am not, for I could talk on science, education and learning, but why does one need to get saved? Why do I need to be washed in the blood of Jesus?"

Big, fine looking men say, "Why did Jesus have to die in order for me to be saved and get to Heaven? What is the idea? Why did He have to die for me to be saved?"

Why! Why! Why! We are so full of "whys." But we are going to try to make everything as plain as that Scarlet Thread which drops from the dome of the building tonight.

First, we must always go back to the book of beginnings. In the beginning God made His people sinless. He placed them in the Garden of Eden and there He walked with them day by day. But Satan, who had once been seated near the Throne of Heaven, but had been cast out because of proud and haughty manners, had never repented and now saw his chance to "get back at God."

He had always wanted to, but had never found a chance until one day when looking into the garden he saw Adam and Eve walking among the trees with God. Then he cried, "Ah ha, now I see how I may get even with God. He threw me out of Heaven and cast me down as a fallen star, but I see how I can get back at Him. He loves these children. They are the apple of His eye and He hates nothing so bad as sin."

Then in came Satan—tiptoeing along. His garments were all shimmering and shining with light as he approached Eve. In a voice all soft and enticing he said, "Yea, hath God said that the day ye eat of this fruit ye shall die? It is a mistake. Help yourself and eat."

Eve was deceived by this dazzling creature, the most beautiful of all the field, and succumbed to his pleasing manner. Immediately she touched the forbidden fruit;

she became disobedient, an unbeliever, and she realized it all as she ate the apple. Her eyes were opened, but as she was a generous sort of soul she immediately gave some to Adam, too. And then instead of him saying, "Eve, you are wrong," he just took hold and ate of the apple also. He, too, became a sinner.

God came once more in the cool of the day to walk with His children, but darkness had fallen in the garden. Man had sinned and was to be cast out because of his unbelief and hopeless despair. They had shut themselves away from God's smile. They had sold themselves to the devil. It seemed as though they were shut out on every hand with death facing them. Then God spoke and gave them a mighty promise. *The seed of woman should bruise the head that had bruised His heel.* In other words God promised that He so loved this world that He would give His only Son to die for us. Man had sold himself and was under sentence of death for "his you are whom you promise to obey" and "the wages of sin are death." God was a just God who could not look upon sin with the least degree of allowance. Even then they did not repent. They saw themselves naked and unclothed. They tried to make themselves a fig-leaf apron, but it was of no avail. Our own good works of usefulness will never cover us from God's eyes.

God left them for a moment and soon in the distance a little cry was heard. A little lamb had died at the hand of God. He took its life. The blood of the first thing in the world to die went streaming down and He took the skin and formed coats for Adam and Eve to wear.

This first shed blood was part of the Scarlet Thread, bespeaking that our own righteousness of fig leaves and excuses will not do, that through the blood of the Lamb we must put on the righteousness of God.

Cain and Abel, the sons of Adam and Eve, were once making an offering unto God. Cain had brought the fruits of the field, fruits and vegetables–the best he had to offer. The other came with the blood of the slain lamb, the innocent, spotless gift.

God looked down on the gifts Cain brought but He couldn't smile upon them for they were things of the earth, earthly. They would not do, for if our own good works would do, God's Son would not need to die for us. Upon an altar Abel made a better offering than his brother Cain, and God's smile came streaming down. He honored the little, white, soft, innocent lamb.

If the little lamb, laying there so prone, could but speak, it would say, "I am but a type of the Lamb of God which takes away the sins of the world."

Days passed swiftly by, and down in Egypt's land the hearts of the Children of Israel were hardened against God. Yet at the same time they longed to get back into the sunshine of His smile. Came the day when God told them that He would pass over the land that night and all the firstborn should die. He told them that if they would take the blood of a lamb, put it over their doorposts and down the sides thereof, that when He saw the blood He would pass over them. Hyssop, type of faith, was to be dipped into the blood and sprinkled over the doorposts and down the sides.

Dear Jewish friends, how can you explain what your Scarlet Threads meant in any other way?

Why was the blood put there? It was but a type of the door of your heart. The lamb that was slain is but a type of the Lamb of God.

The night on which the Lord was to pass through the country came, and darkness fell swiftly. It was deep darkness, too, very dense and black. We will picture a typical home that night.

The family have gone to bed. Almost in the middle of the night comes the voice of Junior. "Daddy."

"Yes, son, what is it?"

"Are you sure the blood is over the door?"

"Yes. Go to sleep. It is all right for I told the servant to put it there."

Silence for a little while, then, "Daddy, are you sure that the servant put it there?"

"Yes, he is a good servant and I am sure he put it there."

"But daddy, I can't sleep. You know it means my life. Do you mind getting up and looking to see if it is there?"

To satisfy the child more than anything else, the father gets up and looks. To his horror he finds there is no blood there. It is only five or ten minutes to the midnight hour. The father runs quickly and kills the lamb. The blood is brought and sprinkled upon the door. Then when the Lord passed over the land and the firstborn of the Egyptians were slain, that house where the blood was sprinkled on the door was saved.

When, at the stroke of twelve should the angel come to your door would it be well with your soul? If so, you can lie down in peace and safety.

One day a father and son were commanded of God to make a certain sacrifice and were on their way up a hill in obedience to His command. The father's name was Abraham and the son's Isaac. Abraham had been commanded by God to make the offering of his own son. The son did not know of this and on the way he turned to his father and said in a rather plaintive voice, "Father, here is the wood and here is the fire, but where is the lamb for the offering?"

Abraham answered, "My son, God will provide Himself a lamb."

What a Lamb! What a pure, spotless, innocent Lamb He provided in Jesus Christ!

When at last they reached the top of that hill, the altar was built, wood laid upon the altar and Isaac bound to it. Seems I can see him there now, tightly bound with the Scarlet Thread. Abraham lifted his hand, raising it high toward heaven. Although with a broken heart, he was determined to obey God, even when it took his dearest and best. Just as the hand was coming down, and God saw he was willing to do it, God said, "I see you love your son and yet are willing to do this for Me. But look you, Abraham. There in the thicket is a ram caught by the horns. Just put him in the place of the boy."

That ram took the place of Isaac; but how different it was with Jesus Christ. When He reached the top of the hill, and the soldier was ready to drive the spear home, there was no ram to take the place of Jesus Christ. There was nothing that could suffer in His place and the blow fell.

There are many other Scarlet Threads. Let me paint another picture for you. It is in the days of the Children of Israel.

Here is the leper. The dread spots of the horrible disease are covering his body. Realizing that death is facing him he comes to the priest for cleansing.

"O priest, look at me. I am a leper. Is there anything that will cleanse me?"

"Yes, indeed—the blood. Bring hither quickly two doves." Then the priest took the two doves, killed one and caught its blood in a laver. The Scarlet Thread that leads to Calvary was being formed. As the leper stood looking, the blood of the dead dove went dripping down into the basin. Then the priest did a peculiar thing. He dipped a sprig of hyssop down into the blood of the dead dove. Then he sprinkled it upon the live one, upon the leper, and up toward God. The priest then loosed the living dove and it went sweeping up, up, up on crimson pinions into the sky above. As the leper watched it go soaring up into the heavens, he was cleansed. Read the story for yourself in Leviticus 14:4.

This is a type of Jesus Christ. It always takes two of anything to represent Him. He is the dead dove and the living dove. He is the dead lamb and He is the living lamb.

Hallelujah! Jesus, our living dove, has spread His snowy pinions crimsoned over by His own blood and has ascended into the heavens to show Himself in our behalf before the throne of God.

Now comes the sixth Scarlet Thread in the Old Testament. It is found in the story of Rahab. Jericho's walls were to be overthrown. Death was stalking through the land and when she said, "How shall I escape when the city of sin is overthrown?" they answered, "There is only one way."

"I am a terrible sinner. My life has been spent far from God."

"Yes, you are a sinner but you can be saved if you will take a Scarlet Thread and bind it in the window," which she did.

I have been right down through that city and seen the remains of the wall. Rahab was spared and the little house in which she lived still stood because of the scarlet line in her window.

This old world is a Jericho of sin, wickedness and heartache and the soul that sinneth shall surely die and stand before God. There is only one way to escape. Bind the blood of Jesus in the window of your soul and when all else fails, He will never forsake nor leave you.

There are many Scarlet Threads running through the Old Testament, but I would like to bring you just one more. We read that as a sheep before his shearers He was dumb and opened not His mouth. "He was bruised for our iniquities and wounded for our transgressions." How glorious to know that it was Jesus Christ of whom Isaiah spoke and not of himself or some other!

Now we pass from the Old Testament into the New. The Scarlet Thread runs on and on. Jesus is born now. He is thirty years of age and ready to begin His ministry. John is baptizing in the Jordan when Jesus steps down to be baptized. Seeing Jesus Christ approaching he lifted up his eyes and said, "Behold the Lamb of God that taketh away the sins of the world."

That was really the passing from the Old Testament to the New. Jesus lived and died for His people. For three years He preached to them, healed them, cleansed and forgave them. He fed the multitude, calmed the seas, blessed the little children, raised the dead, cleansed the lepers, taught His disciples to go on with His work and when at last He was to die He distinctly said, "For this cause came I forth."

He didn't need to die. He could have backed down on His Message and compromised. Even that last night in Gethsemane He could have gone down to Jericho and passed over into another region beyond the Jordan. But no, He set His face toward Jerusalem. That night as He stood in the midst of His disciples, the fruit of the vine was there typifying His blood and He said, "Drink ye all of it. For this is the New Testament in My blood. Except ye eat My flesh and drink My blood ye are none of Mine."

They looked at Him in horror and could not understand, but we understand now. It was the Scarlet Thread.

Then came the dark shadows of Gethsemane. In anguish of heart and soul Christ was praying in the Garden for you and for me. He sweat great drops of blood, and they went dripping down upon the carpet of leaves on the floor of the Garden. Yes, that was part of the Blood line.

Events run swiftly now. He is taken by the soldiers before Pilate and shouts of "Crucify! Crucify Him" go out through the hall, resound through the corridors and echo out into the streets. Then He is taken to the whipping post and the lash falls upon His back, fulfilling the prophecy, "By His stripes we are healed." A crown of thorns is placed upon His brow and the blood goes dripping down.

He is taken up Calvary's brow. The hammers and nails are brought and the nails are driven through those beautiful hands and feet. From whence these bright red drops? They are working out the Scarlet Thread, that thread which leads us out of the wilderness of discouragement and unbelief to that place where the light shines in the Father's window.

The blood is dripping from His hands, His feet and

His brow, but the glory of the Lord is in His heart and He says, "Father, forgive them. They know not what they do."

Behold! A soldier is coming. He is one of the last of the threads of the crucifixion as he comes, carrying in his hands a great spear. He draws it back and plunges it into the heart of Jesus Christ, and we read that blood and water flowed and mingled forth. As the blood went dripping down onto the ground it formed a fountain in which the sins of all the world may be washed away, if we but believe and trust Him. The sky overhead grows black, and darkness reigns many hours. What is the meaning of it? Clouds cover the face of the sun, and a storm is coming. Thunders are heard in the distance. Lightning begins to flash. The sun hides its face entirely. In that awful hour the Scarlet Threads are being bound together at Calvary.

The mocking crowd below the cross didn't know what it meant. They knew it must mean something, but they didn't understand the real typological significance of it. Suddenly the light struck the place where Jesus hung, and He cried, "My God, My God, why hast Thou forsaken Me?"

Then His last words, "Into Thy hands I commend My Spirit." And He gave up the Ghost and died. At that moment the veil in the Temple was rent from top to bottom. Praise the Lord! it was torn away. The storm abated and the blessed cross shone on through the gloom and is shining yet tonight. Down that cross the precious blood of Jesus Christ was flowing—flowing into the fountain of an ever troubled stream where the sorrows of the world are buried and Christ is enthroned in the heart.

Hallelujah for the cross! There is power in the blood of the Lamb. It doesn't matter who you are or how great your sin, Jesus can wash you and make you whiter than the driven snow. See Him hanging there for you! Believe Him! Receive Him! Open your heart and say, "Lord, I will."

He gathered all those Scarlet Threads together at the cross of Calvary. They were lifted to the very top of His cross, and there was healing for this old sin-torn world, healing for body, healing for soul, and healing for the spirit. Yes, healing for the nations.

We sinned, but Jesus died for us. We were sentenced to die, but He died that we might live. We were condemned, but He bore our condemnation. Glory to His name!

Then they took Him away and buried Him in the earth, but He said, "Though I die, yet shall I live again." And on the third day He was raised from the dead. He stood upon His feet and came forth–Jesus, the glorified Lord.

When He arose from the dead He bore in His hand just one more Scarlet Thread. It was the glorious thread which He was to take to the Father's throne that we might have an anchor within the veil.

What does that last Scarlet Thread mean? It means that all the lambs, goats, bulls and heifers and doves; all the blood that was ever shed on Jewish altars could never wash man's sin away, or make the vilest sinner clean; but when Jesus died, the Lamb of God, He died once for all. He shed His blood and it is finished–glory to God. Everyone that believes Him and receives Him shall come into the family of God, shall become a newborn son of God and a brother of Jesus Christ. Hallelujah!

Jesus knew when He arose from the dead that we would have an accuser which would say, "You old rascal! You sinner! Look at that woman, see what she did?" He took the last thread and today He stands before the throne and shows His hands, His feet and His wounded side to the Father.

The old devil comes along and says, "Lord, look at Mr. Jones. He is without the fountain. He has turned you away for years. He will never be saved."

But up there beside the throne, Jesus is saying, "Behold My hands and My feet! Father, I died for that man. Spare him, Lord, and also that woman in her sins. If they just plunge beneath this crimson stream, their sins are gone."

One says, "Don't let that woman live any longer. She is fifty years old now and, I declare to you, this is the thousandth sermon she has heard, and with every sermon she turns Jesus down. What is the use of letting her live any longer? Snuff her life out tonight."

Then Jesus, still holding this last thread between heaven and earth, says, "But, Father, I died for her. Although she has heard one thousand sermons, and turned Me away as many times, let her hear just one more message—behold My hands and My side."

The Lord has spared you until this hour, and my message is almost finished. Take hold of the Scarlet Thread and let it guide you safely homeward.

You say, "I am lost."

That may be, but you need not remain lost. I don't know who you are or where you have gone, but Jesus Christ will bring you home if you will just let Him.

Sinner, backslider, professing church member without the real glory in your hearts, get hold of the Scarlet Thread. Millions have knelt at the foot of the cross. Your mother knelt there. Your father knelt there, and you must kneel there. You must find your way to the foot of the cross, for the way of the cross leads home.

Chapter II JESUS CHRIST THE BAPTIZER

John the Baptist in his ministry as the forerunner of Christ introduced the Lord Jesus both as the Saviour from sin and as the baptizer with the Holy Spirit.

One day John glimpsed Jesus walking in his direction and exhorted the people in his company to behold the Saviour. His exact words were, "Behold the Lamb of God, which taketh away the sin of the world" (John 1:29). Again the next day John, while standing with two of his disciples, pointed toward Jesus and exclaimed, "Behold the Lamb of God!" (John 1:35).

Earlier even than these encounters, however, Christ's forerunner had encouraged his hearers to behold the baptizer! Luke 3:16 pictures Jesus as such, even as John 3:16 portrays Him as Saviour. John the Baptist announced, "I indeed baptize you with water; but one mightier than I cometh, the latchet of whose shoes I am not worthy to unloose: he shall baptize you with the Holy Ghost and with fire." The other Synoptic Gospels present the same introduction of Jesus by John in almost identical words (Matthew 3:11; Mark 1:7-8). The Baptist proclaimed that Christ would take away the sin of the world and would baptize the converts with the Holy Ghost.

Shortly after John's presentation of Jesus, Christ commenced His public ministry. For about forty months He traveled back and forth through Galilee, Samaria and Judaea. He granted forgiveness of sin and salvation to penitents. He healed the sick. He cast out demons. He performed mighty miracles, stilling the shrieking tempest, walking on the water, multiplying loaves and fishes. But not once during this period of about three and one-half years did the Lord Jesus Christ baptize anybody with the Holy Spirit!

The time for His death approached. The authorities arrested Him. The Sanhedrin tried Him. Pilate sentenced Him to death. And Roman soldiers crucified Him. Jesus died without once performing the promise of the forerunner, "He shall baptize you with the Holy Ghost and with fire."

Of course, Jesus arose from the dead. Foursquaredom insists on faith in His literal, bodily resurrection. For about forty days after Easter Jesus continued His ministry on earth. But during those weeks, He still did not baptize anyone with the Holy Spirit! He finally ascended to heaven without fulfilling John the Baptist's presentation of Him as the baptizer with the Spirit.

Do you wonder why? Why did Jesus save sinners and heal the sick during His earthly sojourn, but not baptize anyone with the Holy Spirit? The incident described in John 7:37-39 furnishes the answer:

> "In the last day, that great day of the feast, Jesus stood and cried, saying, If any man thirst, let him come unto me, and drink. He that believeth on me, as the scripture hath said, out of his belly shall flow rivers of living water. (But this spake he of the Spirit, which they that believe on him should receive: for the Holy Ghost was not yet given; because that Jesus was not yet glorified.)"

The parenthetical explanation came from the evangelist's pen and not from Jesus' lips. So far as we have any record, Christ did not Himself explicitly discuss His eventual ministry as the baptizer with the Holy Spirit until the night before His crucifixion. But then He presented this truth at some length. He promised His disciples, "And I will pray the Father, and he shall give you another Comforter, that he may abide with you forever" (John 14:16). But Jesus would not only pray for the coming of this Paraclete, He would also have a part in sending the Spirit: "But when the Comforter is come, whom I will send unto you from the Father, even the Spirit of truth, which proceedeth from the Father, he shall testify of me" (John 15:26). "Nevertheless I tell you the truth; It is expedient for you that I go away: for if I go not away, the Comforter will not come unto you; but if I depart, I will send him unto you" (John 16:7).

As the moment of His ascension neared, Jesus reiterated the imminence of His entrance into His baptizing ministry as John had proclaimed. Moreover, He commanded His disciples not only to expect, but also to seek this experience: "And behold, I send the promise of my Father upon you: but tarry ye in the city of Jerusalem, until ye be endued with power from on high" (Luke 24:49). Mark quotes Christ as commissioning His followers about the same time, "And these signs shall follow them that believe; In my name . . . they shall speak with new tongues" (Mark 16:17), while Acts 1:4-9 takes us up to the very lift-off of the ascension and reports as Jesus' very last words a reference to this baptism:

> "And, being assembled together with them, [Jesus] commanded them that they should not depart from Jerusalem, but wait for the promise of the Father, which, saith he, ye have heard of me. For John truly baptized with water; but ye shall be baptized with the Holy Ghost not many days hence. When they therefore were come together, they asked of him, saying, Lord, wilt thou at this time restore again the kingdom to Israel? And he said unto them, It is not for you to know the times or the seasons, which the Father hath put in his own power. But ye shall receive power, after that the Holy Ghost is come upon you: and ye shall be witnesses unto me both in Jerusalem, and in all Judaea, and in Samaria, and unto the uttermost part of the earth. And when he had spoken these things, while they beheld, he was taken up; and a cloud received him out of their sight."

Jesus' very last words, therefore, coupled the promise of power with the purpose of power. "Ye shall receive power, after that the Holy Ghost is come upon you" and "Ye shall be witnesses unto me." Moreover, by brushing off the politically-motivated question of His disciples about the restoration of Jewish national independence, Jesus eloquently enforced the truth that the mission of His church was ever to be preeminently spiritual. This is God's will according to God's Word. The message of the church is the witness unto Jesus Christ!

Now as many as 500 disciples may have been present at the time of Christ's ascension to hear His encouragement to believers to expect the baptism with the Holy Spirit "not many days hence." Paul mentions that Jesus "was seen of above five hundred brethren at once" (I Corinthians 15:6). He does not tell us where or when that crowd met Christ, but some authorities suggest it may indeed have been at the occasion of the ascension. If this is true, the number of believers who actively sought the promised baptism was significantly smaller than the company which heard Jesus enforce the importance of the experience, just as today only a comparatively small minority even of professedly evangelical Christians obeys the same injunction to receive the same baptism! At any rate, after Jesus ascended from Olivet, about 120 believers descended from the same mount to gather in an upper room in Jerusalem to wait for the promise of the Father.

The company in the upper room represented the broad spectrum of Christ's followers. The eleven apostles were there. Women were there. Scores of believers whose names never reached the pages of the New Testament assembled with the more prominent disciples. As they waited, they meditated and prayed and even transacted business such as the selection of Matthias to replace Judas as an apostle. Days passed. And then it happened. No re-creation by modern author could improve the account of Luke:

> "And when the day of Pentecost was fully come, they were all with one accord in one place. And suddenly there came a sound from heaven as of a rushing mighty wind, and it filled all the house where they were sitting. And there appeared unto them cloven

tongues like as of fire, and it sat upon each of them. And they were all filled with the Holy Ghost, and began to speak with other tongues, as the Spirit gave them utterance" (Acts 2:1-4).

The Lord Jesus Christ had now, early on this particular Sunday morning in Jerusalem, begun baptizing believers with the Holy Ghost and with fire. For the first time He fulfilled the forerunner's forecast; but of course, not for the last time, for He has continued His ministry as the baptizer with the Holy Spirit to this very day!

Foursquaredom proclaims not only the experience of the baptism with the Spirit but especially the fact that this is a divine act of Jesus. We emphasize *Jesus* as the baptizer with the Holy Ghost! Peter declared Him thus on that pristine Pentecost of the church. When anyone receives the baptism with the Spirit, it is Jesus who baptizes him! Whenever this experience is repeated, right up to the moment of Christ's Second Coming for His church, the explanation Peter gave in Acts 2:33 will remain valid: "Therefore being by the right hand of God exalted, and having received of the Father the promise of the Holy Ghost, he [Jesus] hath shed forth this, which ye now see and hear." Jesus is Himself personally ever the baptizer with the Holy Spirit! This blessing comes from heaven!

In modern times people not in sympathy with the perpetuation of the Pentecostal experience, have suggested sinister sources for the present phenomena. Far too many churchmen imagine erroneously that we are offering strange fire on the altar of the church when we seek to rekindle the flame of Pentecost there.

Thus critics contrive pat explanations, presuming that Spirit-filled Christians work up what in reality believers have prayed down. One of the commonest charges is that the experience of the baptism with the Holy Spirit is induced by hypnotism! In that case, however, should we not investigate the question, "Who is the hypnotist?"

Who hypnotized seventeen-year-old Aimee Elizabeth

Kennedy? She was alone in a house in Ingersoll, Ontario, Canada, when the Lord baptized her at five o'clock in the morning!

Who hypnotized Paul Morris, pastor of Hillside Presbyterian Church of Jamaica, New York? He had commenced seeking the Lord to rid him from his briar pipe, and one night in bed he suddenly started speaking in tongues (cf, *Christian Life Magazine,* Jan. 1959, pp. 16-17).

Who hypnotized the present writer? His eyes were closed long before Sister McPherson stood in front of him to lay hands on him and declare, "Receive the Holy Ghost." How many cases of hypnotism can be cited where the victim had his eyes closed for the treatment?

If this experience results from hypnotism we must conclude that the hypnotist must be–and this is meant reverently–the hypnotist must be none other than the blessed Baptizer Himself!

But of course hypnotism cannot possibly explain the baptism with the Holy Spirit. So critics construe other suggestions to repudiate this miracle.

Some flirt with the unpardonable sin by denouncing this experience as a work of the devil. To this rash and reckless remark it is enough to reply that if such were indeed the case, then the devil certainly must seem to have become soundly converted! For the fruit of this experience–and Jesus declared that by their fruit ye shall know them–the fruit of this experience normally fosters increased love and devotion to Jesus and almost always encourages an intensified expectation of the soon coming of Christ, with resultant attention to the baptized believer's walk and witness!

Only one reasonable explanation exists for the Pentecostal experience, and that is that its cause is Christ. Peter proclaimed this in Acts 2:33. Foursquaredom reiterates it today. Jesus Christ baptizes believers with the Holy Spirit. This phenomenon originates in heaven at the throne of God.

Some have wholeheartedly agreed that the experiences described in the book of Acts were valid for the apostolic age, while questioning whether the church has any reason to expect them to continue. Others oracularly dismiss present phenomena with the announcement, "The day of all miracles is past for the church."

AN EXPERIENCE FOR ALL TIME

Now the Scriptures state that Jesus Christ is "the same yesterday, and today, and for ever" (Hebrews 13:8). He is still the baptizer with the Holy Spirit, as He is still the Saviour. However, the Bible puts the perpetuation of Pentecost not merely as an inference of logic but as an explicit pronouncement. Peter promised the penitents on the day of Pentecost, "ye shall receive the gift of the Holy Ghost. For the promise is unto you, and to your children, and to all that are afar off, even as many as the Lord our God shall call" (Acts 2:38-39).

Careful scrutiny of this scripture demonstrates conclusively that there is not a believer of any generation or location who is excluded from the scope of this promise.

To whom did Peter offer this baptism? To the Jew first, to be sure. "The promise is unto you, and to your children" extended the availability of this experience to every Israelite. But Peter widened the offer with the words, "and to all that are afar off." The expression "afar off", as applied to people, represented an euphemism employed by Jews to describe Gentiles. Jews believed they occupied a position nigh to God, while everybody else wandered afar off. Paul contrasts the terms "afar off" as indicating Gentiles and "nigh" as describing Jews in Ephesians 2:17. So in promising the gift of the Holy Spirit to "all that are afar off," Peter was promising this baptism to all Gentiles. If you're not a Jew, you are a Gentile. In any case, the promise is unto you. But Peter made the universality of this gift even more certain, by extending the offer to "even as many as the Lord our God shall call." That extension removes any doubt any believer might mistakenly entertain concerning whether this gift is for him. If God has called you to salvation, Jesus will fill you with the Holy Spirit. There is no statute of limitations on the promise. As long as God calls, Jesus baptizes!

MANIFESTATIONS PERSIST

The manifestations which accompany the outpouring of the Holy Spirit prove a stumbling block to some. This was true even on the birthday of the church. Mockers beholding the strange behavior of the 120 believers snickered, "These men are full of new wine" (Acts 2:13). Evidently the epithet "Holy Roller" can be traced back to the day of Pentecost! A veteran Foursquare minister, the late Arthur Goble, commented, "Even the devil has to admit we're holy, and I'd rather roll into heaven than stagger into hell."

While considerable excesses have plagued the Pentecostal movement from time to time in this matter of manifestations, the truth remains that when God works mightily through human nature, unusual phenomena generally accompany the divine afflatus. Charles G. Finney, whose writings suggest he was a nineteenth century "Pentecostal Presbyterian," offered this explanation:

> "God has found it necessary to take advantage of the excitability there is in mankind, to produce powerful excitements among them, before He can lead them to obey. Men are so sluggish, there are so many things to lead their minds off from religion and to oppose the influence of the gospel, that it is necessary to raise an excitement among them, till the tide rises so high as to sweep away the opposing obstacles. They must be so aroused that they will break over these counteracting influences, before they will obey God" (sermon reprinted in the *Prairie Overcomer*, Nov. 1953, p. 338).

The facts of history testify that there have been few,

if any, mighty revivals of Bible religion which have not witnessed unusual manifestations and even a tinge of wildfire. The proper attitude will never reject the genuine because the counterfeit appears. John Wesley used to pray, "O God, send us a revival without fanaticism if you can. But at any rate send us a revival." In order not to restrain that revival, the early Methodists put up with many manifestations which the most enthusiastic Pentecostal today would be likely to deplore. The mainstream of Methodism on the American frontier in the first half of the nineteenth century would make the wildest Pentecostal of today look respectable in comparison. Indeed, scoffers even coined an epithet to describe one of the features: "Methodist fit" was how they mocked at Methodists' emotional conversion experiences ("Autobiography of Peter Cartwright," p. 89).

Presbyterians had their problems with fanaticism too. Some Presbyterians more or less spearheaded America's first famous camp meeting, the historic protracted revival at Cane Ridge, Kentucky, in the early 1800's. Archibald Robertson, son of Louisville Baptist Seminary's celebrated Greek scholar, the late Dr. A. T. Robertson, wrote in his book, "The Old Time Religion," concerning the proceedings there:

> "At no time, witnesses have reported, was the ground at Cane Ridge less than half covered with the victims of religious experience. 'Some lay quiet, unable to move or speak.' For these, rescue squads, known as 'bearers of the slain,' were organized, to move them out of the way, where they would not be hurt, until they came to. 'Some talked but could not move. Some beat the floor with their heels. Some, shrieking in agony, bounded about like a live fish out of water. Many lay down and rolled over for hours at a time. Others rushed wildly about over stumps and benches, and then plunged, shouting, 'Lost! Lost!' into the forest. Many 'talked in tongues,' as at Pentecost. Upon some the 'holy laugh' descended. In the 'barks' the votaries fell upon all

> fours, forming groups which loped and gathered at the foot of a tree, yelping, barking, and snapping like dogs; this experience was called treeing the devil!" (Pages 50-51).

No responsible leader in the Pentecostal movement today would endorse many of those reactions, but the moving of the Holy Spirit proved mightily present at Cane Ridge, in spite of almost outrageous excesses. Archie Robertson gives an objective appraisal of the commotion at Cane Ridge which Pentecostals might well ponder in connection with whatever fanaticism we may encounter nowadays: "The mass hysteria which swept the great crowd in the forest was the wild foam on the surface of the oldtime religion, not the essence of the thing itself" (p. 52).

Now Foursquaredom holds no brief for fanaticism in any form. Our Founder pioneered the concept of keeping in the middle of the road, avoiding coldness on one hand and wildfire on the other. Nevertheless, experience shows that it is almost always easier to restrain a fanatic than to resurrect a corpse. Fanaticism has not hindered the progress of the Christian faith nearly so much as formalism and coldness, especially since what man calls dignity in religion ritualism often proves only a misnomer for spiritual rigor mortis, and liturgy sometimes promotes lethargy.

Still, the question persists even from sincere seekers, is noise necessary in spiritual revival? Now most certainly noise—and especially noise for its own sake—is not power. Dr. B. F. Gurden was right when he wrote, "You know, you get a little lightning before the thunder. A lot of Christians reverse that and have the thunder but not much lightning—a lot of noise but not much power. Noise does not count for anything if you have no power with God" (*Foursquare Crusader,* July 22, 1936, p. 8). However, if you do have power with God, some noise is likely to attend it. There was noise on the day of Pentecost. Nor has God seen fit to alter His methods by providing a "noiseless Pentecost" for the present generation! "God isn't deaf," critics may remind us, and He isn't, but as Dr. Kelso R. Glover used to reply, "God isn't nervous either," while Cline Halsey pointed out, "There is more Bible for a noisy religion than for a quiet one."

Pentecost at the beginning witnessed unusual and mighty manifestations, and Foursquaredom would not want the Bible pattern changed in this day. "What About These Manifestations?" by Aimee Semple McPherson, which follows this chapter, interprets impressively the Biblical perspective of these phenomena.

THE INITIAL EVIDENCE

The ministry of Jesus Christ as Baptizer with the Holy Spirit results in the articulation on the part of baptized believers of languages they have never learned. The Bible evidence of this experience is invariably speaking in other tongues as the Holy Spirit gives utterance. Foursquaredom stands steadfast in proclaiming that this is the indispensable initial evidence of the infilling of the Holy Ghost. On this insistence we dare brook no compromise. We must remain true to the Scriptures.

It is impossible to deny, so far as the cases documented in the Bible are concerned, that speaking in other tongues constituted the initial evidence of the baptism with the Holy Spirit. The facts cannot be gainsaid. The evidence is all on one side of the issue.

The baptized believers at the Jewish Pentecost in Acts 2:4 "were all filled with the Holy Ghost, and began to speak with other tongues, as the Spirit gave them utterance." These were real languages, as is demonstrated by the fact that they were understood by Jewish pilgrims to Jerusalem who lived in at least fifteen different areas of the Roman Empire and presumably represented as many foreign languages!

The next outpouring reported in Acts involved the Samaritan believers who previously had been converted under the ministry of the deacon Philip, as recorded in chapter 8. Peter and John proceeded subsequently to Samaria, laid their hands upon the converts, "and they received the Holy Ghost" (verse 17). Now the account does not add, "and they spoke with other tongues as the Spirit gave them utterance," but virtually all Biblical scholars are agreed that this is what took place. Certainly some spectacular miracle attended the laying on of the apostles' hands, otherwise Simon the Sorcerer would not have coveted the power to communicate the gift. Fenton John Anthony Hort, perhaps the most respected New Testament Greek scholar of all time, held that the reception of the Holy Spirit by the Samaritans, as reported in Acts 8:17, is explainable there, as it is explained subsequently at the household of Cornelius (Acts 10:44), as a reference to the manifestation of the gift of tongues (cf. "Expositor's Greek Testament," Vol. II, page 217). Commenting on the same verse, the modern expositor F. F. Bruce remarks, "The context leaves us in no doubt that their (the Samaritans') reception of the Spirit was attended by external manifestations such as had marked His descent on the earliest disciples at Pentecost" ("Commentary on the Book of Acts," 1955, p. 181). And Dr. A. T. Robertson wrote dogmatically that the account in Acts of the Samaritan Pentecost "shows plainly that those who received the gift of the Holy Spirit spoke with tongues" ("Word Pictures in the New Testament," 1930, Vol. III, p. 107).

Other authorities of unimpeachable scholarship declare the same conclusion, including Matthew Henry, Charles John Ellicott, and Adam Clarke in their monumental commentaries. The reader desiring to pursue this subject further should consult Carl Brumback's volume, "What Meaneth This?" (pages 208-214) for impressive documentation. The fact that so many responsible authorities, who have no connection with the Pentecostal movement, take pains to declare that the Samaritans spoke with other tongues when they received the Holy

Spirit ought to dispel any lingering doubts that such was most certainly the case.

The next reference in the book of Acts to a believer being baptized with the Holy Spirit pertains to Saul who is also called Paul. Ananias approached the new convert in Damascus and announced, "Brother Saul, the Lord, even Jesus, that appeared unto thee in the way as thou camest, hath sent me, that thou mightest receive thy sight, and be filled with the Holy Ghost" (Acts 9:17). From I Corinthians 14:18 we know that Paul spoke with other tongues as the Spirit gave him utterance. There is almost a boastful note in the Apostle's profession, "I thank my God, I speak with tongues more than ye all" which may have meant that Paul spoke with tongues more than "all of you put together," as the *Amplified New Testament* suggests. At any rate, the apostle manifested the Bible evidence of Acts 2:4.

Acts 10 finds Peter ministering to the household of Cornelius, to Romans who lived at Caesarea. Suddenly an astonishing interruption ensues.

> "While Peter yet spake these words, the Holy Ghost fell on all them which heard the word. And they of the circumcision which believed were astonished, as many as came with Peter, because that on the Gentiles also was poured out the gift of the Holy Ghost. For they heard them speak with tongues, and magnify God. Then answered Peter, Can any man forbid water, that these should not be baptized, which have received the Holy Ghost as well as we?" (Acts 10:44-47).

Some have argued that speaking in tongues was a manifestation only for Jews, but all who were filled with the Spirit at Cornelius' household were Gentiles.

Now, exactly what was it that convinced the prejudiced Jews who accompanied Peter to Caesarea that these Gentiles had been admitted to the Christian faith? What incontrovertible evidence assured them that Cornelius' household had received the gift of the Holy Spirit? It was the same identical evidence of the first Pentecostal outpouring of Acts 2:4. The Jews were astonished that the Gentiles obtained the baptism of the Spirit, but they recognized absolutely that the gift had been given them, because "they heard them speak with tongues" (Acts 10:46). And when Peter explained to the church in Jerusalem he reported, "And I began to speak, the Holy Ghost fell on them, as on us at the beginning. Then remembered I the word of the Lord, how that he said, John indeed baptized with water; but ye shall be baptized with the Holy Ghost. Forasmuch then as God gave them the like gift as he did unto us, who believed on the Lord Jesus Christ; what was I, that I could withstand God?" (Acts 11:15-17). Present-day critics of Pentecostal experiences are not as cautious as Peter! To oppose this charismatic experience may very well put one in the position of withstanding God!

The lesson of the house of Cornelius, however, is quite clear. Not only did the baptized believers speak with other tongues, but the witnesses to the outpouring received that utterance as evidence that the Holy Spirit fell on these Gentiles as on the 120 at the beginning, imparting to them "like gift as he did unto us," as Peter expressed it!

The book of Acts describes one more outpouring of the baptism of the Holy Spirit. Greeks are the recipients in chapter 19. Paul challenged a small congregation of Greeks whom he recognized as believers in Ephesus, "Have ye received the Holy Ghost since ye believed?" (Acts 19:2). Some interpreters who profess that a person receives the gift of the Holy Spirit simultaneously with conversion insist that the translation of the Revised Version is preferable: "Did ye receive the Holy Ghost when ye believed?" Foursquare believers, along with all Pentecostals, can live with either translation, for the answer to the question is the same in either case. The Ephesian believers had not received the Holy Ghost since they believed, and they did not receive the Holy Ghost when they believed. They were entirely unaware that the Holy Ghost had been given (cf. Revised Version, Acts 19:2). But later "when Paul had laid his hands upon them, the Holy Ghost came on them; and they spake with tongues, and prophesied" (Acts 19:6).

Thus at the Jewish Pentecost in Jerusalem in Acts 2, at the Roman Pentecost in Caesarea in Acts 10 and at the Greek Pentecost in Ephesus in Acts 19, Luke emphasizes that believers who were baptized with the Holy Spirit spoke with other tongues as the Spirit gave them utterance. In the Pauline Pentecost in Acts 9 the same evidence prevailed, as is proved by the Apostle's testimonial remark of I Corinthians 14:18. Paul spoke with tongues. And at the Samaritan Pentecost in Acts 8 Luke implies some spectacularly supernatural manifestation which Bible scholars with virtual unanimity identify as speaking in tongues. So at every occasion reported by Luke where Jesus Christ baptized believers with the Holy Spirit the initial evidence was this *glossolalia* or speaking with tongues! The apostolic Christians accepted the evidence of tongues in recognizing that fellow believers had really received this infilling. The Bible way to receive the baptism with the Holy Spirit involves this speaking with tongues. Only of him who has spoken in tongues can it be said, "The Holy Ghost fell on him, as on the apostles in the beginning" (cf. Acts 11:15, Acts 10:45-46).

But what shall we say to the Christian who professes, "I have received the baptism of the Spirit, but I did not speak with tongues"?

It is unbecoming to argue heatedly with such a person. However, he occupies the same untenable position of people who claim they are Christians but who have never been born again! A pastor of one of America's largest Protestant denominations asked this writer, "What do you mean by 'born again'?" And one of the leading ministers in Portland, Oregon, shocked a company of his colleagues by announcing, "I don't know what you mean when you talk about being born again, and I'm afraid that if you explained it to me I wouldn't want it."

Now if we are going to stay true to the Bible, we must insist that no one is really a Christian who is not born again! And similarly, no one has really been baptized with the Holy Spirit if he has not spoken with tongues! He may have put his foot to the threshold, but he has not yet fully entered in, if he has not exercised glossolalia. He may have been blessed abundantly, but he is not yet baptized, if he has not spoken with other tongues as the Spirit gives utterance. He may have been sprinkled with the Spirit's anointing, but he has not been immersed in the Spirit's fullness, unless he has spoken with tongues!

Yet it rarely accomplishes anything to argue the issue with one who claims the baptism without tongues. Probably the best answer to such a party is to point out in Christ-like kindness, "You may have what you call this baptism, but you have not received what the Spirit-filled believers in the New Testament received. You do not have the full New Testament experience, for believers there all spoke with tongues when Jesus baptized them!"

Every church in the apostolic age was a Pentecostal church. Every congregation was a *Full Gospel* congregation. There weren't any churches in Bible days where Pentecostal phenomena failed to prevail. St. Paul testified to the Romans how Christ wrought through his apostolic ministry with "mighty signs, and wonders, by the power of the Spirit of God; so that from Jerusalem, and round about unto Illyricum, I have fully preached the gospel of Christ" (Romans 15:18-19).

Some have wondered why more is not written about the Pentecostal experience in the epistles of the New Testament. This bewilderment overlooks the fact that for the most part the epistles were penned to counteract either prevailing ignorance of spiritual truths or to correct faulty doctrines or practices. Apparently the charismatic exercises proceeded normally in all but two churches addressed in epistles, for in only two does Paul discuss them. The Corinthian church presumably was carried away with preoccupation with spectacular manifestations. Chapter 14, which more than any other passage in the Bible informs us about the proper purpose and operation of tongues, interpretations, and prophecy, corrects the abuses which disturbed the Corinthian church.

If the Corinthians tended to veer from the middle of the road to the extreme of unbridled manifestations, the Thessalonians apparently veered in the other direction, toward too rigid regimentation of the operation of charismatic gifts. Therefore, Paul prescribed for them the exercise of intensified rejoicing, prayer, and praise (I Thessalonians 5:16-18), and particularly commanded the believers, "Quench not the Spirit. Despise not prophesyings" (I Thessalonians 5:19-20). It is instructive to note how more recent translators have rendered verse 19. The *Amplified New Testament* has it, "Do not quench (suppress or subdue) the (Holy) Spirit," but it is the newest official Roman Catholic edition, the *Confraternity Version*, which delivers the most forceful meaning, for that translation adds to its rendering, "Do not extinguish the Spirit," the explanatory footnote that Paul's command means: "Make use of the charismatic gifts such as tongues and prophecy. Cf. I Corinthians 12-14."

Church history testifies that glossolalia long outlasted the apostolic age, prevailing for centuries on a large scale in the church. Of course, as revival waned and worldliness infiltrated ecclesiastical institutions, the charismatic manifestations grew rarer, but by no means did they ever altogether disappear from the church. Pentecostal believers might do well to remember that even the most erudite authorities can be guilty of formulating fallacies of hasty generalization. Scholars sometimes say a certain thing never happened, when the truth is that it happened but rarely.

John Wesley rebuked a contemporary controversialist for such a fallacy. Dr. Conyers Middleton had written regarding speaking with tongues, "After the apostolic time, there is not, in all history, one instance either well attested, or even so much as mentioned, of any particular person who had ever exercised that gift, or pretended to exercise it in any age or country whatever."

"Sir, your memory fails you again," contradicted the founder of the Methodist church. "It (tongues) has been heard of more than once, no further off than the valleys of Dauphin." Wesley was referring to phenomena among the French Huguenots (Protestants) in the province on that country's southeast frontier.

Wesley could as easily have mentioned numerous other instances between the apostolic age and his own era when people professed to speak with other tongues as the Holy Spirit gave them utterances. There has never been an age or era of church history where the phenomena have been altogether absent. Whenever revivals of religion upset the artificial equilibrium of the church, generally glossolalia was heard. We could subpoena such authorities as Ignatius, Irenaeus, Tertullian, Origen, and Augustine to attest the continuation of the gift throughout the period called the patristic age. During the Dark Ages, that thousand years of apostasy some have called "the devil's millenium," believers in isolated communities experienced the apostolic gifts. The Albigenses and Waldenses spoke with tongues. There is some documentation to the effect that Martin Luther exercised this and other charismatic gifts. *Encyclopedia Britannica* vouches for the practice among the Jansenists of the seventeenth century as well as among the mendicant friars of the thirteenth. The early Quaker Burrough wrote concerning the meetings of the Society of Friends, "We spake with new tongues as the Lord gave us utterance, and as His Spirit led us." And a visitation of this manifestation swept a meeting of the Y.M.C.A. in London following an address by evangelist Dwight L. Moody, and that was before the Azusa Street outpouring which God used to spearhead the present Pentecostal movement!

•

THE VALUE OF GLOSSOLALIA

But what is the value of speaking with tongues? How does the baptism with the Holy Spirit benefit the believer?

Jesus declared that the Holy Spirit would confer upon believers power to witness unto Him. The dramatic difference the experience made in Peter, transforming the apostle from a denier of his association with Jesus to a bold champion of the cause of Christ, furnishes a pattern for present-day believers. When early Christians prayed for boldness to speak the word, God filled them with the Spirit afresh and they spoke the word with boldness (cf. Acts 4:29-31). The upper room experience will endue the believer with power for service. Its purpose is not primarily to bless the recipient but rather to make him a blessing to others! You don't kindle a fire in a stove just to keep the stove warm! God puts His fire from on high within believers that they might warm others.

But what is the purpose of *tongues*?

Those who declare that the gift was given to make possible missionary propaganda in Bible days certainly miss the whole point of Acts 2. The multitudes from almost a score of nations heard the 120 speaking in tongues, but were not evangelized thereby. When Peter preached, they understood his sermon. Being Jews the pilgrims would understand Aramaic. And throughout the inhabited world of that time almost everybody spoke the *Koine* Greek. The apostles did not need to preach in native dialects. Their audiences all understood Greek. So a miracle was not needed to enable Christians to witness the word to foreign audiences without learning foreign languages. An international tongue prevailed throughout the world of that time.

Of course, tongues operate validly in conjunction with the gift of interpretation in according supernatural illuminations to the church (cf. I Corinthians 14:3-5). However, the apostle Paul seems to point out that the greatest value of this exercise is in private devotions, in prayer and praise. Paul spoke with tongues more than all the Corinthians, yet he suggests he rarely did so in public gatherings (I Corinthians 14:18-19). The devotional use of tongues he recommends as having great value: "For he that speaketh in an unknown tongue speaketh not unto men, but unto God: for no man understandeth him; howbeit in the spirit he speaketh mysteries" (I Corinthians 14:2). "He that speaketh in an unknown tongue edifieth himself" (I Corinthians 14:4). If it be objected that the pursuit of self-edification represents selfishness, we must reply that before a believer can edify others, he needs to be edified himself.

Harold Horton seems almost to scale the third heaven in extolling the glory of this devotional experience of tongues! The quotation is lengthy but altogether significant:

> "Every consecrated believer must have felt at times a consuming desire to open his heart to God in unspeakable communication and adoration inexpressible. There is a deep in the spirit of the redeemed that is never plumbed by the mind or thought. That deep finds expression at last in the Baptism of the Spirit, as unaccustomed words of heavenly coherence sweep up to the Beloved from the newly opened well of the human spirit—flooded as it is with the torrential stream of the divine Spirit. Only deep can call unto deep at the noise of God's full flowing cataracts. 'He that speaketh in a tongue speaketh not unto men but unto God: for no man understandeth him; howbeit in the Spirit he speaketh divine secrets' (I Corinthians 14:2). The Gift of Tongues sinks a well into the dumb profundities of the rejoicing spirit, liberating a jet of long-pent ecstasy that gladdens the heart of God and man. Blessed fountain of ineffable coherence, of inexpressible eloquence! Have you never in the presence of Jesus felt inarticulate on the very verge of eloquence? This heavenly Gift will loose the spirit's

tongue and burst upon the speechless heart with utterance transcending sages' imaginings or angel rhapsodies. Have you never wept to think how helpless your words are to express emotion in the presence of Him whom your soul loveth? Other tongues alone can give you utterance equal to the holy task. Other tongues will give you Names for Jesus that even revelation has not vouchsafed. Other tongues will capture the escaping thought, the elusive expression, the inarticulate longing, lending worthy and soul-satisfying utterance to profoundest gratitude and worship . . .

"And what a rest to weary mind and nerve, to relax from mental concentration in praying and praising, and break forth in effortless utterance in the Spirit. Notice the blessed connection in Isaiah xxviii, 11, 12: 'With stammering lips and another tongue will He speak to this people . . . This is the rest wherewith ye may cause the weary to rest; and this is the refreshing'! What heavenly rest in spiritual exercise has the Lord designed in these heavenly tongues! Hallelujah!" (Horton, Harold, "The Gifts of the Spirit," 1953 edition, pp. 152-153, 156).

Foursquare believers must be diligent not only in perpetuating our Pentecostal faith but also in persisting in our Pentecostal experience. As early as the time of Timothy a tendency developed to neglect the charismatic gifts. Paul wrote to his son in the faith, "Stir up the gift of God, which is in thee" (II Timothy 1:6). Believers sometimes pray, "Lord, you stir me," when God is waiting for them to stir themselves. Even in Old Testament times a prophet had reason to complain, "And there is none . . . that stirreth up himself to take hold of thee [God]" (Isaiah 64:7). On occasion David had to encourage himself in the Lord, and the same exercise brings blessed results in divine visitation today. Some complained that Smith Wigglesworth was crude when he explained his constant anointing by declaring, "If the Spirit does not move me, then I move the Spirit," but the Bible continuously calls on men to exercise themselves in the things of God. Moreover, the believer who has an experience is never at the mercy of the man who only has an argument. Jesus is the baptizer with the Holy Spirit. This is an experience subsequent to salvation which endues the convert with power for service, and especially for witnessing. The discussion of this phase of the Foursquare Gospel occupies more space than the chapters about Jesus as Saviour, Healer, or Coming King, but not because this subject is of greater importance. It must be reiterated strongly that nothing Christ does is as great as His work of salvation. However, the baptism with the Holy Spirit represents the phase of the Foursquare Gospel which is most misunderstood by outsiders, and for that reason we have discussed it more exhaustively than the rest, though the theme has itself been far from exhausted in these pages! For a more complete treatment of this thrilling subject, the reader is referred to Aimee Semple McPherson's book, "Fire from on High."

May every reader ponder Paul's question, "Have ye received the Holy Ghost since ye believed?" If the answer is negative, may he obey the same apostle's command, "Be filled with the Spirit" (Ephesians 5:18). Anyone whom God has called unto salvation is extended the promise, "Ye shall receive the gift of the Holy Ghost" (Acts 2:38).

Sermon

THE BAPTISM OF THE HOLY GHOST

That the positive, conscious knowledge of the Spirit's incoming was really beyond question in apostolic days, no one can doubt. "And they were all filled with the Holy Ghost, and began to speak with other tongues as the Spirit gave them utterance." They had received a definite indisputable experience upon the solidity of which they could step out confidently, and speak with positive assurance.

The outpouring and baptism of the Spirit had been foretold by prophets and talked of by sages centuries before. "For with stammering lips and another tongue will He speak to this people. To whom he hath said, this is the rest wherewith ye may cause the weary to rest and this is the refreshing, yet they would not hear," declared the prophet Isaiah. "And it shall come to pass afterward, that I will pour out my spirit upon all flesh; and your sons and your daughters shall prophesy . . ." said God through the prophet Joel; "Be glad then, ye children of Zion, and rejoice in the Lord your God: for he hath given you the former rain moderately, and he will cause to come down for you the rain, the former rain, and the latter rain in the first month. And the floors shall be full of wheat, and the vats shall overflow with wine and oil." And thank God this prophecy is being fulfilled today before our very eyes. If you had been here this afternoon at the after service you would have seen these floors filled with wheat–the slain of Lord were many.

Then came our Jesus, of whom John the forerunner cried: "I indeed baptize you with water unto repentance; but He that cometh after me is mightier than I . . . He shall baptize you with the Holy Ghost and with fire." Not only did Jesus speak frequently of the coming Holy Spirit, but He emphasized the necessity, and utmost importance of receiving Him when He did come. Toward the end of His ministry, with ever increasing forcefulness Jesus continued to emphasize this truth in such passages as:

"Nevertheless I tell you the truth: It is expedient for you that I go away: for if I go not away, the Comforter will not come unto you; but if I depart, I will send him unto you." "Howbeit when he, the Spirit of truth is come, he will guide you into all truth: for he shall not speak of himself; but whatsoever he shall hear, that shall he speak: and he will shew you things to come. He shall glorify me" (John 16:7, 13-14).

"And I will pray the Father, and he shall give you another Comforter, that he may abide with you forever: Even the Spirit of truth: whom the world cannot receive . . . But the Comforter, which is the Holy Ghost, whom the Father will send in my name, he shall teach you all things, and bring all things to your remembrance" (John 14:16, 26).

"Go ye into all the world, and preach the gospel to every creature . . . And these signs shall follow them that believe; In my name shall they cast out devils; they shall speak with new tongues" (Mark 16:15, 17), etc.

"And, behold, I send the promise of my Father upon you: but tarry ye in the city of Jerusalem, until ye be endued with power from on high" (Luke 24:49).

"For John truly baptized with water; but ye shall be baptized with the Holy Ghost not many days hence . . . But ye shall receive power, after that the Holy Ghost is come upon you: and ye shall be witnesses unto me . . . unto the uttermost part of the earth" (Acts 1:5, 8).

Many of the faithful servants of God in by-gone days had felt the Spirit resting upon them with blessed anointing, but though all the mighty promises of His coming had been given, no human being had ever been baptized with the Holy Spirit.

In Acts 2, we read of the outpouring of the Holy Ghost on the day of Pentecost, and see the curtain roll up on the official opening of this dispensation or "church age." The 120 believing saints who had spent day after day in prayer and supplication were suddenly filled with the presence and power of Him for whom they waited. "And they were all filled with the Holy Ghost, and began to speak with other tongues, as the Spirit gave them utterance" (Acts 2:4).

The Bible is careful to tell us, that the first act by

which the Spirit introduced Himself through the temple in which He had taken up His abode was to speak through them in other tongues (languages they had never learned).

Not only was this the case in Jerusalem, where Jews "from every nation under heaven" were assembled, but also in the house of Cornelius (chapter 10) and at Ephesus (chapter 19) where there were no Jews of foreign tongue, and therefore no seeming external necessity for it. At the house of Cornelius, where Peter was preaching to the Gentiles, his sermon was suddenly interrupted without warning or apology for: "While Peter yet spake . . . the Holy Ghost fell on all them which heard the word. And they of the circumcision which believed were astonished, as many as came with Peter, because that on the Gentiles also was poured out the gift of the Holy Ghost. For they heard them speak with tongues, and magnify God."

Here was an experience which for some reason not even the Jews of the circumcision could doubt, even though it fell in the most unexpected manner, on the most unexpected people. We are told that they knew they received the Holy Ghost: "For they heard them speak with tongues and magnify God."

Could the Word of God have told us in any more striking, and convincing manner that the speaking in tongues as the Spirit gave utterance was the accepted, initial, Bible evidence amongst the Jewish believers everywhere during the eight years which had elapsed since the day of Pentecost? Had there been even a hint of any other evidence being the sign of His incoming, would not the Jews who came with Peter have demanded this evidence, ere their age old racial prejudices against a people they had been wont to look upon as dogs were overthrown like the walls of Jericho?

Yet—though we read of their astonishment that on the Gentiles was poured out the Holy Ghost, we discover not one shadow of doubt in their minds, "For they heard them speak with tongues." This was such conclusive evidence to their minds that there was nothing more to be said.

A few days later when Peter stood before the council in Jerusalem, facing the serious charge of going in to men that were uncircumcised he brought his defense to a close by saying:

"And as I began to speak, the Holy Ghost fell on them, as on us at the beginning . . . [and] God gave them the like gift as he did unto us . . . what was I, that I could withstand God?" (Acts 11:15, 17).

And how did this learned body of men who had been in this Holy Ghost revival ever since the beginning receive the news? Did they receive the speaking in tongues as a conclusive sign that the Gentiles had received the gift, or did they doubt and demand other evidence? (Acts 11-18).

"When they heard these things, they held their peace, and glorified God."

What more was there to say? If the "speaking in tongues" was an accepted evidence, what else was there to do but hold their peace, and glorify God? Upon the acceptance and recognition of this sign, and the testimony of Peter, the Magna Charta of Gentile freedom was prepared. The evidence was so completely sufficient that a delegation of apostles and chief man were sent to Antioch, and a permanent work established.

Again in chapter 19 of Acts, the speaking in tongues is brought to the foreground as an immediate accompaniment of the baptism. Paul had been preaching to the disciples at Ephesus; but something must have seemed lacking about them. Perhaps they did not have the great welling "Hallelujahs" and "Glory to Jesus," that are so peculiar to the baptized people. Paul must have missed that freedom, love, and transporting glory, which we too find missing in so many professing disciples of today. Anyway he had a pretty good idea where the trouble lay and turning to them he asked the straight question, "Have ye received the Holy Ghost since ye believed?"

and they as frankly answered his question in the negative. Some time ago I asked a certain lady whether she had received the baptism of the Holy Ghost. She said she didn't know what that was but she was sure she had received it anyway, as she thought she had all God had for her. This, I am sorry to say, is the attitude of many people. They are ashamed to candidly confess that there are experiences they have never had, and depths they have never fathomed. Had the Ephesians Paul met been of this class I doubt whether the revival power would have ever fallen upon them. "Woe unto you who are full now, for ye shall hunger hereafter."

Humbly, simply, frankly they acknowledged their lack and said: "Why, no, we have not so much as heard whether there be any Holy Ghost." "And when Paul laid his hands upon them, the Holy Ghost came on them; and they spake with tongues, and prophesied" (Acts 19:6). If any one ever tells you the speaking with tongues in the Bible times was merely to converse with foreigners, ask him whether there were any foreigners at Ephesus or Caesarea. They all spoke in other tongues, even though outside of its relative connection with the incoming of the Holy Ghost there was no apparent need for it. Paul also tells us plainly in I Corinthians 14:2, that "he that speaketh in an unknown tongue speaketh not unto men, but unto God: for no man understandeth him; howbeit in the spirit he speaketh mysteries." This passage forever explodes the erroneous idea that the "tongues" are given for missionary purposes, though God can and at times has used them so in this present age.

At Samaria (Acts 8) we find a newly converted people, who have received the Word of God and been baptized in water, none of whom have as yet received the Holy Spirit (verse 16). This plainly shows that the Spirit is not received at conversion, for these were converted and baptized, and now ready for the promise of the Father.

Peter and John were sent to pray for them that they might receive the Holy Ghost. "Then laid they their hands on them, and they received the Holy Ghost." So real, so definite (not only to themselves, and to Peter, John and Philip, but even to Simon the Sorcerer) were the signs attending their filling; so joyous and desirable, that Simon himself was delighted, and thought he had found the way to make a fortune. For surely every one would want such a wonderful, happy, rapturous, heavenly experience as that which took place before his eyes. But ah! Simon, this gift cannot be purchased with money, but by prayer, consecration, and yieldedness to the will of God.

The context does not say in so many words that they spake in tongues but it is clearly implied, and practically all Bible scholars are unanimous in this belief. If the miraculous sign (which this sorcerer himself recognized as supernatural, and could not gainsay) was not the "speaking in tongues," what was it? Love? Blessing? Peace? No, it could hardly be one of these for these he could not see or hear. This wondrous baptism of the Holy Ghost is too precious, too vitally important to the spiritual growth of the church and individual to be left without some unmistakable, outward sign whereby both the recipient and spectator may know when He has come in to take up His abode.

In our meetings today, so many are receiving the Holy Ghost that to mention in every case that the individual spake in tongues would be superfluous. For instance, when I say, "this morning six received the baptism of the Spirit, twelve received this afternoon, and eighteen last night," standing as I do for the recognized Bible evidence of the baptism, would it not be needless repetition to say each time that they all "spake in tongues?"

If, however, some one doubts that a certain party received, and the news seems almost too good to be true, we say, "Oh yes he did, for we were all there and heard him speak with tongues." Take this dear holiness preacher here for instance; he received the baptism this afternoon, though for years he had claimed to have all he needed. Today he went down under the power (just like the most ordinary of us) and received the baptism.

A sister came running in with an incredulous look and said: "Sister, you don't mean to say that minister is receiving the baptism?"

"Yes, dear," I replied. "Listen a minute and you'll hear him for yourself, he is speaking in tongues and magnifying God."

Therefore, you see, while it is superfluous and unnecessary to mention the speaking in tongues in every instance, when there is any doubt about one's receiving the gift, we instantly go back and produce the Bible evidence, just like Peter did in the case when the Gentiles' baptism was disputed. We know for we heard them speak with tongues.

Your uncle dies, leaves you his property through a perfectly legitimate will. I come along and say, "What right have you to this property? I don't believe you own it and I would like to put you out and move in myself." Would you not run and get your papers and say:

"You are mistaken, this is my land, it is rightfully mine and here is the legal evidence to prove my statement."

Hundreds of thousands are enjoying this blessed Bible experience of the indwelling Holy Spirit. The latter rain is falling and "the promise is unto you, and your children, and to all that are afar off, even as many as the Lord our God shall call" (Acts 2:39). God has not changed His pattern, nor discarded the old-fashioned evidence as no longer necessary. Don't you want to receive this great gift in the Bible way, so that you too can speak definitely, and authoritatively that He has come?

Remember that the receiving of the Holy Spirit is only the beginning, just the triumphal arch through which you enter into a new life of union, fellowship, praise, worship, prayer, love and service such as you have never known; a life endowed with power from on high, which will enable you to add your voice to those of the host who are witnessing of His coming, to the uttermost parts of the earth.

Sermon

THE GIFTS OF THE HOLY SPIRIT

Jesus commanded His disciples saying, "Receive ye the Holy Ghost." Then on the day of Pentecost "they were all filled with the Holy Ghost, and began to speak with other tongues, as the Spirit gave them utterance" (Acts 2:4). Believers are today being baptized with the same Spirit in the same way.

The baptism of the Holy Spirit, instead of being the apex of the Christian's experience, however, is but the beginning–the gateway that leads into a veritable Canaan, as it were. And there, stretched out before him, lies a land bathed in God's own sunlight, flowing with milk and honey, and filled with vines that hang low with an abundance of fruit.

Having enjoyed the milk of the Word, as a babe in Christ, the child now growing into manhood longs for the strong meat, or deeper teaching of spiritual truths, and to know the purposes, object and result of the mighty incoming of the Third Person of the Trinity.

Let us turn together to I Corinthians 14, a chapter filled with meat, misunderstood by many, but readily acceptable and comprehensible to those who possess the key of the Spirit.

So closely interwoven is the chapter with the twelfth and thirteenth, that the three are often called "The Sandwich Chapters"–the meat of love being in the center, *as it were, the bread at either side.* To get a correct understanding of chapter 14, it is therefore necessary to acquaint ourselves with those immediately preceding.

In chapter 12, verses 4-11, Paul has just enumerated nine gifts of the Spirit, the word of wisdom, the word of knowledge, faith, gifts of healing miracles, prophecy, discerning of spirits, tongues and interpretations, which are distributed through the church to various saints and members of the body, by the selfsame Spirit who divides to each man severally as He will. And after an earnest, inspiring exhortation in which the necessity and importance of every gift and member of the body being in its proper place is set forth, the Apostle closes chapter 12 with the earnest appeal, "But covet earnestly the best gifts."

Then, as though set in parenthesis, comes the glorious unfolding and expounding of the first and most important fruit of the Spirit—Love, reminding his hearers that though they may have every gift but are minus love—they are nothing.

But thank God, through the Apostle the possibility of having both the gifts and fruits manifested in the church is made plain. The one does not stand in the way of the other, for the same Spirit who bestows the gifts "severally as He will," is the very One who causes the fruit of the Spirit to grow and thrive upon the branches of the Spirit-filled believer. Thus it is that after completing the beautiful parenthesis on love, with which he punctuates his treatise on the gifts of the Spirit, their operation, importance and workings in the church, Paul takes up and resumes the subject of spiritual gifts.

The fourteenth chapter opens with the words: "Follow after love and desire spiritual gifts." Follow after love AND: don't stop short there, however, for just as the gifts need to be attended and completed by love, so love needs as a complement the gifts of the Spirit, that the ministrations of the church may be followed and confirmed by signs and wonders.

How closely that little conjunction "and" binds "love" and "spiritual gifts" together! How eloquently it sets forth as unscriptural the erroneous teaching of men today who declare that these chapters, references and promised gifts of the Spirit were only for the earthly church, professing that "love" is for the church till Jesus comes, but "gifts" were to be only of short duration and soon vanish away. Surely an order that would countermand the "desiring spiritual gifts" would also countermand "following after charity," for both have their places in the body and could not have been more closely connected by the Apostle.

God's power and the supernatural "sign and wonder" workings of His Spirit know no cessation, limitation or boundary, except that put upon them by our lack of faith. "For the gifts . . . of God are without repentance" (Romans 11:29). It is not only the height of folly to pick and choose among promises of God given in these epistles saying, "this is for today–and that for yesterday," but positively detrimental and injurious to the work of God and the restoration of the church to the fullness of Pentecostal power and perfection which must take place before Jesus comes to take His Bride away.

After enumerating nine gifts and dwelling on the place of each member in the body, Paul draws chapter 12 to a conclusion by the exhortation–"But covet earnestly the best gifts." Now if we covet a thing, we desire it very intensely. Some say we should not seek the gifts but the Giver, but there is no such intimation given by Paul. He is addressing the Spirit-baptized Christians who have the Giver, and advising them now that they have the Giver to covet the best gifts (chap. 12:31), and seek that they may excel to the edifying of the church (chap. 14:12).

"Covet earnestly the best gifts." Here emphasis falls on the word best and, from its use, we conclude that there must be certain gifts which Paul considers of even greater importance for edification, exhortation and comfort than others. And now after his parenthesis on love (love is a fruit, not a gift), he takes up the thread of his discourse and selects from the nine gifts, three (prophecy, tongues and interpretation), which he evidently considers of such importance that an entire chapter, some forty verses long, is devoted to weighing and enunciating their different values. These three gifts which Paul brings so prominently before the church are the ones whereby God speaks to people through people by His Spirit.

Here in this chapter 14 of First Corinthians, Paul with his splendid, logical, analytical mind enlightened and inspired by the Spirit, draws a line down the center—forms a balance sheet, and sets forth in order the values—on the one side of the balance sheet, of prophecy; on the other side, of tongues and interpretation.

To fail to read this chapter in the same analytical, logical, balanced way and in the same spirit by which Paul wrote it, or to pick out a verse here and there to be used as a club against the operations of the SPIRIT is something like the man who believed in opening the Bible and taking the first command his eye fell upon as his guidance for the day. One day he opened to the verse: "Judas went and hanged himself." Thinking this could not be for himself, he opened the Word and tried again. This time his eyes fell upon the words, "Go thou and do likewise." Let us not make this mistake, but rather read the verses in order.

"Desire spiritual gifts, but rather that ye may prophesy." Tell us please, Brother Paul, what is there about these three gifts that makes them so desirable? and what is there about prophecy that makes it even more desirable than the gift of tongues—unless the gift of tongues be coupled with interpretation, thus putting the two on one level (see verse 5).

"Well, it's like this," says Paul, "he that speaketh in an unknown tongue speaketh not unto men" (this explodes the erroneous idea that tongues were only for the day of Pentecost and for use only among foreign speaking people), "but unto God: for no man understandeth him; howbeit in the spirit he speaketh mysteries" (I Corinthians 14:2).

In other words, it is not the person alone that is praying, for he knows not what he asks, neither is his own mind framing the words of the petition—he knows not what to ask for as he should—but now the indwelling Spirit helps his infirmities, praying through him with groanings that cannot be uttered.

Jesus said: "Ask and you shall receive," but our receiving capacity is limited in a great degree to our asking capacity. When the indwelling Spirit prays through us, however, His praying is not bound by the shackles and limitations of our human mind and desires. He prays through us in Heaven's own language and soars into the very ethereal realms and presence of God; then we are but the channel through which intercession is made.

Why Paul, that is wonderful! Do you mean to say that at times you pray in the spirit without understanding what you say?

"Oh yes," answers the Apostle (verses 14 and 15). "For if I pray in an unknown tongue, my spirit prayeth, but my understanding is unfruitful. In other words, I know not what I say. The Spirit speaking through me addresses Himself not unto men but unto God, for no man understands Him, howbeit in the Spirit He speaks mysteries. This is a private line between the Spirit and His God and cannot be listened to by man or devil."

And do you pray with the spirit all the time, Brother Paul?

"What is it then?" answers the Apostle, "I will pray with the spirit," (which is not understood), "and I will pray with the understanding also: I will sing with the spirit" (which is not understood), "and . . . with the understanding also. Else when thou shalt bless with the spirit, how shall he that occupieth the room of the unlearned say Amen at thy giving of thanks, seeing he understandeth not what thou sayest? for thou verily givest thanks well, but the other is not edified."

"For this reason I pray not only with the spirit" (which you note he puts first), "but with the understanding also, that others may understand and say Amen."

Now "he who prophesieth," Paul explains, "speaketh unto MEN, to edification, exhortation, and comfort."

It is of great importance indeed that the Spirit speak

through you unto God. It is also of great importance that He be able to speak through you to men. And the Spirit who speaks unto God in the unknown tongue in mysteries is the same Holy Spirit who speaks through a yielded vessel in prophecy. Both tongues and prophecy are spoken by the same Spirit, under divine anointing—the difference between the two being that a message to the congregation (see verses 27 and 28) given in an unknown tongue needs to be accompanied with interpretation before it, like prophecy, can be spoken unto men to edification, exhortation, and comfort, while prophecy is spoken to men directly in the language of speaker and audience and has therefore no need of interpretation.

This gift of prophecy referred to by Paul is not the gift of preaching, teaching, or expounding the Scriptures from knowledge or doctrine as some have claimed; but is a direct inspired message given by the Spirit through His temples "and holy prophets spake as they were moved by the Spirit." Insomuch that "out of our innermost beings" (not out of our heads), "shall flow rivers of living water—this spake Jesus of the Spirit whom He would send."

Prophecy is not a cut and dried sermon studied and thought up, but an opening of the mouth that He may fill it, an involuntary flowing forth in streams of beautiful language and teachings of which the Spirit Himself is the author.

But would not such inspired utterances add to or make another Bible? might be asked.

Not at all—one man in the Bible had seven daughters, another had nine daughters that prophesied, but we read of no such accusation being made. Moreover, God plainly declared through the prophet Joel that in the last days He would pour out of His Spirit upon all flesh and the sons and the daughters should prophecy, (Joel 2:28).

This, points out the Apostle, is a gift (not something studied or acquired in a seminary) of paramount importance, and should be coveted by the Spirit-filled saint. Through its use not only are men edified, exhorted, and comforted (verse 3), but also convinced of all, and judged of all insomuch that the secrets of his heart are made manifest, and falling down on his face he worships God, and reports that "God is in you of a truth" (verses 24-25).

God gives great benefits to the individual and to the church through the ministry of these vocal gifts of the Holy Spirit.

"He that speaketh in an unknown tongue edifieth himself" (verse 4). It is impossible to have the blessed Holy Spirit abiding within, speaking (verse 2), praying (verse 14), singing (verse 15), praising (verse 17), without being edified, built up, strengthened, and encouraged; and it is indeed wonderful and necessary to be edified oneself. In fact, one must be edified himself before he can edify another, if it be true that it is impossible to lift another higher than we are ourselves. The husbandman must be first partaker of the fruit.

But though 'tis true that "he who speaketh with an unknown tongue edifieth himself," says Paul, yet don't stop there–go on–covet to prophesy, "for he that prophesieth edifieth the church."

Verse 5–"I would that ye all spake with tongues, but rather that ye prophesied."

But Paul, tell us why, even though you "would" (or wish) that we all spoke in tongues, you would rather that we prophesied?

"I have told you already"–read the rest of the verse–"for greater is he that prophesieth" (as far as speaking unto men unto edification is concerned) "than he that speaketh with tongues, except he interpret."

Up to this time Paul has been speaking of the blessing derived through the Spirit's speaking with tongues, even without interpretation–such as speaking unto God in prayer, giving thanks well and a sign to the unbeliever. But now he is gazing upon and weighing this gift from another angle–namely, that of edifying the church. He points out the evident fact that prophecy (which can be understood in the mother tongue) is of greater edification in church service than speaking in tongues, which cannot be understood, and therefore cannot edify except when accompanied with the gift of interpretation.

This counterpart (interpretation) being added, however, completes the whole, making tongues plus interpretation equal to prophecy in speaking unto men.

Now, after showing how handicapped tongues without interpretation are, when looked upon from the angle of edification to the church, the Apostle gives us the keynote, substance, and solution of the whole matter in verses 12 and 13: "Even so ye, forasmuch as ye are zealous of spiritual gifts, seek that ye may excel to the edifying of the church. Wherefore let him that speaketh in an unknown tongue pray that he may interpret."

Many great preachers of today through whom the Spirit has spoken in a language other than their own, seem to be ashamed of the fact. Compromising, they never mention the fact, lest they should lose position in their churches.

Dear old Paul was not ashamed of the fact that he spoke in tongues, and in verse 18 says, "I thank my God, I speak with tongues more than ye all." My what a lot Paul must have talked in tongues! and how uncomfortable he would be made to feel should he stand in the center of some of the great churches of today and admit the same!

But Paul, wasn't this experience something to be a little fearful and ashamed of?

Ashamed–oh no, rather something to thank God for! "I thank my God I speak in tongues more than ye all: Yet in the church" (or in preaching, when it comes to edifying men) "I had rather speak five words with my understanding, that by my voice I might teach others also, than ten thousand words" (without interpretation), "in an unknown tongue."

Just after Paul had penned these words, I think perhaps the thought might have dawned upon him that some of these twentieth century doubters and Scripture twisters, would misconstrue what he had said, for he immediately adds the words:–

"Brethren, be not children . . . but in understanding be men. In the law it is written"—and you know how careful God has always been to fulfill every jot and tittle of the law—"In the law it is written, With men of other tongues and other lips will I speak unto this people; and yet for all that they will not hear me, saith the Lord. Wherefore tongues are for a sign, not to them that believe, but to them that believe not: But prophesying serveth not for them that believe not, but for them which believe" (verses 20-22).

So that in no way is the speaking with tongues even without interpretation underestimated, for it serves purposes which prophecy cannot serve. Besides being a direct line of communication with the Throne (verse 1), a means of edification to oneself (verse 4), a channel of praise (verse 17), it is a wonderful sign to the unbeliever and a direct fulfillment of the prophecy of Isaiah 28:11.

And now, Paul, after showing us that tongues, even without interpretation, is a wonderful blessing in our private devotional life, in prayer and praise, and in the assembly, too; when instead of praying at all times with the Spirit, we pray with the understanding also (verse 15); you tell us that tongues as a sign to the unbeliever, can be of little edification in the assembly unless accompanied by interpretation. On the other hand you declare that while prophecy, though not serving as a means of prayer—speaking to God, or as a sign to the unbeliever, is of great edification, exhortation, and comfort.

Now, after showing the importance and edification to be derived from both these gifts, when exercised by the Spirit, in their proper places, how would you regulate and define their usage in the assembly?

In verses 26 to 31 the apostle Paul not only answers this query but sums up the whole chapter in six verses, and sets down in order, the only church program recommended for use in the Christian Church of the New Testament. He did not say,

"How is it, brethren, when you come together, you have every bit of your program cut and dried, days in advance, your psalms hung on a board by the organ, after fifteen minutes song, have ten minutes prayer (read from notes and rehearsed beforehand), swelling with such eloquency and oratorical power that the congregation will say, 'My, what a fine prayer he made,' then after the announcements for the oyster supper, Tuesday night, and the box social Wednesday, the young peoples' games and concerts Thursday, and the bridge and dance Friday, take the collection, have the trained prima donna (who sings in the theater during the week, and whose heart is far from God) sing with culture and refinement, let the preacher be sure his notes are all in order, ere he wades through the intricate labyrinths of social reform, community uplift, and the strides of politics, then sing the doxology, repeat a stiff little formula of dismissal, and go home to the waiting ministerial chicken dinner."

No, indeed, that isn't what he said. Let us read his words and ask ourselves whether this is the way in which our meetings are conducted?

"How is it then, brethren? when ye come together, every one of you hath a psalm, hath a doctrine, hath a tongue, hath a revelation, hath an interpretation. Let all things be done unto edifying.

"If any man speak in an unknown tongue, let it be by two, or at the most by three, and that by course; and let one interpret. But if there be no interpreter, let him keep silence in the church; and let him speak to himself and to God.

"Let the prophets speak two or three, and let the other judge. If any thing be revealed to another that sitteth by, let the first hold his peace. For ye may all prophesy one by one, that all may learn, and all may be comforted" (I Corinthians 14:26-31).

The same rule of restriction is placed upon both "prophecy and tongues." They who speak in tongues are to speak by two or at most by three, and that by course, letting one interpret; while the prophets are also to speak two or three and let the other judge.

Paul does not say—take every word purporting to be given in prophecy as direct from God—but bids us listen, judge and compare it with the Word of God. Does it edify, exhort, comfort? This rule may always be applied to determine the genuine from the false.

The same rule by which prophecy is to be judged in order to determine whether or not it be of God, might well be applied to tongues and interpretation—does it edify, is it an exhortation, does it bring comfort?

And the spirit of the prophets is subject to the prophets, for God is not the author of confusion, but of peace, as in all churches of the saints. He who set the sun, the moon and the stars in the firmament of heaven, causing each planet to rotate and revolve upon its axis without friction or confusion will also set His holy church in order. He will set each member whether it be eye, ear, foot, or hand, in his or her place, divide the gifts of the Spirit to each man severally as He will and give the manifestations of the Spirit to profit withal.

There is a wonderful dynamic power in the Holy Spirit. And power to accomplish good results must be directed along the proper channels, or havoc and disaster will be wrought. You purchase, for instance, a certain electric appliance. With it comes a book of instructions, explaining how the power must be operated and utilized. Obey instructions, and there is perfect order and satisfaction. Disobey orders, or disregard instructions—a short circuit, an electric shock, or some disaster is wrought. Few machines are made absolutely "foolproof."

Just so with the administrations, manifestations and operations of the Holy Spirit (who is much more powerful than electricity), the workings and operation of His power must be directed along certain channels and controlled according to the book of directions—God's Holy Word, or dire results will follow.

"Wherefore, brethren, covet to prophesy, and forbid not to speak with tongues" (I Corinthians 14:39). Believe God's Word, and do not stand in the way of the manifest power of the Holy Spirit. Today every prophecy and sign predicted to take place before the coming of the Lord is being fulfilled in the earth and sea and sky. The coming of the Master draws nigh. The Bride, the Lamb's wife, is putting the last touches to her Heavenly trousseau, filling her lamps with Holy Spirit oil, binding her sandals tightly upon her feet in readiness for that day when she shall be brought to the King in raiment of fine needlework, and stand before Him in gold of Ophir.

The work of preparation is not complete till each bridal adornment, each gift, and grace, and jewel is in its place.

O lift no longer doubting hands, or incredulous voice nor think such power, such signs and wonders were only for the days of the apostles. We still live in the dispensation of the Holy Ghost, which opened on the day of Pentecost, and will not close till Jesus comes. This is the last day, and true to His Word through the prophet Joel, God is pouring out of His Spirit upon all flesh. Instead of opposing His divine plan, let us rather bow low at His feet beneath the sheltering blood, and falling in line with His divine purpose and decree, ask of the Lord rain in the time of the latter rain, till showers and torrential downpours of His Spirit shall transform the desert into a watered garden, wherein the eyes of the blind are opened, deaf ears are unstopped, and the lame man leaps for joy, as we await our Lord's appearing.

Sermon

WHAT ABOUT MANIFESTATIONS?

God's power was falling everywhere in the tent, sinners being saved, believers baptized in the Holy Spirit with the Bible evidence of speaking in tongues. Sick bodies had been healed. Some were leaping, dancing, and praising God. The slain of the Lord were many. My heart felt full to the bursting with joy at the sight, and with uplifted hands I was walking up and down the aisles amongst the audience, praising my wonderful Redeemer for the way in which He was working.

Suddenly I felt a restraining, kid-gloved hand laid upon my arm, and a dignified, silk-gowned lady drew me down beside her. Her husband, a fine, dignified type of man, was seated beside her. They had snow-white hair, both of them, every well-tailored line of their faultless apparel bespeaking refinement and culture. This dear lady seemed so sweet, and I was so filled with joy, that I remember I could scarcely resist throwing my arms around her and kissing her and shouting, "Glory to Jesus!" Her troubled, agitated look checked this impulse, however, and as she began to talk to me in her rapid way, her chest was rising and falling with her quick breathing (I was going to say "indignation," but hardly think that would be the word to apply to such a sweet and proper personage).

As she spoke, she alternately gazed through her lorgnette, which hung on a slender thread of gold from her gown, and pointed to some manifestation, for the saints were dancing, shouting, and praising God, or tapped lightly upon her book for emphasis:

"Of course, I believe in the power of God," she said, but oh, the noise, these awful manifestations! What is the good of them, anyway? Did not Paul say that all things were to be done decently and in order? Now, take, for instance, that dancing and shaking, it seems like confusion, and is not at all necessary. And that falling on the floor and lying for an hour. Do you think that looks dignified or proper?" she demanded. "As for this leaping and shouting, why cannot these people praise God in a quiet, orderly way in their heart and give expression to their worship soberly in a quiet hymn of thanksgiving? You know the world would think far more of them," she added, "and stop criticizing and persecuting if only they would put down these awful manifestations. Oh! Oh! I am so disturbed. Do tell me, what about these manifestations?"

Knowing that many honest Christians are asking the same questions, might it not be well to look at this important matter from the standpoint of God's Word today? Let us begin with verse 7 in chapter 12 of I Corinthians, which says, "The manifestation of the Spirit to profit withal."

Quoting the whole context we read as follows: "Now there are diversities of gifts, but the same Spirit. And there are differences of administrations, but the same Lord. And there are diversities of operations; but it is the same God which worketh all in all. But the manifestation of the Spirit is given to every man to profit withal." "Yes, but what is the good of these manifestations?" you ask. Why "to profit withal," answers Paul.

"Well, but what can be the profit resulting from manifestations such as shouting, dancing, shaking, or falling under the power?" you ask.

In a moment, and we will take these things up one by one, but first let me say that when the power of the Holy Spirit is upon a person or a church you can no more stifle the manifestations without quenching the power of the Spirit than you can shut off all air from a fire without extinguishing it, or turn off the water faucet without stopping the flow of water, or turn off the electric light switch without putting out the lights, or cutting the telephone wire without breaking the connection. Wherever there is living, vital, tangible power, there is bound to be a manifestation.

Turn on the gas jet of your stove, apply a match to it and there will be a hot flame. The greater the gas pressure the greater the flame.

Then take down your shining teakettle that has stood filled with cold water on the shelf, quiet, cold and orderly enough to please any church member; put it over the hot flame, keep it there a few moments, and the first thing you know, it will just be obliged to break forth into singing. If the fire burns low, singing may be as far as your kettle will get, but keep it on the hot fire and soon steam and vapor will rise like praise from a heart that is warmed by His love. The hotter it gets, the more manifestations there are in the kettle, till at last it is bubbling and dancing and boiling all over.

If you do not like manifestations, dear believer, turn the gas or power off and you will not be bothered with the manifestations very long, your particular kettle will soon sit still enough and cold enough to suit even your most rigid ideas of propriety and order.

We repeat that where there is power there is a manifestation of that power. Put your church or self on the hot flame of Jesus' love and the Spirit's power, and you, like yonder kettle, will soon break forth into singing, and the vapor of praise will rise, not from outside sources, but from within the innermost depths of your being, and as the fire burns brighter there will be a bubbling and dancing in your soul. Try to put the lid on tightly if you will, but 'twill only boil over through the spout. Stop up that and keep it on the fire and there will be an explosion that will blow the cover off, and the bubbling and dancing will go on as long as the kettle stays on the fire.

The wind is invisible, but there is a power there, and when it blows through the trees there is a manifestation, the leaves begin to shake. The harder the wind, the more the power, the greater the manifestations. The branches, limbs, and even the trunk sway. I have known greater trees than you to be slain prostrate beneath this visible power of the invisible wind.

We might mention many more instances wherein the workings of nature are analogous with the workings of the Spirit. Let us turn, however, from these comparisons in nature to the Word of God. Let us ascertain what saith the Scriptures pertaining to the subject of manifestations, and let them be the authority on the subject.

DANCING IN THE SPIRIT

Is dancing in the Spirit scriptural in the light of God's Word? Yes, the Word is full of it. Dancing belongs to the Lord. The devil has simply tried to imitate it and has made as poor an imitation of this as most of the other things he has tried to counterfeit. If you read carefully what the Scripture says about dancing you will find that singing, music and dancing have their place in the Lord's church. I am wondering if you who disapprove of dancing in the Spirit today disapprove also of Exodus 15:20-21, where "Miriam the prophetess . . . took a timbrel in her hand; and all the women went out after her with timbrels and with dances. And Miriam answered them, Sing ye to the Lord, for he hath triumphed gloriously." The whole multitude of women, Miriam, the prophetess and leader, went forth praising the Lord with dancing, shouting and music.

I am wondering if you approve of Moses, who also led the hosts in the same way, with music and dancing; whether you approve of David in II Samuel 6:14, where "David danced before the Lord with all his might." His wife disapproved, you remember, as she stood behind her window. I have always believed, however, that if she could only have been outside where the full tides of praise were flowing, could she but have heard the music, she, too, would have wanted to dance and praise the Lord. Oh, come outside of the window of self and formality and remember that David's wife was stricken with barrenness to the day of her death because she disapproved and fought manifestations. Did you ever know of an individual or congregation who fought the manifestations of the power of God without being stricken with barrenness and leanness? I never did. Remember, too, they who laid their hands upon the ark to steady it were consumed immediately by the indignation of God.

Psalm 149:3 says: "Let them praise his name in the dance: let them sing praises unto him with the timbrel and harp." Psalm 150:4, "Praise him with the timbrel and dance." Jeremiah 31:13, "Then shall the virgin rejoice in the dance, both young men and old together." Acts 3:8 tells us that when the lame man was healed "he leaping up stood, and walked, and entered . . . into the temple, walking, and leaping, and praising God."

This same redeemer which was theirs is ours today. He heals in the same way. How can we keep from dancing and praising such a Saviour?

SHOUTING

It seems almost impossible that any Bible student would question for a moment the right of the children of the Lord to shout His praises, the Word is so filled with it. You recall that "When the ark . . . came into the camp, all Israel shouted with a great shout, so that the earth rang again. And when the Philistines heard the noise of the shout, they said, What meaneth the noise of this great shout in the camp of the Hebrews?" (I Samuel 4:5). Again we read that "David and all the house of Israel brought up the ark of the Lord with shouting, and with the sound of the trumpet" (II Samuel 6:15). Psalms tell us "O clap your hands, all ye people, shout unto God with a voice of triumph."

"There's a shout in the Camp. Hallelujah!
Glory to God!
There's an echo in Heaven. Hallelujah!
Glory to God!"

Truly, "the children of the Lord have a right to shout and sing." We are in the same battle today that we read of in Joshua 6:5, where it came to pass that when they made a long blast with the ram's horn, and heard the sound of the trumpet, that all the people shouted with a great shout and the wall of the city fell down flat. There will be a wonderful shout some of these days, for we read that "The Lord Himself shall descend from heaven with a shout, with the trump of God." Why, even the Lord shouts, and He is our great example.

Truly, we have something worth shouting over. Joy always manifests itself. The shouts at ball games, races and political celebrations are accepted as a usual and expected thing. The day would be considered tame and with something radically wrong and missing without it. Remember how the announcement of peace was met right here in our own country, how they tied down the horns and the whistles, how every conceivable noise-making device was brought forth to swell the sound of jubilee. Now we have heard the proclamation of everlasting peace, from the King who has won the greatest battle ever fought. How can we keep from shouting? There are so many shouting for the devil with none to hinder that we thank God for those who shout for Jesus.

When shouting is in the Spirit it comes from such depth and rings so true and genuine that none can mistake it. The devil will try to imitate the shout in the camp of the Hebrews, but there will be a hollow, forced sound that does not ring true. There are many who do not like the noise of the shouting, but we advise all such to let Jesus fill them with the same power and glory, to put a shout in their soul, for this is by far the quietest world they will ever live in. In heaven John heard the shouting and praising of the multitude as they cried, "Holy, holy, salvation and honor and dominion belongeth unto him, till the voice and shouting of the people was as the sound of many waters, and as the voice of great thunder." Surely those who dislike shouting would dislike heaven, or must learn to join the song. O, how can you look upon such a wonderful Saviour without shouting His praise? And as for those who are cast into hell, "There shall be weeping and wailing and gnashing of teeth." That will surely be a noisy place, and I would much rather hear the noise of shouts and rejoicing than weeping. Wouldn't you?

O, beloved, thank God for the shout and the dance and the sound of joy. Let us never be ashamed of it.

How many denominations once had God's power resting on them in this same way and became too proud and haughty and dignified to remain yielded to His will. Soon the power left, the amen corner left, and, as Joel 1:12 puts it, "The vine is dried up, and the fig tree languisheth; the pomegranate tree, the palm tree also, and the apple tree, even all the trees of the field, are withered: because joy is withered away from the sons of men." Each of the churches that once had power and glory of God resting upon it, and later fought this power, is barren today. The enemy would like Pentecost to do the same as those who have gone before, but if we ever do this thing God will cause the cloud of glory to lift from us and call another people who will be willing to go on and who are not ashamed to let Him have His way. We will be left our creeds and ceremonies and forms as surely as were our predecessors.

The outpouring of the Holy Ghost on the day of Pentecost, Acts 2:4, stood for a mighty manifestation of the power of God; men and women reeled, staggered, talked in tongues, were accused of being drunken. Did it turn the people away? No. Three thousand souls were added to the church that day. If we call ourselves Pentecostal, if we have the sign "Foursquare" over our church door, let us stand behind all that it means, or else change our name, take the sign from our door, and go back to church forms and ceremonies. The Holy Spirit never intrudes nor forces His way and manifestations where He is not wanted. Many flourishing churches, once filled and swayed by the power of God, have quenched the Spirit, criticized and checked manifestations until today they have no manifestations to quench or to bring reproach upon them. It is not difficult to rid a church of this outward working of the supernatural power of God. Just a little criticism and disapproval and the gentle dove will spread His wings and pass on to some other abode where He can find a people humble enough to let Him have His way, and not ashamed of the manifestations.

Thank God we have not come to the place where we

have to try to be popular or pleasing to the world. Even if we are a gazing-stock, or a spectacle, let God and His Spirit have the right of way, whatever the cost may be.

SHAKING AND TREMBLING UNDER THE POWER

As for the shaking and trembling under the power, very often when the great power of the eternal, omnipotent, almighty God comes in direct contact with, or moves upon a weak, earthly frame, there is quaking and trembling, not of fear as men count fear, but of power. Moses said, "I do exceedingly quake and tremble." In Acts we read of one place where the house wherein they sat was shaken.

Hebrews 12:26 says, His "voice then shook the earth: but now . . . once more I shake not the earth only, but also heaven." See Acts 9:9, how Paul trembled in the presence of the Lord. Daniel tells us that he did exceedingly quake and tremble, and in speaking of those who were with him, says that a great quaking fell upon them. Sacred history tells us that this manifestation has not been uncommon all down through the ages, and coming to modern days we note that the Quakers came by their name because of the way they shook and quaked under the power of God. We might mention also the shaking Methodists. This is the same power which we see in our midst today.

BEING PROSTRATED UNDER THE POWER

What about this being slain, prostrated, lying under the power? You do not think it looks at all dignified or proper, you say. I wonder whether Peter looked dignified or proper when he lay in the trance on his housetop and saw the vision of the sheet let down (Acts 10:9-16), or John, on the isle of Patmos, when he lay at Jesus' feet as one dead, or Daniel, as he lay in a vision, or Saul, when he fell from his horse in the dust of the road as Jesus revealed Himself to him. It was as though

Jesus, when He conquered, got both of Saul's shoulders to the ground, and he surrendered there and then. 'Twas not at all dignified or anything for the "flesh" or "pride" to boast over, I agree. In fact they were so ashamed and mortified they gave up in despair and died there and then; but O, the Spirit life of humility and knowledge of God's power that took their place!

We might go on to mention Isaiah, Jeremiah and others who fell prostrate before Him. We might mention the prostrations in the early Methodist church, the Salvation Army, the Welsh Revival, and today, throughout the world, wherever God is pouring out His Spirit, and when I get to heaven I expect to see angels and men before Him prostrate fall as they "bring forth the royal diadem and crown Him Lord of all."

SPEAKING IN TONGUES AND INTERPRETATION

In Isaiah 28:11 we read, "For with stammering lips and another tongue will he speak to this people." Jesus Himself said, "And these signs shall follow them that believe . . . they shall speak with new tongues" (Mark 16:17). In Acts 2:4 those who were filled with the Holy Ghost began to speak with other tongues as the Spirit gave them utterance. Likewise Acts 10:46, Acts 19:6, and Paul tells us (chapter 14 of I Corinthians), " . . . let him that speaketh in an unknown tongue pray that he may interpret," and that, in the congregation, "If any man speak in an unknown tongue, let it be by two, or at most by three, and that by course; and let one interpret."

Are manifestations of the Spirit scriptural? Y-E-S. Are all manifestations scriptural? N-O. How can we tell the difference? It is easy to discern, in the Spirit, between the real and the counterfeit. There is a different shine on the face, a different ring in the voice, a majesty and holiness. There will be that which edifies and builds up. (But just here remember that your conception of edifying manifestations and that of God may vary. Had you seen the 120 reeling and staggering like drunken men (Acts 2:13, 15), you might not have thought it edifying, yet God was in it, and Peter said they were filled with the Spirit, and 3,000 souls were added to the church that day.)

But do we claim that all manifestations are in the Spirit? you ask. We answer No, for the devil has tried to imitate manifestations as he has everything else. There are also some manifestations in the flesh by those who are anxious for God to manifest Himself and use them, who run before the Lord.

But what shall we do in our church when we find manifestations that are not of God? Shall we quench the Holy Spirit for fear of that which is not of the Spirit? Not at all. Do as Aaron did when the enemy sought to counterfeit; you remember, he threw down his rod and it became a serpent. Straightway the magicians threw down their rods and immediately they became serpents. Did Moses and Aaron begin to wail and regret that they had obeyed God, thus giving the enemy an opportunity to manifest himself? Why, no, their God was bigger than the devil. Their serpent opened up his mouth and swallowed up all the other serpents until they were out of sight completely; so will the true Holy Spirit, if we let Him have His way, swallow up and spoil every trick and tactic of the enemy. If you let Him have His way you will have no need to fight in this battle. He will do it all, and get greater glory to Himself then as though there had been no struggle. The counterfeit makes the genuine to shine the brighter. When the Ark is in the midst all earthly gods must fall and be broken before it. Hallelujah!

Many leaders seem to fear the enemy so much that they almost act as if they had to protect "poor little God" from the onslaughts of the "Great, Big DEVIL"; but Oh, dear ones, our God is Great and Big and High and Wide. He sitteth in the heavens, the earth is His footstool, the seas are in the palm of His hand, the mountains are but as the small dust in His balances. He is more than a match for the enemy. Let Him have His way when

He will, where He will, how He will, and the earth will quake and His enemies be scattered before Him as clouds before the whirlwind.

He is getting a sign-and-wonder people today, a people who are a gazing-stock to the world. The Holy Spirit is His own advertising agent today as He was on the day of Pentecost when the multitude came running together crying, "What meaneth this?"

There is going to be a great manifestation some of these days, dear ones, a greater shaking, a greater leaping and shouting than ever you have heard or imagined before. The graves of those who died in the Lord are going to be shaken open wide and with them the liberated souls of those who remain are going to leap so high that they will not return to this earth again for a long, long time, and shouting! Oh, what a triumphant, victorious, joyful shout will rend the sky as our eyes behold the Bridegroom descending out of heaven, clad in power and might. What a manifestation there will be that day! Every band, every stringed instrument in heaven will be there. Every mouth will be filled with the shouts of His praises, as the saints are swept into His presence. They will come with songs of everlasting joy upon their heads.

In the meantime, dear heart, let Him have His way with thee, quench not the Spirit, but let Him move upon the waters as He will, for from Genesis, the first chapter, when He moved upon the waters, saying, "Let there be light, and there was light," there was a manifestation. From the moment that at His Word the moon and the stars sprang into being, down into the present day and on into eternity, where God is, where God moves, and where God speaks, there will be a manifestation of His presence and of His power.

Chapter III JESUS CHRIST THE HEALER

Is Jesus Christ the same yesterday and today and forever?

The Bible says He is (cf. Hebrews 13:8).

You cannot believe the Bible and deny that Jesus ministered as the healer during His lifetime on earth and throughout the period described in the book of Acts. Indeed, we see Jesus healing the sick through Paul's prayers in the very last chapter of Acts!

Now if Jesus healed yesterday, and He is the same today, surely the church should be preaching and practicing divine healing! Nevertheless, millions in Christendom suppose that divine healing is a novelty, a passing fad which some churchmen have concocted to add some new gimmick to the gospel! Some have criticized Foursquaredom for promoting this imagined innovation.

Anyone who nurses that misconception needs to ponder this pronouncement by a noted religious leader: "There is nothing new about the miracle of healing!"

Those words could have been spoken by Aimee Semple McPherson or Dr. Charles Price or Smith Wigglesworth or Oral Roberts or any of the evangelists who have attracted attention in recent generations by their healing ministries. But none of these Pentecostals was responsible for the statement, "There is nothing new about the miracle of healing." Instead these words were spoken by a high official of the oldest Protestant denomination in the English-speaking world. It was Dr. Austin Pardue, the Episcopal Bishop of Pittsburgh, who declared, "There is nothing new about the miracle of healing!" Dr. Pardue has been practicing a healing ministry in accordance with chapter 5 of the epistle of James for many years!

Of course, the final authority vindicating the fact that

divine healing is not a new innovation in the church is not the word of any individual minister but rather the Word of God itself. From the first book of the Bible we behold the Lord at work in healing physical afflictions.

HEALING IN THE BIBLE

Who is the first man on record who prayed for the healing of another? It was none other than Abraham, the father of the faithful himself. Genesis 20 tells how the distinguished founder of the nation of Israel prayed for the household of Abimelech, and God delivered! That was about 4,000 years ago. Of course, there is no reason to doubt that others before Abraham prayed for the sick with gratifying results. We just have no record of such occasions.

The Old Testament's covenant of healing appears as early as Exodus 15:26. Not long after Moses led the Israelites out of Egypt the Lord revealed Himself as the God of healing: "If thou wilt diligently hearken to the voice of the Lord thy God, and wilt do that which is right in his sight, and wilt give ear to his commandments, and keep all his statutes, I will put none of these diseases upon thee, which I have brought upon the Egyptians: for I am the Lord that healeth thee." More will be said about this revelation later in this chapter.

Ensuing books in the Old Testament report remarkable miracles of healing. Israelites bitten by fiery serpents recovered when they looked at the brazen serpent on a pole Moses erected, a symbol Christ applied to Himself in John 3:14. "And as Moses lifted up the serpent in the wilderness, even so must the Son of man be lifted up." David could testify that the Lord not only forgave all his iniquities but also healed all his diseases (Psalm 103:3). Elisha gave directions to Naaman which, when obeyed, brought healing from leprosy to the celebrated Syrian general. Isaiah ministered to Hezekiah and the king recovered from his critical illness. Finally, the Old

Testament canon closed with Malachi's marvelous prophecy of the coming Christ: "But unto you that fear my name shall the Sun of righteousness arise with healing in his wings" (Malachi 4:2).

Christ's inauguration of public ministry prompted a spectacular revival of the miraculous wherever He itinerated. Years later Peter could capsulize his Lord's career with the statement, ". . . God anointed Jesus of Nazareth . . . who went about doing good, and healing all that were oppressed of the devil" (Acts 10:38). It is no exaggeration to declare that every disease capitulated to Jesus' healing virtue. The blind saw. The lame leaped. The deaf heard. The dumb spoke. The maimed became whole. Jesus cleansed lepers, restored paralytics, delivered the insane, and cast out demons. Indeed, Matthew reports, "And Jesus went about all Galilee, teaching in their synagogues, and preaching the gospel of the kingdom, and healing all manner of sickness and all manner of disease among the people" (Matthew 4:23).

Jesus not only healed the sick Himself, He commissioned His disciples to minister healing to the afflicted as well. The gospel of Luke records the things which Jesus began to do and teach during His earthly lifetime. But Jesus continued the same ministry, including the healing of sick bodies, after His ascension through His apostles and disciples and believers! Peter, John, Philip the deacon, Paul, and countless other Apostolic Christians not mentioned by name in the Bible carried on this ministry with remarkable results. Jerusalem witnessed a mighty stirring when people "brought forth the sick into the streets, and laid them on beds and couches, that at the least the shadow of Peter passing by might overshadow some of them" (Acts 5:15). What happened then? "They were healed every one" (Acts 5:16).

Miracles were ordinary, everyday affairs, it seems, while Paul resided in Ephesus. Otherwise why would Luke describe certain wonders as "special miracles"? Yet we read, "And God wrought special miracles by the hands of Paul: So that from his body were brought unto the sick handkerchiefs or aprons, and the diseases departed from them, and the evil spirits went out of them" (Acts 19:11-12).

Some have wondered why, if healing was so prominently ministered in New Testament times, this ministry disappeared from the church at large to the point that its re-emphasis in modern times has prompted accusations that an unscriptural innovation is being promoted in Christendom by those who champion divine healing in our generation.

Of course, as is eloquently explained in the sermon, "Lost and Restored," divine healing was by no means the only scriptural truth to vanish from prominence in the church. The fact that God will heal the sick in answer to believing prayer is only one of the many precious truths which were submerged under the tidal wave of apostasy which inundated Christendom through the Dark Ages, to be recovered to the church only after centuries of neglect! Martin Luther's emphasis on justification by faith was just as much a novelty in his day as has been the revival of faith in Jesus as the healer in our times! The Foursquare Gospel is fostering no new doctrine when it exalts Jesus Christ as the great physician. For as Episcopalian Bishop Pardue insisted, "There is nothing new about the miracle of divine healing."

That the Lord Jesus is the healer of sick bodies today is assured by the promises of Scripture, by the atonement of Christ, and by the nature of God!

HEALING PROMISED IN SCRIPTURE

The promises of the Bible furnish a firm foundation for faith for physical deliverance. When Jesus declared, "*What things soever ye desire, when ye pray,* believe that ye receive them, and ye shall have them" (Mark 11:24), the phrase which appears in italics includes healing of sick bodies. Do you desire to be made whole from your diseases? Do you plead that petition in prayer?

Then believe that you receive healing, and you shall have healing!

Again, when Christ proclaimed, "If ye shall ask any thing in my name, I will do it" (John 14:14), the words "any thing" includes healing. Ask, and Jesus will act. Ask, and you shall receive! The Bible's promises that the Lord will answer prayer generally afford strong grounds for confidence that Jesus will heal any and every disease. Even if there was not one single definite promise in the whole compass of Scripture which mentioned physical healing, any Christian believer would still have the right to ask the Lord for healing on the basis of the Biblical revelation that God hears and answers prayer! Passages like Philippians 4:6 command Christian believers to pray about everything. Everything includes the needs of health.

However, we have specific, definite promises of divine healing, besides those passages where God declares He will answer prayer generally. From the Old Testament come Deuteronomy 7:15: "And the Lord will take away from thee all sickness"; Jeremiah 30:17: "For I will restore health unto thee, and I will heal thee of thy wounds, saith the Lord"; and Isaiah 33:24: "And the inhabitant shall not say, I am sick." The New Testament abounds with healing promises. Jesus incorporated the healing ministry into His great commission, proclaiming, "And these signs shall follow them that believe; In my name . . . they shall lay hands on the sick, and they shall recover" (Mark 16:17-18). If the command to go with the gospel persists in force to this day, the promise of healing attending that evangelization must also continue in force to this day. Then there is the New Testament healing covenant of James 5:14-15 which will be discussed later in this chapter. Undeniably God's promises in the Bible to answer prayer generally and to heal the sick specifically constitute a sound support for faith for physical healing.

HEALING PROVIDED IN CHRIST'S ATONEMENT

But more than the promises of Scripture encourage this belief. The atonement of Jesus Christ contributes confidence that the Lord will heal. Jesus provided a double cure for a double curse. Sin and sickness intruded together in human affairs at the fall in the Garden of Eden. Deuteronomy 28 includes sicknesses specifically in the curse. Jesus bore our sins to the cross, and He bore our sicknesses to the post—the whipping post.

Isaiah beheld Jesus as both Saviour and Healer! "But he was wounded for our transgressions, he was bruised for our iniquities: the chastisement of our peace was upon him; and with his stripes we are healed" (Isaiah 53:5). Just one verse before the prophet proclaimed, "Surely he hath borne our griefs, and carried our sorrows." The last phrase of Isaiah 53:5 and the first phrase of Isaiah 53:4 both prophesy of healing in the atonement of Christ!

Some, however, object, "It means spiritual healing only. Isaiah was not speaking of physical healing."

How can we know for sure? How can we determine whether the prophet meant healing of sick bodies or healing of sinful souls?

The Bible is its own best interpreter. And by interpreting scripture by scripture we can establish beyond doubt that physical healing is meant in the opening statement of Isaiah 53:4, thus making the presumption unassailable that when healing is mentioned in the next verse, the reference there is to physical healing, too.

But how can we demonstrate that healing of the sick is prophesied in Isaiah 53:4: "Surely he hath borne our griefs, and carried our sorrows"? This appears clearly in the application the New Testament makes of this Old Testament prophecy. At the end of a great day of healing in Jesus' ministry Matthew reports,

> "When the even was come, they brought unto him many that were possessed with devils: and he cast out the spirits with his word, and healed all that

were sick: That it might be fulfilled which was spoken by Esaias the prophet, saying, Himself took our infirmities, and bare our sicknesses" (Matthew 8:16-17).

Consider carefully how Matthew interprets Jesus' fulfillment of Isaiah's forecast of chapter 53 verse 4. He "healed all that were sick." Jesus healed sick bodies! Physical healing rather than spiritual healing is cited by the evangelist as the fulfillment of the ancient prophecy. Note moreover how Matthew quoted the Old Testament passage: "Himself took our infirmities, and bare our sicknesses." "Infirmities" represents the meaning of the Hebrew word used in Isaiah 53:4 better than "griefs" which appears in the Authorized Version in that place. And "sicknesses" more truly represents the meaning of the Hebrew word translated "sorrows." Rotherham, probably the most literal of all Bible translators, renders the verse, "Yet surely our sicknesses he carried. And as for our pains, he bare the burden of them." Now these sicknesses are physical, otherwise Matthew would have erred in describing the healing of sick bodies as the fulfillment of this prophecy! And every time Jesus heals the sick in our generation, He enhances the fulfillment of Isaiah's prophecy.

But how does this relate to divine healing in the atonement?

The terminology is convincing. Jesus not only heals the sick, but He is said to have borne our sicknesses and carried our pains. As the Lamb of God He took away the sins of the world. He also bore the burden of our sicknesses. The Lord laid on Christ the iniquity of us all. Jesus also shouldered our diseases.

Moreover, the conjunction of salvation from sin and healing of sicknesses in Isaiah 53:4-5 unites these provisions in the same sacrifice of Christ. Now Peter paraphrases Isaiah 53:5 in his first epistle: "Who his own self bare our sins in his own body to the tree, that we, being dead to sins, should live unto righteousness; by whose stripes ye were healed." Of course, the change of the tense of the verb "healed" in the two passages appears significant. Isaiah used the present, "We are healed," while Peter used the past tense, "Ye were healed." The atonement was not an accomplished fact when the prophet wrote. The Saviour's sacrifice was still future. By the time Peter penned his paraphrase, however, Jesus had already died on the cross for men's sins and He had been whipped at the post for their healing! The cruel Roman lash had broken His body, splattering walls and floor and ceiling with chunks of Christ's lacerated flesh. Jesus' ordeal at the whipping post had no effect on sinners' salvation. His crucifixion at Calvary would completely provide atonement for sin. To redeem fallen men did not require the breaking of Christ's body, only the shedding of His blood. Why then was Jesus whipped? The Bible proclaims the answer: "By his stripes ye were healed."

Jesus incorporated this element into the Holy Communion which He instituted as a memorial of His atoning sacrifice. The Lord's Supper serves two elements, not just one. The cup signifies the blood He shed to save us. The bread symbolizes His body which was broken for our healing. St. Paul emphasized to the Corinthians the importance of discerning the Lord's body. Born-again believers are not likely to fail to discern the Lord's blood. But many fail to understand the significance of His broken body. They need to understand and experience the truth that "by his stripes ye were healed." Because the Corinthian believers neglected to discern the Lord's body as broken for their healing the Apostle informed them, "For this cause many are weak and sickly among you, and many sleep" (I Corinthians 11:30). The implication is that these victims could have had health if they had discerned the Lord's body which had been broken for them. Divine healing is more than a promise of God. Healing is a provision of Christ's atonement.

HEALING AND THE NATURE OF GOD

But there is even further support for faith for divine healing! The Bible reveals that healing is an expression of the nature of God! The Old Testament healing covenant of Exodus 15:26 climaxes with the divine disclosure voiced by Jehovah Himself: "I am the Lord that healeth thee." Here divine healing is included in the name of God, and what is in God's name is in His nature! "I am the Lord that healeth thee" constitutes a revelation that it is the nature of God to heal, that our Lord is the God of healing!

One day the Lord that healeth took human flesh. As T. DeWitt Talmadge put it dramatically, "Omnipotence was sheathed in his arm, and omniscience strung in his optic nerve." Jesus "went about doing good, and healing all that were oppressed of the devil" (Acts 10:38). The Lord that healeth spoke to a leper, "Be thou clean," and the leprosy left. The Lord that healeth rebuked the fever that prostrated Peter's wife's mother, and that raging fever fled. His presence radiated such power that the sick had only to touch the hem of His garment in order to be made whole. And Jesus Christ is still the same today. He is still "the Lord that healeth thee." Healing remains an expression of the nature of God. Christ is the Great I Am, not a great has-been. The day of miracles is not past, because the day of the miracle worker is not past. Foursquaredom believes in divine healing because we believe in the divine Healer, who is the Lord that changes not, the same yesterday and today and forever, for whom nothing is too hard and with whom nothing is impossible! We base our faith for physical deliverance on the promises of the Bible, on the atonement of Jesus Christ, and on the immutable nature of our God! Promises proclaim, "Jesus heals." The atonement announces, "Jesus heals." The very nature of God reveals, "Jesus heals."

NEW TESTAMENT HEALING COVENANT

Now the New Testament covenant of healing appears in James 5:14-15:

> "Is any sick among you? let him call for the elders of the church; and let them pray over him, anointing him with oil in the name of the Lord: And the prayer of faith shall save the sick, and the Lord shall raise him up; and if he have committed sins, they shall be forgiven him."

Some have sought to explain away this particular passage by arguing that the epistle of James was just for the Jews, that it has no authority for Gentile Christians. They appeal to the first verse to substantiate this limitation: "James, a servant of God and of the Lord Jesus Christ, to the twelve tribes which are scattered abroad, greeting."

However, this method of limiting scriptures, if applied wholesale to the Bible, would remove the authority of almost every passage. James' address of his epistle "to the twelve tribes which are scattered abroad" no more limits his letter's application to them than do Paul's epistles addressed to the Romans or Corinthians or Galatians limit Paul's letters to those peoples!

Do not be deceived. James 5:14-15 is a message to Christians in churches, not to Jews in synagogues. James did not suggest that the sick summon the rabbis of the synagogue but that they call for the elders of the church! And of course, the gospel of Jesus is the same for all races. There is not one message for Gentiles and another for Jews!

Three parties participate in this New Testament healing covenant, the sick person, the elders, and the Lord.

James inquires, "Is any sick among you?" He does not limit healing to a favored few. Rather he boldly extends the promise of help to *any* sick person. As whosoever will may come and be saved, any sick may appropriate the Lord's healing ministry. The responsibility of the sick party is to call for prayer. "Let him call" is in the imperative mood. This is a command. When a person becomes ill, he should at once call. He should not expect the elders to know he is sick. He should not wait for the elders to offer their services. The initiative here is with the suffering believer. God expects him to send for the ministers.

Having been summoned, the elders' responsibility is to come to the bedside and pray for the sick, anointing him with oil in the name of the Lord Jesus.

This oil is not, as some have imagined, a medicine. If it were a medicine, why would it be administered by elders of the church? You consult a physician to obtain medication. The oil is not a medicine. The oil does not heal. It is rather a means of faith or as modern evangelists sometimes call it, point of contact. God has employed numerous other means in ministering healing, such as the laying on of hands (Mark 16:18), the spoken word (Matthew 8:8-10), contact with healing cloths (Acts 19:11-12, cf. Matthew 9:21), a look (Numbers 21:18), Hezekiah's poultice, Naaman's seven dips in the Jordan, and various others. These means are not necessary in the sense that they have any organic connection with the recovery. Just as Jesus employed the loaves and fishes to feed the multitude, though He could as easily have done so without them, so God can and often does heal without means. But God has appointed anointing with oil as the sign of this healing covenant. When the sick summon the elders, the elders should pray and anoint with oil.

From that point on the responsibility passes to the Lord. The promise proclaims, "The Lord shall raise him up." It is never the minister who heals, it is always the Lord. Nor has Jesus abandoned this ministry in our age because of the tremendous strides of medical science. Medical men abounded on earth at the time Jesus went about healing all manner of disease, for Mark tells us there were "many physicians" (Mark 5:26). There are many more physicians today, but they have not destroyed sickness and disease. Foursquaredom has never reflected a negative attitude concerning medical science. In a sermon entitled "Living Epistles" delivered in Angelus Temple on March 23, 1924, Aimee Semple McPherson said, "Thank God for every hospital. Thank God for every doctor and physician and all the skill that they have! I never cease to thank God for alleviation of suffering that earthly physicians have been able to give." But even with all that doctors can do, the need for the healing ministry of Jesus is just as great or greater today than in Bible times. And Jesus heals today. The testimonies, authenticated by medical examination in countless cases, are irrefutable! As the Spirit-filled Presbyterian pastor, James Brown, put it, "I don't argue about divine healing. I've seen God touch people. The argument is over. When you meet Jesus Christ you have to get out or get in. It's not 'pull up a chair and let's discuss this, brother'."

The expedients to which deniers of divine healing resort to, to prove that divine healing is not for today, remind us of a debate in Greece in the fifth century, B.C. An old Sophist teacher by juggling the laws of logic proposed to prove that it is impossible for a man to walk. The philosopher on the other side of the question did not offer any verbal argument. He simply got up and walked around the room. That ended the debate dramatically.

As in the case of the baptism with the Holy Spirit, so also in healing, the man who has an experience is never at the mercy of the man who only has an argument. Hundreds of thousands, probably millions of Christians have experienced divine healing and testify to recovery through faith in Jesus Christ as their great physician. Jesus not only saves the sinner's soul and empowers his spirit with Holy Ghost baptism, He also heals the sick body.

This truth is a fundamental of Foursquare faith, for the third phase of this gospel exalts Jesus Christ as the divine healer! Faith in Him today will bring the same deliverance like faith secured in Bible days. Jesus still says to believers, "Thy faith hath made thee whole" (Matthew 9:22). He still says, "As thou hast believed, so be it done unto thee" (Matthew 8:13), because He is "the same yesterday, and today, and forever" (Hebrews 13:8). It is man's part to seek the Healer's ministry in faith. Then Jesus will do His divine part and raise him up to health!

Sermon

THE HEALING CUP

My eyes fill with tears and my heart grows warm as I consider the healing cup that I have had the privilege under God of humbly bearing to hundreds of thousands during the years of my ministry.

Divine healing is quite well known today. I read an article in the *Ladies Home Journal* about divine healing and was impressed by the commonplace and yet very beautiful way in which the author spoke about it. What a change, I thought! The article, which mentioned some of my meetings, as well as those conducted by James Moore Hickson of the Episcopal Church, Dr. Charles Shreve of McKendree Methodist Church of Washington, D. C., and others whose names I have forgotten, described the manner in which divine healing is being practiced.

It is not uncommon now to hear Mr. Smith say to Mr. Jones on the street, "Did you hear about my wife? She's been healed in answer to prayer." But years ago when I first began preaching the gospel divine healing was not as well known as it is now. Even when we came to Los Angeles the message of divine healing was not generally known. When I first began to pray for the sick here, it caused an excitement and somewhat of a furor.

Two ministers especially made it the subject of their sermons for four weeks, preaching against divine healing and declaring there was nothing to it. Finally they became very excited. I think probably their people went back and asked them to pray for them. If I could pray for the sick, why couldn't they do it. From reading the articles I decided they must have come here and procured names and addresses of the people we had prayed for, then they had called on them in their homes.

"Look here," they said, "didn't Mrs. McPherson pay you?"

On the one hand they accused that I paid the people to testify, and on the other hand they charged that people had to pay me to get healed! So it was sort of a paying proposition both ways! At any rate, many could not believe that Jesus was actually healing sick bodies in this present generation.

Finally I became rather weary of the attacks. I asked my people, "What do we have to *prove* that Jesus heals the sick? We have the Bible, yes, but a lot of people will not believe that. I have your word—your testimonies, but they say you are mistaken. It is often charged that most of the diseases for which healing was claimed•were imaginary. People imagined they had a cancer or were paralyzed. In case of fire or accident or some other emotionalism they would be able to 'snap out of it,' using the critics' expression, as though nothing had happened." So I determined I would be a very practical, level-headed woman and see whether I could prove, outside of the Bible and outside of faith, just from a matter-of-fact standpoint, that Jesus did heal the sick. As a result we had a photographer come over and photograph each person before he was prayed for. We made some questionnaires and had them filled out. We had the person seeking healing go to his doctor and get a doctor's certificate and fasten it to the back of the questionnaire.

We continued this for about eight months. At the end of that time we had thousands of questionnaires filled and thousands of pictures. In many instances we sent the people back to their physician for a clean bill of health after they were prayed for and had their pictures taken again. Myrtle Terry came, with her lips cut, her face swollen, bruised. She had been an epileptic for ten years, biting her tongue so that the blood spurted from her lips. Thin and broken she was when she came and the first picture was taken. Afterwards she had a new picture and a complete bill of health. No more epilepsy! Jesus had made her whole. In addition to abandoned wheelchairs, crutches and braces, we kept these written testimonies.

At the end of that time I went on the radio and calmly but firmly announced that if the next preacher who was going to preach against divine healing would just let me know forty-eight hours in advance and reserve 1,000 seats for us, that I would march 1,000 people to his door with crutches and X-rays, with their doctors' certificates and a proof that Jesus heals the sick!

There really is no "bunkum" about it. Jesus Christ is really the Son of God. He really came to this world to die for lost sinners, and not only by the precious blood have we redemption from sin, but with His stripes at the whipping post we are healed. When Christ was here upon earth He carried in His hand, as it were, a healing cup. Wherever He went He put it in the hands of needy ones. One day He saw a blind man tip-tapping his way along through life, hopeless, his mouth all drooped at the corners, his face seamed with loneliness.

"Wait a moment, man," said Jesus. "I am going to make you whole."

He stooped down and got some clay to put on the poor man's eyes. I suppose the Lord was trying to teach us a lesson when He did that. Maybe somebody there did not believe in His power to make the blind to see, so the Lord took clay and put it on his eyes. I wonder if He didn't mean by that an illustrated sermon. You know, the Lord made man out of clay in the beginning, and if the Lord can make man out of clay, breathe in his nostrils and give him the breath of life, can He not restore him?

Jesus touched the man's eyes with clay, then said, "Go, wash in the Pool of Siloam." The man went tapping to the pool, he washed his eyes, and he came, seeing. All along the way people shouted at him. "Why, is this he that used to sit and beg? It looks like him." "Yes," someone else said, "it is the man who was once blind." The man went jumping, shouting down the street, saying, "Hallelujah! Once I was blind, but now I see." And you know the preachers came around—I mean the scribes and Pharisees and high priests came round and said,

"Who made you whole? How did this happen?"

"Why, a man came and touched my eyes with clay and said, 'Receive your sight and by faith you are made whole.' "

"Was it this man Jesus?"

"Yes, it was Jesus."

"This Jesus is a sinner, a hypocrite, a rogue, a winebibber. This Jesus speaks against the government. This Jesus is this, and that, and the other!"

"Well, I don't know about that—I haven't had time to read all the papers and all you say about Him and all the priests say and all the Pharisees; I have not been able to see very well, I don't know much about Him one way or the other; I have not been so interested. But one thing I do know now: whereas I was blind, now I can see! Hallelujah!"

And he went singing and shouting on his way down the streets, being from that hour fully restored.

Jesus took the healing cup and passed it on.

"I am going home to be with the Father," He said to the disciples, "to prepare a place for you and to make intercession for you and to send My Spirit out upon you; but you go into all the world and preach this same gospel to every creature, and as you go, preach the gospel, cleanse the leper, heal the sick, raise the dead; freely you have received, freely give. Take the cup of healing wherever you go to preach."

Peter had it one day when he was going up to pray in the temple with John. As they came to the gate Beautiful just outside the temple, a man sitting there had been lame from birth, never could walk. He asked alms from Peter and John, in the old, whining voice he had always used.

"Why, man, you have asked the wrong people—we are preachers," was their reply as Peter and John looked down at him. "Silver and gold have I none, but such as I have give I unto thee. In the name of Jesus Christ of Nazareth, rise up and walk."

They took him by the right hand and lifted him up, and immediately the man drank from the healing cup which they bore in their hands. (The Bible is the healing cup. "He sent forth his word and healed them.")

As Peter and John went into the temple, they saw the man they had prayed for dancing joyously down the aisle of the temple.

I cannot keep people's feet on the ground when the Lord heals them. They jump and praise the Lord till I can get hold of them and say, "Sit down now and be quiet."

"Oh, I can't! My pain is all gone! That old paralyzed leg is healed! I can hear out of that ear I have not heard out of for forty years."

It is hard to keep people quiet under those conditions.

Down the aisle of the temple in Jerusalem came that man, leaping and shouting. "Oh, Glory! Glory! Glory! I have touched the healing cup; I have quaffed the healing virtue, and I am made whole. Glory!"

Paul received the healing cup. While he preached he noticed a poor man who had been lame for a long while and was unable to walk. His legs were helpless. He heard Paul preach, and while Paul preached, the lame man had faith born in his heart that Jesus could make him whole. And Paul, perceiving that the man had faith to be healed, stopped his sermon and the man was healed.

You know, you can perceive faith. Faith lights up

people's faces like an electric light inside a shaded window.

"In the name of Jesus of Nazareth, stand up on thy feet!" Paul commanded as he perceived that the lame man had faith to be healed. And the man stood and was made whole.

The healing cup comes down to my hand. The healing cup comes down to the hand of every preacher and elder and worker who will take hold of it. Here is the healing cup for us: "Is any sick among you? Let him call for the elders of the church; and let them pray over him, anointing him with oil in the name of the Lord: and the prayer of faith shall save the sick, and the Lord shall raise him up; and if he have committed any sins, it shall be forgiven him . . . Pray one for another that you may be healed . . . The effectual, fervent prayer of a righteous man availeth much."

And so the healing cup is still in our hands. Little did I think I would ever be praying for the sick. It certainly is not a life I would have chosen. I do not suppose there has been a time for years that I have walked around the places where I have been preaching that someone hasn't touched me on the arm and said, "Sister, I wish you would pray for me. I am so sick." "Sister, I wish you would pray for my aunt. She has just broken her leg." "Sister, I wish you would pray for my uncle. He has a cancer."

You put yourself in a young woman's place for years; maybe you would not just choose that life. I am surrounded always with the sick, the dying and the needy. And yet after many years in the service of the King, I am glad and happy to say that there is no imagination about it, laying the religious side of it aside for a moment—there is no imagination about it, Jesus Christ really works miracles and the blind see. I have seen cataracts melt like a little fleck of snow on a window pane. I have seen goiters go down as you would break a balloon and watch the air slowly ebbing out of it. I have seen tumors pass away in answer to prayer. I have seen people whose bones were decayed with tuberculosis of the bone restored, put away their crutches and stand up. I have seen legs that were three inches short grow until they were of the same length as their mates, and the crippled ones could walk. I have seen people straightened who were born with curvature of the spine and always walked bent over.

Jesus really does heal the sick. This is a practical gospel. It is not just talk! It works!

"Well, I don't think divine healing is very important," someone says.

You would, though, if you were sick. We all agree that salvation is the more important, of course. We all agree that, good as divine healing is, it has its weaknesses. The worst thing I know about divine healing is that it does not last. I am very frank to admit that divine healing is only temporary, it does not last forever. People get sick again and die. Healing may last ten years, or twenty years, or fifty years—or even 100 years; but if Jesus tarries, you will die at last and go to be with the Lord. Even the people Jesus healed in Bible days died.

The work that is done for the soul, however, does last forever. It lives forever in the world beyond. But, meantime, divine healing comes in pretty handy. That woman who was eighteen years in the wheelchair got plenty tired of it. Myrtle Terry would not care to have her epilepsy back, and have those awful spells down on the street.

"Sister McPherson, just a minute now. Don't you think God makes us sick to make us better Christians?"

No, I do not. I would never break my son's leg to make him stay home. I would never give my daughter blindness so that she would not go away. I would not try to hold them by force if I could not hold them by love. I do not believe sickness draws people closer to God. It is hard to pray when one is sick; one's spirits, vitality and faith are low. Jesus didn't think that. He said, "This woman whom Satan hath bound." "Thou deaf and dumb spirit, come out." And He is just the same today.

So I bear to you, humbly in the name of Jesus, the healing cup. There is a simple little step or two you must take before you can drink from it. The first thing you must do is be converted. Jesus didn't have any preparatory meetings, but He plainly said He could do no mighty works because of their unbelief, and He said, "According to your faith, be it unto you." You must build on a rock. The first thing to do is to confess your sin, get on your knees, be born again. Even if you are a church member and a Sunday School teacher, if your heart is cold and you are not living in the glory of the love of Christ, get right with God and be filled with the real, old-time spirit of it.

The next thing to do is let Jesus go home with you and clean up your house. Take your theater tickets, your tobacco, your dancing slippers and any unfit literature and put them in the stove. Get out your Bible and wipe the dust off. Set up a family altar. Pay what you owe. Ask the people whom you have injured to forgive you. Really cleanse your heart, cleanse your home, make preparation. Then come up and say, "Lord, here I am, sick and broken. Jesus, heal me now and I will give this strength I have derived from Thee back to Thee for Thy service."

I believe that will bring you right in under the healing cup and the golden showers will come down upon you. You will not look for the evangelist to make you whole, but you will say, "O Jesus, I come with faith in my heart," and you will be healed from that very hour.

Some people who come for healing, experience a mighty emotional and even physical stirring as they are prayed for. A man who came when I was preaching at a Methodist Church in Philadelphia was all bowed over on his crutches with rheumatoid arthritis. His joints were all drawn together. There were a lot of preachers around me. I prayed very quietly and this man fell under the power. I thought the preachers would hold him up, so I didn't do anything about it, but to my amazement they let him down. There he lay under the power of

God. We went on praying. Several porters were there. Their eyes looked as though they would pop out when they saw the man go down. "Has he fainted?" they asked. I assured them that it was the old-fashioned power of God. After a few minutes, during which time we were praying for others, that crippled man sprang to his feet. God had evidently taken him on His operating table. His knees that had been drawn were straight. His elbows were straight. He threw down his crutches and went off the platform praising God! I met that man years later. He had become Sunday School superintendent in that church and was leading many to Jesus Christ.

Not everyone who is healed, of course, shakes or shouts or falls under the power. Many healings come quietly, like the still dew on the roses. But whether it be with the rushing wind, or with the fire, or with the earthquake, or with the still small voice, the great thing to know is that it is the Lord and we are ready for His touch. He would forgive all our iniquities, and He would heal all our diseases.

Chapter IV JESUS CHRIST THE COMING KING

Three of the four cardinal emphases of the Foursquare Gospel concerning the ministry of the Lord Jesus Christ pertain to present experiences. Jesus saves believers now, in this day and age, in this church dispensation. It is an everyday occurrence. The Lord adds to the church daily such as should be saved (cf. Acts 2:47, esp. *Weymouth's* translation). Likewise, Jesus is baptizing a host of believers in the Holy Spirit daily, no doubt, as well. The same may be said of Christ's healing ministry. The Lord ministers constantly at the present time as Saviour, Baptizer, and Healer. However, He has not yet commenced His career as *coming* King. But He will, and the Word of God encourages believers to expect that coming to be soon!

There can be no doubt that Jesus Christ is coming again. Angels announced it. Prophets predicted it. Christ Himself promised it. God guarantees it. He will send His Son the second time from heaven. The greatest news story of all history is bound to break in due season. "In every newspaper shop the largest size headline type—a type so big that in most cases it has never been used—" explained Hugh B. Patterson, Jr., while publisher of the *Arkansas Gazette,* "is called 'Second Coming type.' This is not irreverence, but rather stands as evidence of our recognition that the return of Jesus would be in fact the greatest news story in all history." Someday composing rooms will employ "Second Coming type" to headline the eventuality that gives it its name. Jesus Christ is definitely coming again.

Surprisingly enough in view of the secularization of American society and the rampant unbelief and agnosticism which prevails in most educational institutions, public opinion polls reveal that rank-and-file citizens cling to a faith, albeit hazy, in Christ's second coming. Dr. George Gallup's "American Institute of Public Opinion" sometime ago released a report stating, "A majority of the public believes that Christ's promise to return to the world will someday be fulfilled." The Gallup Poll had its reporters interview a cross section of persons of all faiths in all areas of the nation. Here is the first question asked and the results: "Do you think Jesus Christ will ever return to earth?" The replies were Yes, 55%; No, 31%; and No opinion, 14%. The dispatch continued, "The expectation of the early Christians was that the return of Christ was close at hand. Since that day various interpretations have been made among religious groups as to when this would occur. Some maintain that Jesus has returned already—in the hearts of believers. Other groups have designated exact dates for the return of Christ in person. To determine what people in present-day America believe concerning the Second Coming, the Gallup Poll asked the following question of those who stated a belief in the Reappearance: "When do you think this will happen?" Of those persons who selected a specific point in time, about one-half expected the return of Christ to be within the next 100 years.

Some statesmen have been driven to the conclusion that only the second coming of Jesus Christ can solve the problems plaguing this world and this age. Kenneth de Courcy, the proprietor of Britain's "Intelligence Digest," "World Science Review," and "The Weekly Review," told three visiting American clergymen of a significant interview with Winston Churchill. The former Prime Minister walked into de Courcy's home in Eton Place in London one evening and exclaimed, "De Courcy, I'm a changed man in my older years. I want to talk tonight about the immortality of the soul." And Churchill framed the question, "What will happen when the Almighty becomes weary of man's perpetual arrogance and his rebellious nature?"

During the course of the ensuing discussion between editor and statesman, Winston Churchill repeated eight or nine times, de Courcy told his guests, the statement, "The only hope of the world is the coming of Jesus."

While crises and conflicts and crime prompt harassed citizens to ask in despair, "What is this world coming to?", Christians know that the solution to all problems lies in who is coming to this world, and that is Jesus Christ.

SCRIPTURE PREDICTS THE SECOND COMING

The fact of the second coming of Christ, however, is not established by the opinion of any majority or by the hope of harried humanitarians or politicians. The fact that Jesus Christ will most certainly return rests upon the revelation of God's infallible Word!

The main thrust of the Old Testament message focused upon the first coming of God's Son. Yet it is estimated that there are about twice as many prophecies in the Old Testament pertaining to Christ's second coming than to His first! Jesus Christ came to earth, His birth like a wedge splitting time into the years B.C. and A.D. He fulfilled the prophecies of His first advent. Surely He will fulfill the Old Testament forecasts of His second coming!

However, the New Testament adds over three hundred references to that second advent. About one out of every thirty verses in the New Testament concerns this great and glorious theme. Paul's epistles, for example, refer to water baptism about thirteen times but to the second coming fifty times!

Let us survey some of the Biblical authority for faith in the return of Jesus Christ.

Old Testament prophets forecast the second coming. Isaiah's proclamation in chapter 40 verse 10 is strongly reminiscent of Revelation 22:12, the next to the last reference in the New Testament to Christ's return. Isaiah prophesied. "Behold, the Lord God will come with strong hand, and his arm shall rule for him: behold, his reward is with him, and his work before him." The same prophet declared of Christ, "For . . . the government shall be upon his shoulder . . . Of the increase of his government and peace there shall be no end, upon the throne of David, and upon his kingdom, to order it, and to establish it with judgment and with justice from henceforth even for ever. The zeal of the Lord of hosts will perform this" (Isaiah 9:6-7).

If, as is generally assumed the two men in white apparel of Acts 1:10-11 were actually angels (for angels are sometimes called men in the Bible), then angels add their voices to those of inspired Old Testament prophets in announcing the second coming. Jesus had just disappeared into the heavens at His ascension forty days after His resurrection. The disciples' gazes still stared skyward, "And while they looked steadfastly toward heaven as he went up, behold, two men stood by them in white apparel; Which also said, Ye men of Galilee, why stand ye gazing up into heaven? this same Jesus, which is taken up from you into heaven, shall so come in like manner as ye have seen him go into heaven" (Acts 1:10-11).

Jesus Christ Himself insisted that He would come the second time. On the eve of His crucifixion He pronounced the words which still thrill believers, "In my Father's house are many mansions: if it were not so, I would have told you. I go to prepare a place for you. And if I go and prepare a place for you, I will come again, and receive you unto myself; that where I am, there ye may be also" (John 14:2-3). The occasion of His return was often on His lips during His ministry on earth, and even after His ascension to heaven. Christ's very last statement in the Bible is a reiteration of His return. The last promise of Scripture quotes Jesus as proclaiming, "Surely I come quickly." These last red letters in red-letter editions of the Bible do not appear in the gospels or the first chapter of Acts. Jesus speaks them from heaven on the final page of the Scriptures in Revelation 22:20.

The Lord's apostles emphasized this second coming in their preaching and in their inspired writings. God "shall send Jesus Christ, which before was preached unto you: Whom the heaven must receive until the times of restitution of all things, which God hath spoken by the mouth of all his holy prophets since the world began," proclaimed Peter in Jerusalem a few days after Pentecost (Acts 3:20-21). And the same apostle alluded to Christ's return in his sermon before the household of Cornelius when he declared that God has ordained Jesus "to be the Judge of quick and dead" (Acts 10:42). John the Revelator envisioned the second coming in chapter 19. And perhaps the classic passage of Paul's fifty references to the event is I Thessalonians 4:16-17:

> "For the Lord himself shall descend from heaven with a shout, with the voice of the archangel, and with the trump of God: and the dead in Christ shall rise first: Then we which are alive and remain shall be caught up together with them in the clouds, to meet the Lord in the air: and so shall we ever be with the Lord."

Now not only do prophets, angels, apostles, and the Coming King Himself emphasize the second advent, the prayer life of Christians anticipates that return, or should anticipate it. Everytime a person repeats the Lord's Prayer he is petitioning–consciously or unconsciously as the case may be–for the second coming of Jesus. For we pray, "Thy kingdom come, thy will be done, in earth as it is in heaven." But how can there be a kingdom without a King? The kingdom will come in its consummation only when the King comes to earth. So we pray for Christ to come when we pray for His kingdom to come. Moreover, the very last prayer recorded in the Bible constitutes a petition to our Christ to return: "Even so, come, Lord Jesus" (Revelation 22:20).

So Jesus Christ will surely come again. He will come in person. He will come literally. The Old Testament prophecies of His first coming were fulfilled literally. The Word was made flesh and dwelt among men. Since the promises of His first coming were fulfilled literally, we must expect the promises of His second coming to be fulfilled literally likewise.

Foursquare believers reject every formula which would explain away the literal fulfillment of Bible promises and prophecies of Christ's second coming. To those who claim that Christ's second coming occurred on the day of Pentecost we point out that a real person descended there with great power upon the disciples, but this person was not the Lord Jesus Christ but the Holy Spirit whom Christ sent from the Father in heaven. To those who assume the destruction of Jerusalem in 70 A.D. represented the second coming of Jesus, we point out that according to Bible prophecy Christ's coming will be accompanied not by the destruction of Jerusalem but by its restoration and exaltation (cf. Isaiah 2:2-4). Moreover, the signs predicted to accompany that advent did not occur in 70 A.D. No graves were opened. No dead believers arose.

Still, others claim the second coming occurs at conversion when Jesus indwells the believer's life. However, at salvation, the focal coming is the coming of the sinner to Christ. And the New Testament extends to the already converted the promises of Jesus' return. If His second coming took place at their salvation, how could they continue to expect a second advent?

Some maintain that the death of the believer is the occasion of the second coming. But here again, the believer goes to be with Christ, absent from the body, at home with the Lord, while the second coming according to the scriptures involves in its unfolding those who are already "dead in Christ" as well as all who are "alive and remain" (I Thessalonians 4:16-17). If death were the second advent, Christ would be coming again to earth hundreds of times every day. As Sister McPherson put it, "No, bless the Lord, the coming of the Lord will not mean death, but life,—not a going down into the grave but a coming up out of it in a resurrection bright and fair" (Aimee Semple McPherson, "The Second Coming of Christ," Los Angeles, 1921, p. 17).

Every effort and expedient to spiritualize or explain away the literal second coming of Jesus comes into direct collision with the teachings of the Word of God. Jesus Christ will come again. He will come in person. He will come literally. Foursquare believers confess this faith in number 36 of our Creedal Statements which preface our By-laws and Articles of Incorporation. "We believe," this statement declares, "in the personal, literal, bodily pre-millenial coming of Jesus Christ."

THE RAPTURE OF THE CHURCH

Moreover, our Founder unequivocally proclaimed not only the pre-millenial coming of Jesus Christ but also the pre-tribulation rapture of the church. Any study in depth of the printed articles and sermons of Aimee Semple McPherson will document this emphasis. The following quotations come from a series entitled "Foursquare Fundamentals" published under her by-line in the *Foursquare Crusader* between February and June, 1933:

> "The second coming of our Lord and Saviour, Jesus Christ, is divided into two parts: His coming for His people, or the Rapture, and His coming with His people to reign, or the Millenium" (March 22, 1933, p. 2).
>
> "The ministry of Jesus for this dispensation began with a wedding at Cana of Galilee and it will end with a wedding and a marriage feast at the Home of the Bridegroom" (March 29, 1933, p. 2).
>
> "The period between the Rapture and the Return of Christ with His saints, or the revelation, is designated as the Great Tribulation" (April 5, 1933, p. 2).
>
> "The revelation occurs when Christ comes, with His saints (Colossians 3:4; I Thessalonians 3:13) to end the Tribulation by the execution of righteous judgment upon the earth (Jude 14, 15)" (April 12, 1933, p. 4).

The official Foursquare position regarding the Second Coming, therefore, rejects Post Millenialism and Amillenialism and espouses Pre-millenialism. And while the Pre-tribulation Rapture is not explicitly expressed in our confession, this was unquestionably the position of our Founder and remains the position of virtually every Foursquare authority on Bible Prophecy and eschatology.

With these Biblical guideposts in mind, we proceed to survey what the Scriptures state concerning the manner, the time, the place, and the reason for the return of Jesus Christ. How, when, where, and why is He coming again?

How will our Lord return?

The Bible declares that Jesus will come secretly. Christ Himself heralded, "Behold, I come as a thief. Blessed is he that watcheth" (Revelation 16:15). There is a difference between thieves and robbers. A robber does not hesitate to hit his victim openly. A thief takes pains to conceal his act. The very word thief enshrines the idea of stealth. A thief strikes secretly. Jesus will come secretly. "Behold, I come as a thief." He is not a thief, for a thief takes what does not belong to him. When Christ comes as a thief–secretly–He will take only those who belong to Him–"the dead in Christ" and "we which are alive and remain." When Christ comes again He will come secretly–for His church. As R. W. Francis put it, "It is natural that He should come first for His own. When a country makes war on another country, its first act is to withdraw its ambassador, and Scripture tells us we are the ambassadors of Christ. Before the judgments of God fall upon the earth, we shall be taken away." Christ will come as a thief–secretly. That is how He will return.

To answer *when* He will return we may use the adverb *imminently.* That means Jesus may return at any moment. For decades Christians have sung the familiar testimony, "He's coming soon," and that song echoes a personal promise Christ made four times in the book of Revelation—indeed, three times in the last chapter of the Bible! "Behold, I come quickly," He announced in Revelation 3:11. In Revelation 22 He repeated that promise twice (verses 7 and 12) before voicing His very last promise in the sacred volume: "Surely I come quickly." Jesus declares that His coming is surely soon. He may come at any moment. While still on earth He warned, "Watch therefore, for ye know neither the day nor the hour wherein the Son of man cometh" (Matthew 25:13). The early church expected that advent imminently. Paul commended the Thessalonians because they "turned to God from idols to serve the living and true God; And to wait for his Son from heaven" (I Thessalonians 1:9-10). The Corinthians likewise were waiting (I Corinthians 1:7). Christians employed as a greeting among themselves the word "Maranatha" which means, "Our Lord cometh." If Jesus and Paul wanted believers in their day to watch for the second coming, how much more ought we today to cultivate the same outlook. Jesus Christ may come at any moment. "Imminently" is the best available adverb to answer when He will return.

But where is He coming? The Bible locates His secret soon return as "in the air." When Jesus comes as a thief those He takes will "meet the Lord in the air" (I Thessalonians 4:17). This will be the most spectacular rendezvous in space ever scheduled! Jesus will descend from heaven. The resurrected dead in Christ and all living believers will be caught up. Somewhere in the skies there will follow this remarkable rendezvous! Jesus will come and meet His church "in the air"!

And why will He return?

Here is an answer in Christ's own words: "I will come again, and receive you unto myself; that where I am, there ye may be also." The promise of John 14:3 becomes the accomplished fact of I Thessalonians 4:17's final statement, " . . . so shall we ever be with the Lord." Jesus will return to receive us unto Himself! He will also come, He declared, to distribute rewards for faithful service: "And behold, I come quickly; and my reward is with me, to give every man according as his work shall be" (Revelation 22:12). He will reward believers at the judgment seat of Christ (cf. II Corinthians 5:10, I Corinthians 3:13) at the time of His soon and secret return in the air. And we know also that He will come to glorify our physical frames, to change this mortal to immortality and this corruptible to incorruption (cf. I Corinthians 15:53), and to swallow up death in victory by robbing the grave of deceased believers (cf. I Corinthians 15:54). Thus we testify with St. Paul, "For our conversation is in heaven; from whence also we look for the Saviour, the Lord Jesus Christ: Who shall change our vile body, that it may be fashioned like unto his glorious body" (Philippians 3:20-21).

There are other reasons why Christ will come again, but the mention of these three must suffice here: He is coming to receive us unto Himself, to reward us for our service if said service so merits, and to change us into the pattern of His resurrection body.

Thus we have answered the questions proposed. Christ will come secretly, imminently, in the air, and for the reasons just outlined. Our answers represent the truth and nothing but the truth, as given by Scriptures. But we have not yet told the whole truth. For the second coming of Christ as was pointed out earlier, embraces two installments. He is coming for His church. Later He will come to earth with His church. So to understand the how, why, when, and where of the latter event, we again look into the pages of the Bible.

How will Christ return on this occasion? He will come publicly. Jesus Himself proclaimed, "Ye shall see the Son of man sitting on the right hand of power, and coming in the clouds of heaven" (Mark 14:62). Jesus was talking then not to His friends but to enemies, not to believers but to unbelievers. He promised a public vindication of His claims. When He comes for His church, only believers will witness and participate in the blessed hope. But when He comes with His church "every eye shall see him" and "all kindreds of the earth shall wail because of him" (Revelation 1:7). Not secretly, but publicly is how He will return.

Matthew 24:29-30 and Revelation 19:11 certainly seem to remove all doubts about when Christ will return publicly. "Immediately after the tribulation of those days" and the divine judgments consummating that period "then shall appear the sign of the Son of man in heaven: and then shall all the tribes of the earth mourn, and they shall see the Son of man coming in the clouds of heaven with power and great glory." When? Then! Immediately after the tribulation and its concluding prodigies. It is noteworthy that John the Revelator witnesses Christ's second coming after the marriage supper of the Lamb. Christ must come first to claim His church bride. Daniel's seventieth week of tribulation on earth has its counterpart in the church's bridal week, as we might call it (cf. Genesis 29:27; Judges 14:12), in heaven. Both end with Christ's return.

Where will Jesus return when He comes publicly immediately after the tribulation's closing judgments and the marriage supper of the Lamb? Acts I advises that Jesus ascended heavenward from the Mount of Olives. Zechariah 14:4 declares he will return to the same place: "And his feet shall stand in that day upon the Mount of Olives, which is before Jerusalem on the east." With Him will come, arrayed in fine linen, clean and white, the armies of heaven (cf. Revelation 19:14). Their attire is identical with that described as the church bride's in verse 8 of the same chapter, indicating identity with the bride. Even more than Solomon's Shulamite, Christ's bride will be "terrible as an army with banners" (Song of Solomon 6:10).

Finally, why will Jesus come back publicly with His church after the tribulation and take His stand upon the Mount of Olives east of Jerusalem?

Many reasons motivate this return, of course. Christ will come to destroy the Anti-Christ and his system. Jesus will consume him with the spirit of His mouth and will destroy him with the brightness of His coming (cf. II Thessalonians 2:8). Paul's expression "spirit of his mouth" there suggests John's statement, "Out of his mouth goeth a sharp sword, that with it he should smite the nations." Jesus will return to unseat and destroy the beast, the man of sin, the son of perdition (cf. Revelation 13; II Thessalonians 2:3).

And Jesus will come back also to punish the wicked. Paul declares that "the Lord Jesus shall be revealed from heaven with his mighty angels, In flaming fire taking vengeance on them that know not God, and that obey not the gospel of our Lord Jesus Christ" (II Thessalonians 1:7-8).

Jesus will return, moreover, to rule and reign. He will rule the nations "with a rod of iron" (Revelation 19:15). And His saints will rule with Him for a thousand years (Revelation 20:6). This represents the period we call the millenium. Christ's coming will consummate the divine purpose at the divine time to lift the curse which has plagued the earth since Eden (cf. Romans 8:21) and to establish peace under the aegis of the Prince of Peace: Christ "shall judge among the nations, and shall rebuke many people: and they shall beat their swords into plowshares, and their spears into pruning hooks: nation shall not lift up sword against nation, neither shall they learn war any more" (Isaiah 2:4).

Thus we see from the Scriptures how, when, where, and why Jesus will come first for His church and then subsequently with His church. We employ two words to designate these occasions—the rapture and the revelation. The rapture is secret, imminent, and will consummate in the air. The revelation is to be public, after the tribulation, and focus on Mount Olivet. There is nothing a person need do now to prepare for the revelation. In this age of grace our responsibility is to be ready for the rapture, to watch and look for the blessed hope. Christ's public coming will be a terror to those who were not ready for His secret appearing. The proper attitude of the believer was reflected—a bit melodramatically, perhaps, but nevertheless accurately—in the sign a young Christian hung inside his automobile. The sign warned, "Ride at your own risk! I'm leaving at the rapture." And everyone who is not ready for the rapture ought to follow the example of the railroad fireman to whom the engineer—in the days of steam—declared, "I want to teach you how to operate this contraption." "Why?" demanded the fireman, to which the engineer replied, "Because I'm a Christian, and Jesus is coming, and I expect to be raptured out of here." With deep feeling the fireman pleaded, "Don't teach me how to operate this contraption. Teach me how to go with you."

Jesus Christ is coming. The circumstances attending His advent captivate the imagination. But it is more important for a person to know that he is ready for that return than to know how, when, where, and why Jesus is coming. Across the centuries thunder words of Jesus worthy of supreme attention: "Therefore be ye also ready: for in such an hour as ye think not the Son of man cometh" (Matthew 24:44).

There is not a single prophecy in the Bible which must be fulfilled before Jesus Christ comes in the air for His church. There are many prophecies which must be fulfilled during the interval between His coming for the church and His coming with the church, but not one sign or prophecy must come to pass before the rapture. Jesus Christ could come at any moment.

The renowned Biblical scholar and educator, Dr. William L. Pettingill, lectured a class of theological students on this point. Marshalling massive evidence from the Scriptures he emphasized and reiterated the imminence of Christ's return for His church. At the close of the period he quizzed the students on the material he had covered. One question he asked, expecting that no one would volunteer an answer, was, "Who can tell me any sign that must take place before the rapture of the church?" Dr. Pettingill sighed with disappointment when he beheld a man near the back of the classroom raise his hand to reply. "All right, what is the sign?" the instructor recognized the volunteer, masking with effort his tone of disgust.

The student smiled and answered, "The shout." Dr. Pettingill relaxed. "The Lord himself shall descend from heaven with a shout" (I Thessalonians 4:16).

Jesus is coming again. Scoffers may scorn His advent, but the Lord will return anyway. As Vance Havner put it, "The *outlook* may be dismal but not the *uplook*. The second coming of our Lord is a certainty; His soon coming is a glorious possibility. The Bible teaches it. The early church believed it. The signs indicate it. Our Lord said, 'I will build My church,' and He did. He said, 'I will send My Spirit,' and He did. He said, 'I will come again,' and He will. Scoffers ask, 'Where is the presence of His coming?', but the man who says there are no signs is a sign himself, a human placard advertising the very thing he denies! . . .If you are worried about the *outlook*, cultivate the *uplook*! We are not all going to be destroyed by bombs. There will be living saints when Christ comes for His own. Civilization may be headed for ruin but the church is headed for the rapture" (*Moody Monthly*, April 1956, pp. 23-24). So Foursquare believers not only proclaim the gospel of Jesus the Coming King, we also live in anticipation of that advent, "Looking," as St. Paul exhorts, "for that blessed hope, and the glorious appearing of the great God and our Saviour Jesus Christ; Who gave himself for us, that he might redeem us from all iniquity, and purify unto himself a peculiar people, zealous of good works" (Titus 2:13-14).

We are not looking for the Tribulation or coming of Antichrist. We are looking for the coming of Jesus Christ. And "yet a little while, and he that shall come will come, and will not tarry" (Hebrews 10:37). Today? Perhaps!

Sermon

THE WEDDING IN THE AIR

"Let us be glad and rejoice, and give honour to him: for the marriage of the Lamb is come, and his wife hath made herself ready.
"And to her was granted that she should be arrayed in fine linen, clean and white: for the fine linen is the righteousness of saints." Revelation 19:7-8.

"For the Lord himself shall descend from heaven with a shout, with the voice of the archangel, and with the trump of God: and the dead in Christ shall rise first:
"Then we which are alive and remain shall be caught up together with them in the clouds, to meet the Lord in the air: and so shall we ever be with the Lord." I Thessalonians 4:16-17.

Brother, Sister, have you heard? There is soon to be a wedding in the air!

The bride? Her name is the Church. She is composed of many members; but is one body—blood-washed, Spirit-filled, the love-light kindled and glowing in her heart, looking for the coming of the Bridegroom.

The Bridegroom is Jesus Christ—none other than He who was despised and rejected of men, crucified upon the cross of Calvary, whose blood spattered upon the ground, and was caught in a fountain with the healing and the cleansing of the nations in its flow.

The Bridegroom is none other than the Lord Jesus Christ who was raised from the dead, who has ascended on high, leading captivity captive. And one of these days, perhaps sooner than we expect, He is coming back for His bride, the church, who waits for Him with her lamp trimmed, filled and burning bright.

I have heard of people being married on boats, in

airplanes, on the beach; and one night I had a couple who wanted me to marry them in the baptistry.

Wonderful weddings indeed there have been of society people. We pick up our paper and read every detail of the snow-white dress worn by the beautiful bride, her trailing veil, her blushing cheeks and starry eyes; and we say, "Oh, isn't she lovely!"

There have been weddings of international interest and repute. We remember the weddings of kings and queens and with what interest the papers recounted what the bride's dress was to be like.

I remember the day of the coronation in England when the streets were filled with flags, bunting and shouting people, when men beat with canes upon the hollow lamp posts to express their exuberant spirits.

But no wedding festivity, no matter how gorgeous it may be, will ever compare with the glory of the wedding we are on our way to attend—*the wedding in the air.* It is a triumphant theme—it is a most glorious truth—the coming of the King.

Everybody loves a wedding. I know when I have been on the train, traveling from city to city, many times a bride would get on the train. First we would hear the patter of the rice against the windowpane. Someone would say, "Oh, it's a wedding party coming!" And there was one compartment of the train fixed with white ribbons.

Everybody would stop, no matter what they were reading. Businessmen figuring busily would pause. People would look up from their books. Those playing cards would stop, and all would look. That is, everybody would look unless it was an old grouchy bachelor.

"Here comes the bride!"

Today, every Christian loves the subject of the coming of the Lord. It thrills the heart and fills us with joy. He is coming! I want to see Him when He comes!

Some people wonder why we are so happy—why we are always smiling, and why we walk with such a spring. They say, "What makes you so happy? Why do you clap your hands? Why do you hold your hands up when you sing? What is this something you have?"

Why, praise the Lord! It is the fact that we are on our way to a wedding! We are not on our way to a funeral. Some people I know seem to take their religion so sadly, and they sing, "Hark from the tombs a doleful sound." You would think there was no joy in the religion of Jesus Christ whatever. But once men and women get acquainted with the subject of the coming of the Lord, their pulse begins to quicken, their heart to beat faster, their eyes to shine, their voice to ring, their step alilt. They really are new people.

He is coming soon, and we shall see Him in His glory! What a pity—what a tragic pity it is that so many people never hear a sermon on the second coming of Jesus Christ! How pathetic that some, even ministers, do not believe in the premillenial coming of the Lord! Many do not believe we will ever see Him in the clouds. On the other hand they believe that all there is to His coming is that this world will become better and better, and finally get so good that it will be a little heaven right here on earth.

But I don't think that is working out, do you? I don't think, as we see crime and sin on the increase, that that theory holds true. And the Bible says that He is coming in the air.

Now, before there can be a wedding, there must, of course, be a meeting; and this story of the wedding in the air which I want to tell you is really the most romantic story I know. It is the romance of the ages.

We used to read fairy stories about Prince Charming, and how he came galloping upon his steed and rescued his bride from the dungeon and carried her away.

But this is the story of the wedding in the air. This old world was shut in the dungeon of sin and darkness; but Jesus came to her rescue on the galloping steeds of grace and faith, truth and mercy; and then came the meeting.

Will I ever forget when He first came to me—when

first I heard His lovely voice! I had steeled my heart against Him. I had said, "Oh, maybe some day when I am old I will be a Christian, but not now. I liked the gaiety of the world, and I would have to give that up."

I am afraid I was one who wanted to live for the world while I lived, and accept Christ before I died.

Well do I remember the night Jesus Christ smiled upon me that wistful, haunting, sad, sweet smile that revealed to me my sin and told me that I was grieving His heart; that I had wandered so far away, and yet that He loved me so. 'Tis the same sweet story of your own meeting with Him.

And then came the voice. Oh, how He wooed and won my heart. Just as He has won yours! He drew me, and I followed. Just one glimpse of His face, and it seemed earth was so drab and gray and stripped of all glory without Him. 'Twas as though one had gazed upon the glory of the sunset, and then looked away, and the sun was gone and a midnight sky of steel gray and black hung low.

He drew me to Him and won my heart. For three days I set myself against His love, and then I said, "Lord, I would rather be a Christian than anything else in all the world! I would rather have Your love, and feel Your arms about me, and know I am cleansed through the precious blood, than live to claim the highest honors this old world could ever offer."

The trysting place was at the fountain on Calvary's brow. 'Twas there we met. 'Twas there the great miracle took place. 'Twas there the blood was applied, and garments that were black became whiter than the driven snow. Hallelujah!

Oh, today I would like to bring about the meeting of Christ and some poor sinful heart! Today I would like to help Him woo you to Himself!

Then came the betrothal, when I said, "Lord, I will be thine."

"All I have is yours," He promised, "my heavenly home in Paradise, my mansion is yours."

Then I looked down where my hand held the little wilted, faded flower I had to give Him. My lips trembled, and I said: "Lord, it is not much I have to give in return, but all I have is Thine."

He graciously took that little faded flower, all that was left of my wasted, wilted life, and praise His name! by His grace it was a mutual exchange.

After the meeting and the betrothal, the wedding is soon to take place. One would be surprised at the choice of the bride for this great Bridegroom, Jesus Christ. One would suppose He would have chosen people for their beauty of physical body; that He would have chosen them for their social standing and prestige among the high and mighty. One would expect the King of Glory to make His choice among kings and rulers, potentates and moguls, those who were of the highest education, that they might lend grace to His church and to His cause.

But on the other hand, you can never tell where love is going to strike and, wonder of wonders, He loved us! He chose the sinner, who had wandered far away, and drew him to Himself. Instead of loving and singling out those high in this world, He is seeking those of a contrite heart and a yielded spirit—those who have humbled themselves under the mighty hand of God. He is not coming to the powerful, the haughty and the upright as the world considers it; but to the humble, lowly and meek of spirit. These shall inherit the Kingdom, praise God! The broken, contrite people are His choice.

We consider her choice—the choice of the bride. Whom will she choose for the bridegroom? Once her eyes have been fixed upon Him, He is her choice. Not the proud, the arrogant, the unbeliever, but Jesus Christ in all His glory.

Then, if a wedding is to take place, one usually receives the engagement ring—the blessed Holy Spirit—the promise of that great day when we shall be caught up to meet Him in the air.

Came the time of parting, when the Lord Jesus went

home to His Father in the Glory Land. In substance He said: "Now, I am going away–going to leave you for a time. But when I go, I will prepare a place for you that where I am, there you may be also. I am going to see that the streets are paved with gold, the walls with jasper set, the gates made of one solid, beautiful pearl. I am preparing a mansion for you, My bride, in the beautiful world above. Not only will you have a mansion; not only will you have a robe and a crown; but you will sit with Me upon My throne, and reign by My side forever."

Can you imagine anything more wonderful than that? This is the hope of the Church, when we shall see Him again! He has gone home now. We cannot see Him; but the Church is waiting–has waited throughout the centuries.

In the meantime, the Master is doing His part. The mansions are being builded in Glory. Sometimes at sunrise or at sunset, when the heavens open a little bit more than usual, seems I can almost catch sight of the spires, the turrets and the minarets of the Glory Land. Seems I can almost hear, through the rushing of the wind, the splash and play of the Fountains of Life that are ever flowing over there. Sometimes when I look up I am almost sure, for a moment, that I catch the gleaming of the sea of glass where the angels are standing with their golden harps, singing praises unto the King.

The Saviour is preparing the mansion for His bride, and soon He is coming back. In the meantime the Church waits for her Redeemer, waiting, watching and listening. We read of her in the Songs of Solomon: "Who is she that looketh forth as the morning, fair as the moon, clear as the sun, and comely as an army with banners?"

Why is the face of the Church bride pressed against the windowpane of prophecy? Because she is looking forth, confident of His coming. She knows He is near! The bride of Jesus is an alert people, who are awake to the signs of the times. They are listening.

When waiting for someone whom you love, did you

ever notice how your nerves are keyed up, and how bright your eyes, how keen your ears? Every click of the garden gate, and you look to see. Is that the one? Every ring of the door bell and you hasten to see who is there. Every sudden step on the stairs and you spring up. Perhaps this is the one for whom you wait. So the church of Jesus Christ is watching every click of the gate, every footfall, every knock upon the portal of time. She is interpreting every sign of the coming of the Lord.

She hears the click of the gate, and runs to look. They tell us the world is in a most unsettled condition. We pick up our paper. War is feared. Nations are in an uproar. Yes, it is a click of the gate.

They say there is another great earthquake; and the bride hears the step of the Bridegroom.

She hears the newsboy calling "Extra! Extra! Extra! All about the great earthquake!" She finds the thing has struck in our own state; and she hears the click of the gate.

Is this the day? Is this the hour?

There comes another cry of "Extra! Extra! Great earthquake has struck Montana, spreading out over three states!" And there comes a knock at the door. She is listening–listening. These are the signs of the times–the signs of His coming.

We read that another quake has come in a part of the United States never known to have a tremor before. They tell us that somewhere every moment a quake is being recorded.

The Church bride turns to her Book and reads: "Earthquakes in divers places."

We hear of the speakers who are lecturing everywhere upon world peace. We pick up magazines, read articles which cry: "Peace! Peace! Peace and safety!"

Lord, is this a click of the garden gate? Is this a step upon the walk? Is this a tap upon the door?

She takes the sacred page and reads that in the last day men shall cry peace and safety–men shall rise up and be paid to do nothing else but preach peace, peace,

peace. And when they cry peace and safety, the end cometh. He is near, even at the door. And she waits, watching, watching.

Who is this that looketh forth at the window, pale as the moon, comely as an army with banners?

'Tis the waiting church of Jesus Christ. Others may sleep, but she is awake. Wherefore she watches, her eye keen and alert for every sign, that she may see Him when He shall appear.

We see the Jew stepping up to the cashier's window to pass through his bank book.

Lord, is this a click at the gate to say Thou art coming soon, down o'er the Milky Way, to receive us to Thyself?

Yes, this is the time when the fig tree putteth forth its leaves. She looks upon the Jewish nation, and marks the fact that thousands of Jews per month are going back to Israel, back to their own country. She reads of the rebuilding of the walls, the preparation of homes to receive the incoming Jewish families, and she says, "Ah, yes, Lord. This is but a sign of Thy coming, for in Thy Word I read, 'In the last days the fig tree' (or the Jewish nation) 'shall put forth its leaves'."

When other nations have lived within themselves, they have died out. But instead of the Jewish race dying out, it is growing, increasing and spreading.

The little bride reads it and she hears another click of the garden gate, and a step upon the stairs.

The Jews have branched forth until today they own a great part of the money of the world. They are our bankers. They own our great department stores and many of our great newspapers. The fig tree is putting forth its leaves.

The land of Palestine has been given back to them. It was said to be impossible, but God accomplished it by the turning over of His hand, and now they are going home to the land which has been given to them as a free gift just as the Lord foretold. So on every hand the fig tree putteth forth her leaves, and the face at the window is pressed close to the pane.

We read of evolution, modernism, higher criticism, and a great tide of unbelief that threatens to engulf the church.

Is this another step upon the stairs? Thou art coming, Lord?

"Yes, O bride of My heart," He answers back. "This is a sign of My coming. In the last days the love of many shall wax cold. Many shall have a form of godliness, but deny the power thereof. Look up, child! I am coming! I am near, even at the door!"

Then, she is running out to the ends of the earth to preach the blessed gospel, that not one corner of the world shall be in darkness—that there shall not be one little spot into which her light has not flashed.

Why? Because the coming of the Master draweth nigh.

She reads of the great modern inventions. She looks up and sees aircraft soaring like great birds. Is this a step upon the stair, my Lord? I read that in the last days, knowledge shall be increased. Men shall run to and fro, and the vehicles shall jostle each other in the streets.

The world that has seemed so big is only a tiny place now. Men can span it with their voice.

Is this, O Lord, a click of the garden gate and a step upon the stairs? Is this the tapping of Thy gentle fingers at the portal?

I know it is, for this world is only tiny now. Knowledge has increased in the last days. Why did not we have the telephone before? Why did we have to wait these thousands of years? There were just as clever people years ago as there are now. They who had the secret that we cannot discover, of how the pyramids were built, and how the bodies of the dead were embalmed, were just as clever as we. Why did they not bring forth the telephone, telegraph and wireless, the radio and television, the cable, the steam engine and gasoline motors? Why? Because the Lord left them for a sign, a click of the garden gate, a step on the stair, a tap on the door in the last days.

And the pale face at the window looks up through the night and says, "Oh, Lord Jesus, how long?"

"It may be in the morning, when the day is waking."

"Oh, Lord Jesus, how long?"

"It may be at noontide. It may be at even. Watch."

Oh, won't it be wonderful when He comes? God is shaping everything up now for His coming. Then shall be the great day. My, I would not like to be left when He comes! I want to be ready at His appearing.

"How is He coming?" you ask.

I wish I could tell you. I know a little bit about it, but not all. I know suddenly there will be a sound, that the starry floors of heaven will burst asunder, and Jesus will appear. I know that He is coming in mid-air, and that all they who are watching for His coming shall hear His voice, for the Lord Himself shall descend from heaven with a shout, with the voice of the archangel and the trump of God. Then the dead in Christ shall rise first, and those who are living and remain shall be caught up to meet Him in the air. So shall we ever be with the Lord.

"But, Sister, if I did not know He was coming, He would not blame me for not being ready, would He?"

Yes, He would. You have His letter, the Bible, that told you He was coming.

Jesus Christ declares He is coming back. Every sign is pointing to His soon returning. The very winds declare the coming of the Master draweth nigh. Oh God, let us be ready!

Did you ever see folks go up in a balloon? Did you ever notice the sand bags, the ballast to keep them down? If they want to rise, they begin to cast out the sand bags, and then up, up, up they go.

Praise the Lord! That is the way with us. If we want to rise, we must begin to cast off the ballast, and be ready for the coming of the Lord.

"When is He coming?" you ask.

Oh, I would like to figure out the time if I could! He reveals it to His elect as the time draws nigh. Some people begin to figure, and they try to set a date; but that is wrong, though you can't blame the dear souls, because they love Jesus so. Sometimes they bring much censure upon the teaching of His coming because of their mistaken dates. Some dear people have gone out to meet Him. A good many speak so critically of them, and maybe they deserve it. I have always thought, that though I know they are wrong, that the man or woman who does that must be good—they must really love the Lord or they would not sell all they possess and give to the poor, and then go out to meet Him. But they are mistaken.

If the Lord took you into a great room all full of bundles and said, "You can help yourself"; and then you came to one bundle that had big gold letters on it which said, "It is not for you," what would you do?

If all the other bundles were marked with my name, and that one bundle said plainly that it was not for me, I would not touch it. I would take the other bundles, but leave the one that was not for me.

Thus it is with the Bible and its promises. He has given so many great promises, but on one He has said, "It is not for you to know that very hour or that very moment. The Father in heaven knows it; but not even the angels know the exact time."

It is not for us to know that which the Father has put in His own power; but we may know He is coming, and we know He is near, even at the door!

Suppose it were today. Suppose right now we should hear His voice, and the door should begin to open. The sinners would hear some kind of a sound, but they would not understand it.

Suddenly the heavens would open and out, and out in beautiful clouds of glory would come that accompanying angel band. I know a grave over in China that would open, and people would be rising here, there and yonder to meet the Lord for "the dead in Christ shall rise first, then we which are alive and remain shall be caught up."

It will be a day of parting. Two will be sleeping in one bed, and one will be taken and the other left. Two will be grinding at a mill, and one shall be taken and the other left. In another part of the world (you know the Lord knew the world was round long before people did) two shall be working in the field. One shall be taken and the other left.

I recall a vision I had in Framingham, Massachusetts. I was speaking three times a day and working very hard. I had tried to be faithful and to stand by my guns until the last. This was Sunday night, and I was very, very tired and hot, having preached and smiled and tried to cheer up others all day until I felt like a wilted flower.

The last soul at the altar had been prayed for, the last person had said good night, the last light was turned out. But I remained a moment and sat down by the altar, hesitating even then to go. "Oh Lord," I prayed, "I am so tired. I would not tell anybody but You; but I am, Lord. Jesus, dear, I have been trying to be a blessing to others during the day. Would You mind just blessing me a little now? Jesus, tell me that You love me. Lord, just rest me and strengthen me that I may do Your work. Lord, I have been giving out all day. Won't You give to me now the encouragement I need?"

My head dropped over upon the altar, and I lay under the power of the Lord. Seemed that I could hear singing:

> "O Lord Jesus how long? How long?
> 'Til we sound the coming song?"

As they sang, I could hear cries of "Hallelujah!" "Amen!" Seemed that the whole world was praising Him. Round about me the Christians were catching up the song. Then suddenly through the darkness there was a flash of lightning, and the heavens appeared to roll back as smoothly as well-oiled parlor doors. Through the opening I seemed to see the Saviour's feet descending. His robes, His form, His hands, His face, His glory-crowned head. And I stood there enraptured.

In a moment the entire heavens seemed to be filled with millions of angels, tier upon tier, row upon row, with harps and trumpets, praising the Lord. As they came down—Oh, it was beautiful! You can't describe a dream or a vision like that!

Did you ever send up a fire rocket at night, and see it as, having reached its height, it burst and came showering down in myriads of beautiful, shining lights?

So was that beautiful picture of the descending hosts of heaven.

In a moment the Lord uttered a shout, and every angel sounded upon his trumpet. They talk about the lost chord. It will be found when He comes back.

At that shout, the earth trembled, and I seemed to see people rising up, up, up from every direction, and coming in towards the center.

In a moment came another shout, and another holding of that great quivering strain of music—the lost chord that was found again, and at that shout, the people who were alive and remained were caught up. They were taking shape into one beautiful being. Each seemed to have some particular little spot to fill. There was the head, now the shoulders, arms, limbs, feet, the shining face; and round about her floated robes of purest white. Many members were coming to take their place, having their place in the body. So that the eye cannot say to the ear, "I have no need of you"; nor the hand to the foot, "I have no need of you."

"Oh, Lord!" I cried, "Have you forgotten me? Lord, I did want to go!" I was running as fast as I could, running up a hill. And then my toe caught on something, and I fell. But the second time I did not trip anymore. I ran to the top of the hill and instead of going down over the other side, I went on up and up and up. It was the most wonderful sensation, rising through the air!

Even then I began to fret, for I did not seem to see any particular place for me to fill. Then I saw a little place down by the foot, and I just fitted into it. So that was to be my place—to just continue to run with the gospel message until the Saviour comes. The Lord did not say, "Come, you can be the head." He said, "Down at My feet in the lowly place is room for you, child of Mine."

Then in the distance I seemed to see her going up, and the Saviour coming down, and the meeting—His dear arms about her. She was looking up into His face. I saw pearls—they were tears on her cheeks, and He caught up the hem of His robe and wiped them away while the angels sang, "And the Lamb shall wipe all tears from her eyes and there shall be no more death and no sorrow there."

In a moment they were gone. It seemed so dark down here—so bleak—men running to and fro seeking rest and finding none. But up there, just above the clouds, was the Throne with the brightness one could not gaze upon. Leading to the Throne was a great long aisle, and on either side were myriad hosts of angels and up the aisle walking these two—the Bride and the Bridegroom.

Oh, I wish I could only picture the glory in her face! It was as though she was saying, "Oh, I have waited for You for years, and now my eyes behold Thee! Even before I saw You I loved You, 'Whom having not seen we love.' "

It was as though He was looking down and saying, "My child, before you loved Me, I loved you. I have loved you with an everlasting love."

The angels sang, "Behold, I will present her faultless before the Father's Throne, without a wrinkle, without a spot, without a blemish."

Then after the presentation will come the wedding. Praise the Lord! I sat up and rubbed my eyes. It was time I was in bed, but suddenly I was rested and refreshed and ready for the coming week in the Lord's harvest fields.

Oh Brother, Sister, He is coming! There is soon to be a wedding in the air! Is your wedding garment ready? Have you been washed in the blood of the Lamb?

Death has no terrors for the blood-washed soul. It is the opening of the door. It is the call of a familiar voice—the voice of the Bridegroom for whom we have waited.

There is no fear in going to a strange land if we can cling to the hand of a loved one who knows the way. So when we go home to heaven the Bridegroom, even Jesus Christ, shall lead us to the Throne. He shall wipe away all tears from our eyes and we shall all sit down together at the marriage supper of the Lamb.

Now, glory to God! each of us may press our faces a little closer to the windowpane, may watch a little more closely the signs of the times, that when Jesus comes we may be ready, ready, ready to meet Him! And that we may rise with a shout saying, "Glory to God! I am ready! He is coming, but I am ready to meet my Saviour in the air."

PART THREE
THE PRACTICE OF THE FOURSQUARE FAITH

chapter one

DEVOTIONAL EXPRESSION
Sermon: Praising the Lord

chapter two

SACRAMENTAL PARTICIPATION
Sermons: Initiation Ceremonies
The Lord's Supper

chapter three

PRACTICAL DEDICATION
Sermons: Soul Winning
The Greatest Robber in Town

chapter four

PROJECTING THE FOURSQUARE GOSPEL
Sermon: The Lighthouse Foursquare

Chapter I DEVOTIONAL EXPRESSION

Through the ages the church of Jesus Christ has oscillated between what might be called extremes of emphasis upon faith or practice. From time to time the importance of one of these factors has been exaggerated at the expense of the other. Is what a person believes more important than what he practices? Some religionists have so proclaimed, leaving the ecclesiastical world the grotesque legacy of opinion that it matters not how a believer lives so long as he believes correctly. On the other hand, the opposite viewpoint sometimes prevails. Certain theologians insist that what one believes is not important, but rather what he practices. "It does not matter," they affirm, "what a person believes so long as he lives right."

The Foursquare Gospel being, as Sister McPherson insisted, a middle-of-the-road movement, avoids scrupulously the extremities of either of these exaggerations. Foursquare people must believe right and must live right. We dare not neglect faith at the expense of practice, nor practice at the expense of faith. We must champion both exercises. Faith without works is dead, as James insists (James 2:20). And works without faith never generate God's approval, for "without faith it is impossible to please him" (Hebrews 11:6).

Now the practice of our Foursquare faith divides itself logically into three main areas, devotional expression, sacramental participation, and practical dedication. A healthy believer will continue active in each of these areas.

Bible study, prayer, and praise represent major exertions in devotional expression. The tendency appears in some lives to specialize in perhaps one of these practices, but a well-balanced Christian must be strong in the Word of God and thrive both in prayer and in praise.

BIBLE STUDY

Believing as we do that the Bible is God's Word and true from cover to cover, we need to cultivate an ever increasing knowledge of what the Scripture contains between its covers! The Sunday School, with its systematic curriculum affording periodically a complete panorama of the whole Bible, provides an invaluable opportunity none should neglect to learn the teachings of Holy Writ. However, neither the Sunday School nor the Bible Study sessions our churches offer can take the place of individual, personal Bible reading and Bible study. The Word of God is spiritual food. Jesus quoted Moses' declaration, "Man shall not live by bread alone, but by every word that proceedeth out of the mouth of God" (Matthew 4:4, cf. Deuteronomy 8:3). The soul requires spiritual food just as surely as the body requires physical nourishment. One meal a week, or even two or three or four, would hardly sustain a healthy body. Our souls need daily bread just as do our bodies. Fasting from physical food is sometimes recommended in the Bible, but fasting from spiritual food, *never!*

It is impossible to prescribe a manner of Bible study which will suit every believer. There is an abundance of excellent literature available outlining suggestions in this field. This is not the place to discuss at length the variety of methods recommended by Biblical authorities. However, it seems fitting to point out that reading the Bible through in its entirety from Genesis through Revelation will reward the believer amply for his investment of time and interest.

The enormity of this project discourages some Christians when they contemplate the thousand-plus pages of fine print found in the average Bible. The prospect of reading sixty-six books containing 1,189 chapters divided into 31,175 verses overwhelms many believers.

However, if you allow yourself, say, one year in which to complete the reading of the sacred volume, you need read only three chapters on each week-day and five chapters on Sunday. If you commence the project on January 1 you will finish reading the Bible by December 31.

After a Christian has read the Bible through from Genesis to Revelation, he would profit considerably by reading the Scriptures through in the order of their events. The American Tract Society publishes a chronological approach which takes the reader through the entire volume, entitled, "Reading Your Bible in the Order of Its Events." This tract, compiled by A. B. Davis, is worthy of wide circulation, and while scholars will not all agree with all his chronological connections of Scripture, the arrangement is exceptionally accurate in most instances. Thus, for example, you read I Samuel 1:1-16:13, from whence you turn to Psalm 23, before resuming the historical narrative of I Samuel 15:14-19:11, where you interject Psalm 59.

Before leaving the practice of Bible study it must be emphasized that reading the Bible and studying the Scriptures are not necessarily synonymous. A person may read without studying. Of course, no one can really study the Bible without reading it. Believers find it spiritually profitable to maintain a constant habit of devotional reading besides a definite program of studying some section or subject of Scripture in greater detail and concentration than simply reading the Bible requirements.

If Bible study represents food for the soul, prayer and praise provide exercise. In the Scriptures God speaks to us. In prayer and praise we speak to God. And again we need to be careful to maintain a proper balance, neglecting neither one of these indispensable practices.

PRAYER

From a study of the Scriptures we learn that prayer is primarily asking. Bible prayers asked God for specific favors. Probably the only prayer mentioned in the Scriptures which asked for nothing was the expression of the Pharisee in the parable of Luke 18, and Jesus took pains to point out that the Pharisee's prayer was wholly ineffective. The publican in the same parable, however, asked God for mercy and received it!

The Lord invites believers to approach Him boldly in prayer, petitioning according to their needs. "Ask, and it shall be given you; seek, and ye shall find; knock, and it shall be opened unto you. For everyone that asketh receiveth; and he that seeketh findeth; and to him that knocketh it shall be opened" (Luke 11:9-10). In the same context, moreover, Jesus authorized persistence in pressing one's petitions. He reflected with approval upon the importunity of the householder who accosted his neighbor at midnight for three loaves of bread (cf. Luke 11:5-8). Later He would commend the determination not to be denied manifest by the widow who pleaded before the unjust judge (cf. Luke 18:2-8). The evangelist introduced the incident with the explanation, "And he spake a parable unto them to this end, that men ought always to pray, and not to faint" (Luke 18:1). The word "faint" here means "give up." Men ought always to persist in prayer and never give up. Of course, if my petition contradicts God's revealed will or His Word, I must forbear from repeating it. But as a general rule, a believer is entitled to ask God for anything that it is proper for him to want! "Let your requests be made known unto God," exhorted St. Paul (Philippians 4:6). "The effectual fervent prayer of a righteous man availeth much" (James 5:16). God hears prayer. God answers prayer. Some religionists recommend prayer for praying's sake, declaring that though prayer does not change anything, it is good for a person to pray. But believers in Jesus Christ pray to get things from God, and when we pray we do receive an answer.

Sister McPherson used to say that God always answers every prayer, but He does not necessarily answer each petition in the same way. Sometimes He answers *yes.*

Sometimes He answers *no*. An earthly father does not grant his child's every request. Would a loving parent comply with his three-year-old's petition to play with his safety razor? God sometimes says *no*. He denied Moses' petition for reconsideration of the prohibition of the lawgiver's entrance into the promised land (cf. Deuteronomy 3:23-27). When God says *no* there is a good reason which we may not know. But God is not always saying *no* when it seems that His answer is *no*. Often His answer is delay, not denial. Often He is answering *wait*! Did not the angel Gabriel inform Zacharias, "Thy prayer is heard; and thy wife Elisabeth shall bear thee a son" (Luke 1:13)? Zacharias probably had not repeated that petition in years, but eventually the time of waiting ended.

Of course, the Bible emphasizes that faith is an indispensable element in obtaining positive answers to prayer from God. Christians have not because they ask not or because they ask amiss (cf. James 4:2-3). But they also obtain not because they waver in faith. James exhorted concerning the man who prays, "Let him ask in faith, nothing wavering," adding the warning, "For he that wavereth is like a wave of the sea driven with the wind and tossed. For let not that man think that he shall receive any thing of the Lord" (James 1:6-7). When Elijah prayed for rain, he expected a cloud. He looked for a cloud. And a cloud appeared, albeit only the size of a man's hand. Jesus declared, "What things soever ye desire, when ye pray, believe that ye receive them, and ye shall have them" (Mark 11:24). For "faith is the substance of things hoped for, the evidence of things not seen" (Hebrews 11:1).

Now a believer's prayer life—and prayer should be a life, since Paul commanded, "Pray without ceasing" (I Thessalonians 5:17); and Jesus announced, "Men ought always to pray" (Luke 18:1)—divides itself into two sections. A Christian should pray in private (cf. Matthew 6:6). We need to get alone with God and pour out our hearts seeking His face. But a Christian should also pray in the company of other believers, both at church and at home.

Churchmen who are strangers to Pentecostal practice sometimes express bewilderment after witnessing the exercise of prayer in Foursquare services. It is not uncommon in such meetings for the entire congregation to participate in concert in fervent petition at the same time that the minister or some other believer is leading in prayer. Hands are often raised and faces uplifted rather than bowed. Such procedures may seem strange in the light of prevailing ecclesiastical customs of prayer, but they are by no means strange in the light of the practice of believers described in the Scriptures. To lead requires others to follow. If the pastor leads in prayer, does the congregation really follow if the people simply listen attentively? Since prayer is addressed primarily to God, and not to the audience, ought not all to enter in and participate? It is impossible to imagine the events of, say, Acts 4:24-31 and 12:5 as anything but the united intercession simultaneously of most, if not all of the Christians present. In the former passage "they lifted up their voice to God with one accord" (vs. 24). The audible expression even of fervent petition by members of the congregation at the same time that the pastor or another is leading in prayer does not compete with the intercession of the pastor but rather complements it!

But what about this uplifting of hands in the congregation? The practice is thoroughly Biblical, indeed commanded both in the Old and in the New Testaments. The Psalmist exhorted, "Lift up your hands in the sanctuary" (134:2), while centuries later the apostle Paul emphasized, "I will therefore that men pray every where, lifting up holy hands" (I Timothy 2:8). In some way a physical position often contributes to a spiritual blessing. The soul expresses itself through bodily members. Raising of hands and uplifting of faces during prayer, as much as the more conventional kneeling or bowing of head, represent a conscious exercise on man's part to draw nearer unto God. Any position may deteriorate into mere formality, but that abuse is no reason to neglect its use in fervently seeking the Lord.

PRAISE

The expression of concerted praise to God is a conspicuous feature in many Foursquare services. Some believers protest that they need not voice aloud their thanksgiving so long as they nurture praise in their hearts. But the Psalmist testified, "I will bless the Lord at all times: his praise shall continually be in my mouth" (Psalm 34:1). Someone has pointed out that m-o-u-t-h does not spell heart! Vance Havner was right when he reflected concerning the vocal expression of Christian worship, "What's in the well will come up in the bucket!" If praise is truly in one's heart its expression will escape his mouth!

The Bible encourages enthusiastic outbursts of praise. "Make a joyful noise unto the Lord, all ye lands," commences Psalm 100. Some try to limit such Old Testament exhortations to the Jews, but specifically all lands are included in the command.

Concerted praise seems always in Bible times to have constituted an integral part of public worship. "Praise God in his sanctuary," commands Psalm 150. And "everything that hath breath" is encouraged to enter into the exercise (verses 1, 6). God is worthy of praise both for His personal excellencies and for His marvelous works. The praise of the redeemed in heaven sounded so thunderous that John the Revelator compared it to the voice of many waters, the reverberation of mighty cataracts. On occasion he overheard millions of loud voices simultaneously celebrating the divine undertakings. If such praise is proper in Paradise, ought not God's people on earth to voice their thanksgiving heartily together? And of course our hearts should overflow with praise when we are in private as well as in places of public worship.

Because the sermon by Aimee Semple McPherson following this chapter deals in depth with the believer's duty and privilege to praise the Lord, this aspect of devotional expression will not receive further development here, save the testimony of many that they have praised their way through predicaments they seemed unable to pray their way through and the comment of Dr. Herman D. Mitzner, "Prayer is asking, and praise is receiving."

Bible study, prayer, and praise represent indispensable devotional expressions which believers must cultivate faithfully and persistently if they are to experience steady spiritual growth. Believing the Bible will never take the place of reading and studying the Bible. Believing in prayer will never take the place of actually praying. The same is true with respect to praise. We must experience these exercises firsthand. What we believe is of utmost importance. But our practice of that faith is of equal importance. That is why James commanded, "Be ye doers of the word, and not hearers only" (James 1:22).

Sermon

PRAISING THE LORD

Praising the Lord has ever been to me one of the most inspiring and exalting themes. Oh how I love to praise Him and to hear Him praised!

It has been my privilege on hundreds of occasions to witness the never-to-be-forgotten scene of many thousands of saints standing on their feet with uplifted hands, and tears streaming down their radiant faces, praising the Lord with all their might and soul and voice, with one accord, till the great volume of thunderous praises blended into a sound as of rushing mighty waters as it rolled majestically heavenward. It went up as one voice, of one people who were one in heart and adoration of the most high God and His glorious Son Jesus Christ.

It is when praising the Lord thus, as at no other time, that my spirit catches the greatest revelation—the greatest vision of the mighty, omnipotent King of the Ages, high and lifted up. 'Tis then that the very atmosphere seems electric-charged with the mighty power of the great God, and I catch the sound of His chariot wheels leaping o'er the mountains, ever coming nearer as His people continue to adore Him, till I hear the stately steppings of the King in the midst of His holy tabernacle—then, as the cloud of glorious adoration still rises from the hearts of the people, I see Him robed with honor, crowned with glory, seated upon a jewelled throne of adoration which His people have builded for Him by their praises.

The Lord inhabiteth the praises of His people. Where real praise is, there is God.

It is impossible to over-estimate the power, victory, blessing, healing, encouragement and inspiration embodied in this wonderful secret of praising the Lord.

Praise the Lord at all times!

"Oh, but you know that I could never put anything on, I never could praise the Lord unless I feel like it," someone exclaims.

Unless you feel like it! Oh! Is that the gauge by which you measure your offerings of praise? Is that the foundation upon which your Christian experience is based? My dear brother, sister, feelings are a poor and a very uncertain guide upon which to rely when it comes to praising the Lord, or any other Christian experience. Only one man in the Bible that I know of went by feeling; that was dear old Isaac, and you remember how he felt the hands and arms of Jacob, his son, and how deceived he was. Oh, dear hearts, praise Him! Not because you happen to feel like it, but praise Him at "all times," and let His praise be continually in your mouth, because He is worthy.

Begin to praise Him whether you feel like it or not, and you will soon feel like it. Why, it is impossible for me to lift up my hands and begin to praise and adore my Master without a downpour of His blessing that is as rain to the thirsty fields and flowers, or as the anointing-oil upon my head, running down to the borders of my garments.

"Let everything that hath breath praise the Lord." Why, according to David, the only excuse you have got for not praising the Lord is being out of breath!

"Oh, Sister, I praise Him in my heart. I could never shout aloud or be demonstrative. It is not my make-up or disposition."

Beloved, when you have put on your beautiful garments of praise (for no matter how homely you may be to the natural eye, you are beautiful to the Lord when you have put on praise as a garment) you are lifted above your own make-up and disposition, and swing far out into the realm of the Spirit. As for praising the Lord in your heart, why, your heart is no different from anyone else's. When it gets just so full of glorious praises and adoration and He becomes so real, so fair as to be altogether lovely, the chiefest of ten thousand to your soul, your heart will run over and you will shout His praises, and your voice will be blended with the voices of all the other redeemed ones and soar upward to the Lamb that sitteth upon the throne.

I was much impressed while in New York during the first World War by the notices posted on the subway and elevated trains and in other prominent public places, warning the people of the severe penalty awaiting anyone who should try in any way to break the morale of the soldiers by talking of possible defeat, failure, or lauding the strength of the enemy. This should be a warning to Christians also. Do not break the morale of the Christian army!

Two saints attend the same meeting. Probably you have these two saints in your church, for almost every church has them.

One enters with a long face, takes her seat, looks solemnly about, and if the meeting seems a little bound, or in need of a blessing, or lacking in praise, this dear one, meaning well enough, begins to be burdened and sigh, to pray aloud, or exclaim in this manner, "Oh, Lord, what is the matter here! Oh, there is such a binding spirit, such a power of darkness. It seems as though the room were filled with demons. Lord, help." Immediately every eye and every thought is directed to the devil, to darkness and binding spirits, and of course, like Peter when he got his eye on the waves, when we get our eyes on the devil we have them off Jesus.

When we advertise and meditate upon the greatness and strength of the devil, and show fear, we underestimate the power of the great I AM, the mighty conqueror who never lost a battle. Such despondency and burdened agonizing is contagious, and soon everyone is moaning and crying and miserable, and it is not until someone begins to praise the Lord that the cloud lifts.

The other saint enters the same meeting, where it seems that not one breath of the heavenly gales is stirring, feels the same pressure upon the meeting, and refusing to look at or recognize the enemy, says, "This is the time to praise our Jesus. This is the time to see our God arise and scatter His enemies. He has told us that He will do great and mighty things if we will but praise Him, and we know that the enemy cannot lodge or abide in atmosphere that is filled with the praises of the Lord." This saint straightway begins to shout, "Hallelujah! We rejoice in Thee! We glory in Thy might! Oh, our King! Victory and honor ever attend Thy troops. Power and dominion envelop Thee. Thy glory and presence fill the heavens and the earth. It fills my heart just now. It overflows and fills the room. Why, glory to Jesus! Beloved, the Lord is in our midst. Do you not feel Him? Why, this atmosphere is just like heaven!"

Such faith and praise is contagious. The fire of unwavering confidence in God that burns within this temple soon leaps over its parapets, spreads first to those in the seats nearby, then on to the farthest corner of the room, inspiring, encouraging, lifting up drooping heads, strengthening feeble knees, and in a moment every eye is fixed on Jesus, His praises fill the tabernacle, souls are blessed, vessels are filled to overflowing, the latter rain is heard pattering on the roofs, running down the troughs, overflowing the rain barrels, the dry ground is saturated and the wilderness and the desert places are blossoming as a rose!

Where was the difference in the two saints? The one recognized and saw only the power of the devil, and straightway began to bemoan the sad state of affairs, depressing everyone who listened; while the other saw only Jesus in His all-conquering, invincible might and splendor, riding on to sure and certain victory.

The Lord taught me a wonderful lesson in a meeting in Philadelphia, demonstrating the majesty and power of praise. I was seated on the rostrum of my tent during the evening service. Not only was every seat in the big tabernacle filled and crowds standing in the aisles, but all about the outside of the tent hundreds and hundreds stood closely packed together. It was the early days of the meeting and conviction had not yet taken the place of curiosity. Therefore, as a great many of the onlookers were Roman Catholics, and the balance unused to any demonstration of the power of God, the very air was filled with unbelief, skepticism, scoffing and ridicule. The people would listen as long as we sang (or was it because that drowned their murmurings?) But as soon as anyone endeavored to speak, the whisperings and the murmurings would begin until another song was started.

As I stood there on the platform, with my eyes closed, I envisioned the entire tent surrounded with great black demons, with huge, bat-like wings. Each demon seemed to stand about ten feet tall, and as they stood in a circle, completely surrounding the tent, they were so close together that their wings touched tip to tip. They stood close to the border of the tent, and with my eyes still closed, my heart began to cry out, "Oh, Lord, what shall

I do?" And He spoke to me in such a real way, in that calm, undisturbed voice which those who love the Prince of Peace know so well, "Just begin to praise Me. I will do the fighting. You do the praising." So I began to praise Him.

"Praise the Lord!" The first time I said it I noticed the demons seemed to tremble.

"Praise the Lord!" The second time I shouted it. I am sure my voice was heard above every other sound, and I saw each demon take one step backwards, away from the tent. "Praise the Lord! Praise the Lord! Praise the Lord!" Each time I said "Praise the Lord" the demons took another step backwards, until I lost all sight of them in the distance. "Praise the Lord!" The next time I said it I saw in the distance a circular band of angels standing around the tent. "Praise the Lord! PRAISE THE LORD!" Each time I praised Him they took one step nearer, another step nearer, still another step nearer, till at last they stood at the very border of the tent, such tall, wonderful looking angels, with their beautiful white wings spread so wide that the wings of each touched, tip to tip, the ones of the next angel on the right and on the left. Father had sent one of His legions of angels to guard the tent.

Perhaps not another person in the tent saw the vision of this great shining band of angels, yet everyone inside and out must have sensed the presence of the divine for not only did a great peace steal over my soul, but the whole audience was hushed. When I opened my eyes I could see only the people looking with rapt attention, but closing my eyes again I could see the angels just as plainly as I could see the people.

Is it any wonder that I believe that the power of praise drives back the enemy and brings down the blessing!

This incident in Philadelphia furnished the inspiration some years later for the fresco work just under the great dome of Angelus Temple. There you see pictured angels with each out-stretched wing touching its neighbor's.

Jesus says, "What things soever you desire when ye

pray, believe that ye receive them, and ye shall have them." Now, if we ask God to give us a certain answer to prayer, and we then proceed to believe we have it, it is only polite to begin to thank Him for it, in other words, shoot upward through the prayer zone into the praise zone, and thank God beforehand that, according to His word, it is done.

When contending with sickness, trouble, misunderstanding, discouragement or depression, begin to see Jesus. Praise Him with all your heart, and the upward flight of His praises will lift you as with the wings of a great eagle, above the woes of this earth till sorrow and sighing are lost sight of and consolation and joy unspeakable fill their place as you exalt and magnify the Lamb for sinners slain.

"But I do not want to praise Him in the flesh," says someone. Ah, but we walk no more "after the flesh, but after the Spirit," and all this poor flesh of mine is fit for anyway is to praise Jesus, and if you never do anything worse in the flesh than to praise the Lord you will never be displeasing in His sight.

When the Comforter abides and has His way, it is so easy to praise Jesus, for "He, when He has come, He will glorify Me," and "out of your innermost being shall flow rivers of living water."

You may have but little gold or silver, or of this world's goods to offer, but there is no excuse for being sparing or miserly with His praises.

Heap up His praises upon the glowing altar of your soul, and pile His adoration on top of that, crown Him with glory, laud and magnify His name until His burning praises rise in precious frankincense, as a sweet-smelling savor to be caught in the golden censer of the angel who, standing by the altar, offers unto the Lord much incense (praise), with the prayers of all saints upon the golden altar which is before the throne (Revelation 8:3).

Let your heart be tuned up until it shall be as a harp of a thousand strings swept with melody by the fingers of the Holy Spirit.

If you have hung your harp on the willow tree, if the rust of coldness or self or formality has formed upon the strings, or if they are broken or out of tune, go, get your harp! Take it down from the willows, clean away the rust which has gathered from long unuse, let the Holy Spirit tune up each string until again the music will spring forth at His slightest touch. Remember, it takes but a slight jar to put the most costly harp out of tune; walk softly, dear heart, with unshod feet before Him.

Chapter II SACRAMENTAL PARTICIPATION

Considerable misunderstanding exists among evangelical Christians concerning the meaning and use of the world *sacrament*. This term suggests somewhat different concepts to different people, depending largely upon the context of their religious affiliations. Some of the associations of the word seem objectionable to Foursquare believers. However, the primary definition as pertaining to theological usage given by Webster's Collegiate Dictionary (Fourth Edition of the Merriam Series, p. 849) proves altogether acceptable for application to our observance of water baptism and the Lord's Supper: "An outward and visible sign of an inward and spiritual grace."

Both water baptism and holy communion represent exactly that—an outward and visible sign of an inward and spiritual grace.

Water baptism was commanded by our Lord Jesus Christ and communion was instituted personally by Him. Neither was initiated by the church or by church organizations.

WATER BAPTISM

Two of the New Testament versions of the Great Commission include emphasis upon water baptism (cf. Mark 16:15-16; Matthew 28:19). Jesus commanded His disciples to evangelize and to baptize their converts into the name of the Father and of the Son and of the Holy Spirit. Thus for a church to baptize or not to baptize, for a convert to be baptized or not to be baptized, is not a matter left to the option or preference of the individual congregation or believer, but is rather an obligation enjoined both by the example and precept of the Lord of the church Himself!

But *how* should a person be baptized?

For centuries churchmen have debated the mode of baptism. Should a candidate submit to immersion, sprinkling, or pouring? In New Testament times, however, there was no variety. There can be not the slightest doubt that water baptism as the apostles knew it and the early church practiced it was by immersion and only by immersion! The Greek word translated "baptize" is the intensive form of the term meaning to dip, to plunge, to immerse. John the Baptist needed "much water" to officiate in his ordinance (cf. John 3:23). No river is needed to supply water for sprinkling or pouring. A well would do. Jesus Himself was immersed. He came "straightway out of the water" (Matthew 3:16). And when Philip baptized the Ethiopian eunuch both men "went down into the water, and came up out of the water" (Acts 8:38). No one who has not experienced immersion has been baptized in the manner in which people in the apostolic age received water baptism. The Foursquare Church insists on immersion for its candidates for this sacrament.

The question *who* should be baptized has perhaps kindled as much controversy in ecclesiastical circles throughout the centuries as the matter of the mode of baptism. The issue must be settled, however, by investigation of the Scriptures. What does the Bible say?

God's Word seems unmistakably clear on this question. Nothing anywhere in sacred writ authorizes the baptism of any but believers! Jesus commissioned His followers to make disciples and then baptize them (cf. Matthew 28:19). "He that believeth and is baptized shall be saved" (Mark 16:16). Personal saving faith must precede water baptism if that ordinance is to have any spiritual significance whatsoever, because faith and nothing else constitutes the entrance to discipleship. What would happen if an unsaved person submitted to immersion? Nothing! Nothing really! The only effect the baptism would have would be to change a dry sinner into a wet sinner!

So who should be baptized? The answer is believers—believers in Jesus Christ, converts cleansed from their sin through faith in the atoning blood of the Saviour. Every believer, moreover, is obligated by divine command to submit to this ordinance. "Be baptized every one of you," Peter enjoined the candidates for conversion on the day of Pentecost, and that command has never been rescinded, nor have any exceptions been authorized in subsequent Scriptures (Acts 2:38). Any believer who has opportunity to be baptized but refuses or neglects to receive immersion is living in disobedience to our Lord's command!

DEDICATION OF BABIES

Since baptism is for believers according to the Bible, Foursquare churches do not baptize infants. No babies were reported baptized in Bible days. Instead, faithful parents presented their children to the Lord in dedication, as the Scriptures records in the case of Samuel and Jesus (cf. I Samuel 1; Luke 2). Baptism would mean nothing to an infant. He would be altogether unaware of what was happening during the ceremony. He is unaware also of what transpires when he is presented by his parents for dedication to the Lord, as is the practice in our churches, but this dedication is not his act but his parents' act, and they are conscious at the time of their pledge to raise the child for the Lord. Baptism is symbolic of a spiritual work accomplished in the soul of a believer. Since a baby has not believed, he cannot be a candidate for baptism. There is strong Biblical precedent for dedication but none whatever for baptism of infants.

HOLY COMMUNION

While water baptism as a sacrament is administered to the believer only once (and that once ought to be as soon as possible after conversion; on the day of Pentecost the believers were baptized immediately), the Lord's Supper as an ordinance is observed periodically. The New Testament employs the adverb "often" (I Corinthians 11:26) to describe the frequency of the observance, but the Scripture nowhere tells believers how often to participate in the Lord's Supper. Consequently a variety of practices prevail, ranging from once a year observance to once a week. Foursquare churches serve communion once a month, on the first Sunday of the month. We practice open communion, making the elements available to all believers present, irrespective of church affiliation.

In its essence, the Holy Communion commemorates Calvary, as it were, in miniature. The remembrance it enshrines is specifically of Christ's death. He gave His body and blood for our benefit. The bread and the cup symbolize that sacrifice. Foursquare believers look upon these elements not as the very body and very blood of the Lord, as those who hold to transubstantiation hold, but as emblems appointed by Jesus to signify His body and blood.

However, if we regard the Lord's Supper wholly as a retrospect, we miss one divinely revealed aspect of the observance. For the Holy Communion not only points back in retrospect to Christ's cross, it points forward in prospect of His coming: "For as often as ye eat this bread, and drink this cup, ye do shew the Lord's death till he come" (I Corinthians 11:26). Sister McPherson used to liken the communion table to a rainbow linking earthly observance of the sacrament with its heavenly counterpart. Jesus Himself anticipated a celestial communion on the occasion when He initiated the Lord's Supper: "But I say unto you, I will not drink henceforth of this fruit of the vine, until that day when I drink it new with you in my Father's kingdom" (Matthew 26:29).

Consideration of Holy Communion from the Foursquare viewpoint would hardly be adequate without a brief reference to St. Paul's comment in I Corinthians 11 about discerning the Lord's body.

Virtually every believer who participates in the Lord's Supper discerns or understands the Lord's blood. We know that without shedding of blood there is no remission of sin. We know the benefits the blood of Jesus brings to the believer, forgiveness of sins and cleansing from all unrighteousness. But many fail to understand the significance of the bread betokening the broken body of Christ. That body need not be broken for man's salvation. The shedding of the blood was sufficient for redemption from all iniquity. But God provided in Christ a double cure for a double curse. Sickness entered the world in the train of sin. But Jesus Christ is the Lord: "Who forgiveth all thine iniquities, who healeth all thy diseases" (Psalm 103:3). As the cross provided atonement for sin, the whipping post where Jesus suffered flogging provided atonement for sickness, for "with his stripes we are healed" (Isaiah 53:5, cf. I Peter 2:24). At the whipping post Jesus' body was broken. When believers discern or understand this, the element of bread in the Holy Communion affords a marvelous means of faith, and they appropriate the healing our Lord Jesus has already accomplished. The reader is referred to the chapter on Jesus the Healer for further details of this divine provision. And the sermons by Foursquaredom's founder which follow this chapter provide fuller insights into our observance both of the Lord's Supper and water baptism. These are the sacraments or ordinances which our movement practices. They rest on the authority of Jesus Christ and Scripture and not on the authority of any ecclesiastical body. All other religious ceremonies called "sacraments" are man-made and consequently not binding on believers.

•

Sermon

INITIATION CEREMONIES

Initiation ceremonies!

I have never been a lodge member and if I ever were to think of joining one, I would probably be scared out at the thoughts of the "initiation ceremonies." But I do know that when we initiate into "the order of the blood-washed and the firstborn" we have some glorious "initiation ceremonies." Water baptism is one of them.

Now the moment candidates are accepted as members of the various lodges, they find themselves among new people—new systems—new ways of doing things. So much more so do the people of "the order of Jesus Christ" find themselves among a new people, who love the Lord.

At one place where I spoke, there was in the door, a funny, little, round peep-hole, with a slide on the inner side. When there was lodge, the person came up to the door and knocked. The doorkeeper pushed back the little slide and asked for the password. The member said, "Kalamazoo" or whatever it might be, and the doorkeeper on the other side said, "I'll let you through." But if you don't know the password, you can't get in.

I'm so glad there is a door with a blessed, blessed opening through the side of Jesus Christ, for He is the door. If you are going to come into the "order of blood-washed people," you must first come through the door—in through the door of that wounded side, from whence flowed mingled blood and water.

But before you can enter and become a real child of God, in order to get through the door of justification by faith, you must have the password. It goes something like this, "God be merciful to me, a sinner. Lord receive me. Wash me in the precious blood," and the minute you send up from a simple, earnest heart, that password, the door will swing wide open and you are admitted.

Dearly beloved, let us cleanse ourselves and join this new order—"the new lodge of the Lord Jesus Christ," which surpasses all the others put together. To be a Christian most certainly is to belong to the grandest order in the whole world.

When a person joins a lodge, a beautiful cloak or robe is given him. (Some of them are very pretty I understand, being garments of various colors with each color symbolical of something they would show forth.) The robe is thrown over you as you come in. Now when you come into "the order of the firstborn," you will be given the robe of Jesus Christ our Lord. Over your shoulders will be cast a wonderful robe of love and redemption and righteousness.

Of course if you are to be initiated into a lodge, you bow at the altar before "*the grand master.*" Jesus is "*the grandest master*" in the whole world, praise the Lord. You bow before Him and say, "Lord, I will submit myself into Thy keeping. I will follow You blindly. I will never question."

No one in any lodge has taken an oath as strong as those who joined this new order of our Lord, pledging body, soul, life, spirit, all they are or hope to be, to the grand master, Jesus Christ. We are not to reason why, but to do and die as He commands.

Now after you are saved, the next thing is to be initiated. We have repented and believed. We are now born into the church triumphant. It is time to be baptized in water.

"But what," someone asks, "is the reason for baptism?" Everything regarding water baptism is freighted with the deepest significance. *First,* water itself is typical of holiness and godliness. *Second, pure* water is a type of salvation which freely flows. So water baptism is a type of cleansing. The Lord will make us pure without and within.

At the back of the baptistry in Angelus Temple we

can almost see the waters really flowing from the painting of the Jordan, so natural is it with its river receding in the distance that we think it must be as real as the waters which come tumbling down over the rocks into the baptistry. This is symbolical too, as the waters poured out and down into the ancient River Jordan, flowing out of Galilee, and into the Dead Sea, passing between the two. And in this water multitudes were baptized. Christ Himself was baptized there, which is again symbolical.

Why did the water flow from the Sea of Galilee into the Dead Sea? What was the significance of this? O Galilee, blessed Galilee, which ever speaks of Jesus. He walks beside its shores and its waters ever speak of Him as "Jesus of Galilee."

Where do these waters empty? I repeat again they empty into the Dead Sea. By the shedding of His own blood, Jesus of Galilee let water and blood come mingling down to wash away our sins. What has become of them? They have flowed into the Dead Sea and are remembered against us no more. People may remember them. The devil may try to make you remember them and he may remind you of the past, but Jesus never will. For when God forgives us, He forgets.

This is a glorious initiation service. Our baptismal fountain here at the Temple is builded in a shape which bespeaks of the open grave, a watery grave to be sure. This is symbolical of another grave in the garden of Joseph of Arimathaea, where Jesus died and was laid away. This ceremony bespeaks the fact that we who follow the Lord reckon that our sins were nailed with Him on the cross, and now, we reckon that they are buried.

Somebody says, "Sister, why don't you sprinkle?"

I answer, "Because I can't find any scripture for it."

Believers are buried, we read, and raised in a newness of life. What would sprinkling mean? If anybody died, you wouldn't sprinkle dirt over them, you would bury them.

Then someone else says, "Why do you wait until they are old? Why don't you just sprinkle them when they are babies?"

I answer, "We dedicate babies. We want you to know every step you take. You must understand what you are doing and take it with your own consent, initiation ceremonies, if you please."

Take John the Baptist. He baptized them in the river, not at a pump or with a cup or bowl, and we often read of how they moved to a place on the river where there was much water. Now, if they had been sprinkling, a little bit of water would have been enough.

Again, we read of Philip and the eunuch. "And they went down both into the water . . .And when they were come up out of the water, the Spirit of the Lord caught away Philip, that the eunuch saw him no more: and he went on his way rejoicing" (Acts 8:38-39).

This baptistry represents a grave. The old life is gone. Sins are gone, Hallelujah! But the Lord not only was buried but He also was raised up. And as you come up out of the water, it bespeaks Jesus Christ being raised from the dead, alive for evermore, and signifies that you too, shall live with Him in this new order.

It is a wonderful thing to be born again into this new, yet old, order of the Lord Jesus Christ. And if you are a real Christian—a Spirit-filled member of the Lord Jesus Christ, you can't hide it.

This morning when I finished broadcasting the "Sunshine Hour," someone told me, "Sister, there's a telephone call for you. You are invited to attend the luncheon that the Optimist Club is giving today."

I slipped away to the Biltmore Hotel where I found a meeting room filled with business men. They presented me with an armload of beautiful roses. I thanked them, gave them some words of encouragement and told them that I would finish my message over the radio tonight.

I had the privilege of sitting at the table with good company. On one side was a well-known baseball player and on the other side, the Baptist minister, Dr. J. Whitcomb Brougher, who gave a wonderful message on the subject "Play Ball!" to those men.

He told a story which I think would be helpful to those whom we are going to initiate into the service of the Lord.

While Dr. Brougher was in England walking with bared head through Westminster Abbey, his guide pointed to the floor and said, "Here is where we bury our dead."

With a twinkle in his eye, Dr. Brougher said, "In America, we don't bury them, we keep our dead in the pews."

I am afraid some of us are dead ones. O God help us to get next to Him and be alive. Some of you folk have not said "Amen" since you came in here tonight for I have been watching, and you are dead if you haven't a real "Amen" in your heart.

Pat and Mike saw their first serpent over here. They were not used to snakes so they got a club and went after this one. They had beaten the poor thing almost to pieces but its tail kept on wiggling. Pat said to Mike, "Do yez think he is dead?"

And Mike answered, "I certainly think he is, but he ain't aware of it."

Some of us are dead in trespassing and sin, only we are not aware of it. We are just simply sitting up and postponing the undertaker's bill. Lord help us to get awake and get the old man out of the way, bury him in baptism and then rise, walk with the Lord Jesus Christ.

Sermon

THE LORD'S SUPPER

"With desire have I desired to eat this Passover with you before I suffer . . ." It must have seemed strange to the disciples to hear His words, and then, at the end of the Feast, deliberately brush the whole thing aside, as it were, as though to say: "I hereby abrogate that which God hath appointed all these years, retaining as much of it as I see fit, and, hereby, do I place Myself on record and empower this Feast with new life and new meaning."

Who was this Man who sat with the twelve? Who was this One who had such power of presumption that He dared to take that which for thousands of years had been the very heart and center and axis around which the national life encircled itself?

Who was this fearless One? Ah, He was the anti-type of which the Passover Lamb was but a type, He was GOD'S PASSOVER LAMB. He was the very fulfillment of it all, and the light of the world come unto His own. With true Lordship, He swept aside the old order of things and established the new.

The Lord's Supper not only points backward, but it points forward. It not only says, "This is My body, broken for you; this is My blood, shed for you," but, like a rainbow of hope, it points forward to the other end of the table inaugurated by our Lord, and rests in that City over There. It reminds us of a feast we shall have very soon in the Kingdom which is perfect–the Kingdom of our Lord.

"With desire have I desired to eat this Passover." His was an earnest desire for just one last hour of calm before the storm and the mob. Again, His desire to partake of the Passover Feast, and then, at the end of the Feast, establish the Lord's Supper, shows to us His fellowship. He loved His disciples. In spite of their shrinking, timid, faltering steps, He loved to be with them in fellowship. He, too, was parting with His loved ones, and from the depth of His heart He said: "With desire have I desired to eat . . .with you before I suffer."

He wanted them to gather just a little closer to Him, to clasp their hands, and to look into their faces once again. But most of all He desired to establish the Lord's

Supper and bid them commemorate it. How precious His words, "Do this in remembrance of Me!"

The Lord's Supper is, truly, a LOVE FEAST. It is a time to draw closer to Him, to draw near through the avenue of memory. My, how we treasure the memory of one who has left us to go to be with Jesus—perhaps, a dear mother or father, a darling brother or sister—and memory ever lives in the heart, sacred forever.

His desire was not only to partake of the Passover, but to absolutely transform it, to imbreathe it with new hope and thought, for the Lord's Supper is at once a memory and a hope for the future—a symbol of the past when He died, and a symbol of the future when we shall see Him face to face.

Some have taken the Lord's Table and have made it altogether into a sacramental table, teaching it is, indeed, the "Lord's body." This is called the doctrine of transubstantiation. But that is not the teaching of our Lord. The Lord's Supper is for a memorial. Our Lord appointed it thus.

The Passover Feast, commemorated by the Israelites, was held every year that they might remember how the Lord had brought them out of slavery. We, too, who have been slaves to sin remember the sacrifice that set us free as we partake of the Lord's Supper instituted by our Lord.

His was an individual desire to be remembered. Have you ever parted with a dear one who was going to a distant city and heard the words, as with tears they held your hand at parting: "Don't forget me! Remember me when you reach that far-distant country or city."

Sad as it seems, yet it is true that people can forget Jesus. He knew the human heart. He wanted to be remembered, and His words seemed impregnated with longing, as though He had plainly said: "Don't forget me!" What sincere desire is expressed in His words: "This do in remembrance of Me." "This cup is the new testament in My blood, which is shed for you. This is

My body which is given for you: this do in remembrance of Me."

The Lord's Supper, then, is a memorial, and He gives us here the power to recall Him by outward symbol, lest we forget. It is a definite, illustrated sermon.

Did you ever receive or give anything in remembrance of happy days, in remembrance of happy hours? Oh, so many of us have treasures and trinkets that we hold dear. Perhaps, it is a *locket.* On one side is the face of a loved one and on the other side is a lock of hair. The curious may touch the spring of that locket and it opens, and it means nothing, and they say, "I wonder who that is?" But there is someone who knows, someone to whom every line and feature of that face is precious and dear.

Little mother, you have a lock of your little girl's hair or your little boy's hair somewhere in the secret place. It is part of your heart. You do not forget. So Jesus wants to be remembered. He left us the emblem of His broken body and precious blood.

Again, some lovely sentiments have been carved on trees, like two hearts, pierced by an arrow and initials. You may have forgotten the initials carved there, but they form the life of the tree. You may have forgotten the face you carved there when the tree was young, but it is there.

So Jesus, beloved, has carved His Name on the cross-tree of the church by the Lord's Supper. Jesus wants to be remembered.

What a beautiful symbol of an engagement is the Lord's Supper Table! The bride of Christ remembers and longs for that day when she will be united with her Bridegroom. As she partakes of the service, she remembers His words: "This do, till I come!"

Have you ever heard someone say: "I would love to have your picture and your autograph"? So, in the Lord's Supper we commemorate His death and suffering, we have a picture autographed by His blood.

Notice those words distinctly are separate: "This is My body broken for you. This is My blood." Christ denoted the fact He was to die a violent death. He knew every drop of blood was to flow from His body. And that blood, the blood of our Paschal Lamb, avails for sin if we will accept that sacrifice. "Without the shedding of blood there is no remission of sins."

Oh, beautiful symbol—the broken bread—and its meaning so very dear. It means the alabaster box of His precious body must be broken in order that the whole house may be filled with fragrance. How it fills the world with incense and myrrh. Do you remember how the woman anointed the head of Christ with the ointment which she had brought in an alabaster box? Jesus knew the love that prompted that deed, and He said: "Wherever this gospel shall be preached throughout the whole world, this also that she hath done shall be spoken of for a memorial of her."

The Jewish Passover will be commemorated and there will be an empty place at the table. But Jesus said: "I AM the Lamb of which this was only the type. I am the anti-type and you do not need the empty chair, 'Lo, I am with you always, even to the end of the world.' Wherever two or three gather together, there am I in the midst."

"You don't need the empty plate. Come and dine. You do not need the horseradish and the bitter herbs. I have taken your bitterness upon Me to the tree. You don't need the egg for I am the resurrection and the life."

And so, with regal bearing, Our Lord deliberately took the empty chair and canceled and set aside and abrogated that God-appointed divine service of the Passover and instituted the new—THE LORD'S SUPPER. He was the fulfillment of it all. And, seating Himself in that empty chair, He said with authority: "This is My body broken for you. This is My blood."

And as we remember His sacrifice with eyes swimming with tears, may our hearts look up and remember He again will sit with His own, for we have His words: "I will not drink of the fruit of the vine until the kingdom of God shall come."

Chapter III PRACTICAL DEDICATION

Christianity is not all theology and sacrament. Faith manifests itself in action. An absolutely inert body is pronounced dead by physicians. A faith which never implements work is pronounced dead by the Bible. The Foursquare Gospel stresses practical dedication in the stewardship of the believer's time and talents and possessions.

In what areas does God expect Christians to dedicate to Him their time?

CHURCH ATTENDANCE

From the day of Pentecost onward the church has stressed the importance of assembling together for worship and work. So it sounds strange to hear some people today inquire, "Why must Christians attend church services? Can't we be believers in our own homes?"

God help the churchman who does not live his faith at home! However, those who bow to the authority of Scripture recognize that church attendance is absolutely indispensable unless circumstances make it absolutely impossible. Apparently in apostolic times the tendency developed among some to neglect the meetings of the church. Thus Hebrews 10:25 forthrightly forbids the forsaking of such assembling, and adds that this responsibility to be faithful in attendance actually increases as the last days approach. Sometimes people say, "God told me not to go to church." If God actually so advised, He was contradicting His Word, for in the Bible He commands attendance.

Of course, going to church does not make anyone a Christian. Going to church does not make you a Christian anymore than going to a garage makes you an automobile or a mechanic! Neither does church membership make anyone a Christian. The steeple belongs to the church. The organ belongs to the church. But neither are Christians. Some church members—probably some members of Foursquare churches at that—are no more Christians than the steeple or organ. But while attendance and membership do not make Christians, those who are truly born again and living in victory will head for the church as naturally as a duck will head for water!

CHURCH MEMBERSHIP

Many dedicated believers attend Foursquare churches with regularity yet have not become members of the church. Sometimes this circumstance results from neglect on the part of those who are members to invite and encourage the friends to affiliate. Others hesitate to join because of ignorance or misunderstanding of the procedure or qualifications for membership. One prospect actually asked this writer, "What is the membership fee for joining your church?" Of course, there is no membership fee. Neither must new members be voted in by a poll of the congregation.

What then are the qualifications for membership?

To join a Foursquare church a believer must profess conversion through faith in the shed-blood of Jesus Christ. He must confess faith in the Lord Jesus Christ by being or having been baptized in the name of the Father and of the Son and of the Holy Ghost. And he must express acceptance of our doctrinal position as stated in our Declaration of Faith. Believers who meet these qualifications are encouraged to join our congregations in order to be more fully involved in the life and outreach of the church. Only active members may hold offices in Foursquare churches.

Church attendance and affiliation, however, are not ends in themselves. They represent rather springboards for service. Of course, the foremost task of the church is evangelism, and this includes not only the efforts exerted during the church and Sunday School sessions to recruit sinners for Christ but also the efforts which ought to be conducted on a large scale outside the church by all the laymen as well as the ministers, efforts altogether too often neglected in the field of personal soul-winning. The most important project any believer ever accomplishes for God is to win an unbeliever to the faith. But other areas of need require workers, including the Sunday School, the Crusader groups, the United Foursquare Women and Council of Foursquare Men, the usher body, communion boards, elders, deacons and deaconesses. There is work for every member to do, ranging from spiritual emphasis to material and philanthropic efforts. God calls believers to devote to Him a sizable portion of their time and talents.

FINANCIAL RESPONSIBILITY

God in His Word lays claim also to the believer's stewardship of possessions. He expects our tithes and offerings.

Some refuse to tithe because they suppose tithing was initiated under the law, while Christian believers are not under the law but under grace. However, tithing antedated the law by at least four hundred years. Abraham, the man of faith, paid tithes to Melchizedek, whom the Epistle to the Hebrews hails as a type of Jesus Christ. Christian believers have this solemn responsibility to bring all their tithes into the storehouse, which in this dispensation means their local church. Because tithing is discussed at length in the sermon by Sister McPherson following this chapter, there is no need to cover the subject further at this point. Suffice to add, the Bible presents tithing as a duty and encourages additional offerings as a privilege.

Contributions to missions constitute the largest area for free-will offerings by adherents of Foursquare churches. One of the main reasons for our denominational existence is our missionary outreach. We consider missions—both home and foreign—to be our number one task and responsibility. Our people generously support the missionary program through their gifts and faith promises. Crusaders are called upon to give in their sessions on the first Sunday of the month. The Sunday School gives to missions on the second Sunday, while the church as a whole contributes its missionary offering on the third Sunday. Four times a year a "Fifth Sunday" missionary offering for some specific project is received. And the effectiveness of our Foursquare missionaries throughout the world should spur our constituency to increase giving and indeed sacrifice that our outreach may be extended considerably. This is a needy world, and the world needs Jesus more than it needs anything else. When we at home give to missions we make it possible for people abroad to receive Jesus as their Saviour, Baptizer, Healer, and Coming King.

To be a doer of the Word, and not a hearer only, requires involvement in the activities of the church. Attendance is necessary but not enough. Financial contributions are not enough. Every member needs to be a soul winner, a witness for Jesus Christ to lost friends and neighbors and acquaintances. And every member needs to seek a job in the church, even though the task may seem lowly in comparison to the positions of others. There are many one-talent believers, but there are no no-talent believers. Every Christian is capable of doing something for Christ and the church, and rewards are promised for even the most seemingly insignificant efforts. Did not Jesus declare, "He that receiveth a prophet in the name of a prophet shall receive a prophet's reward; and he that receiveth a righteous man in the name of a righteous man shall receive a righteous man's reward" (Matthew 10:41)? And the next verse is equally significant: "And whosoever shall give to drink unto one of these little ones a cup of cold water only in the name of a disciple, verily I say unto you, he shall in no wise lose his reward" (Matthew 10:42).

No one is saved by his works, but all born-again believers in Jesus Christ will be judged and rewarded according to their works (cf. Ephesians 2:8-10; II Corinthians 5:10; I Corinthians 3:13-15; Revelation 22:12). By faithfully serving the Lord with the abilities and talents He has given us, we shall qualify for His commendation and reward at the judgment seat of Christ. The Foursquare Gospel stresses faith in the truths of the Scripture and performance of the duties enjoined in the Scriptures. To a large extent a believer's spiritual condition is mirrored by his practical dedication and service.

Sermon

SOUL WINNING

The moment we have given our hearts to the Lord Jesus Christ we should become soul winners. "Follow Me and I will make you fishers of men."

Oh, the moment I gave my heart to Jesus—how that day stands out as the highlight of my whole life!—there came into my very being a yearning to win souls for Him. It was a longing of such intensity, such white heat, such earnestness, I had never known anything like it before. I wanted to be a soul winner. 'Twas the Lord that kindled that desire in my heart for I never could have put it there myself. But it seemed a discouraging outlook. Who was I? Nothing but a little country girl, a farmer's daughter. How could I be a soul winner? But oh, I did want to win souls so very much for Jesus and even though I was nothing I just determined that I would give that little nothing to the Lord Jesus Christ who has promised to take the things that are naught to confound the things that are. And I cried, "Jesus, make me a soul winner."

Sometimes I was almost discouraged and it seemed as though I never could be one because I was so far away in Canada, so far out on the farm, I did not know where to begin. But oh, if I only could! There would sweep over me sometimes in prayer the fear I would never be a soul winner. I thought that would be the most terrible calamity that could ever befall a Christian and I used to sing that song,

"Must I go and empty handed,
Thus my dear Redeemer meet,
Not one soul with which to greet Him,
Lay no trophies at His feet?"

As I prayed I seemed to picture the harvest day, that great, grand day when the gates of the beautiful city would be opened. I pictured Jesus standing at the gate of that celestial city, the Saviour with whom I had fallen in love, the Master to whom I had given my heart. I used to picture Him standing there welcoming the soul winners home, the angels grouped behind Him ready to crown them with crowns set with many stars, souls they had won for Jesus. And yonder was the Victory Way leading up to the gate. Oh, I could see the warriors coming, Hallelujah! Every one of them was coming with rejoicing, bringing in the sheaves. I thought that I would feel so very badly, my heart would be hurt with a hurt that would never heal should I go to heaven empty-handed, not a soul with which to greet Him, no one that I had won for Jesus while all these other folk were cheering and bringing in their trophies. I feared that should I be empty-handed on the day when the saints come marching in, that I would draw back almost ashamed to go through the gates, and how troubled I would be, and that when He gazed questioningly upon me I would have to say:

"Dear Jesus, I love You. Jesus, I have been serving You, oh, really I have, Lord. I love You better than anything in all the world but I have not won a soul for You. My life has been wasted as far as soul winning is concerned." I determined then and there by His grace to be a soul winner. I never expected to preach, did not expect to do the great things. Oh, if I could but do the little things! I was so in earnest that I remember telling the Lord I would willingly go across the continent from Atlantic to Pacific and say to one sinner, "Jesus loves you," and to lead him to Christ. Oh, thank God that in a little measure at least He has made me a winner of souls.

I think that being a winner of souls is the most blessed calling, the most sacred calling, the highest vocation, the most honorable occupation a man or woman could follow. Have you ever won a soul for Jesus? If not it is not too late. You can begin right now.

"He that winneth souls is wise." Thank God for the opportunity of being a soul winner! It is a wonderful thing to be an artist. It is a wonderful thing to be able to paint great, beautiful pictures on canvas, but it is a much more wonderful thing to be a brave soldier in the army, to be a captain that leads his troops forward into victory, to catch up the flag from the hand of some fallen comrade and plunge forward in the fray winning great victories for one's country. But it is a still more wonderful thing to be a victor for the Lord Jesus Christ, going into the enemy's ranks, taking captive soldiers from its ranks and leading them as love-slaves of the Lord Jesus Christ. I would rather be a winner of souls, a brave soldier for Jesus, than I would to win the greatest earthly conquest and receive great medals.

If you want to be a soul winner you are going to need skill and wisdom, you are going to need the faith and the power and the help of the Lord Jesus Christ. You have all heard the story of the barber who wanted to be a soul winner. He was converted at the meeting so happily. They said, "Now brother, you have been saved but you are not saved to yourself alone. Go out and win other people for Jesus." "Oh, I hope I can," said the man. "Of course you can," they replied. "You have a barber shop and people will be in there all day long.

When shaving a man you have a wonderful opportunity to tell him to prepare to meet his God." "All right," he said, "I will certainly do so."

The next morning a man sat in the barber's chair. All the time his heart was going thumpety-thump, jumpety-jump. How was he to talk to that man about Jesus, what should he say? He took his barber's brush and stirred up the lather, and all the time he was thinking. "What can I say to that man, how can I get up my courage? Here is a man whose soul is worth more than all the silver, all the gold, all the rubies in the world put into one. Lord, give me courage to say something." But he had the man all lathered and had not thought what to say. He took up his razor and began to strop that, getting it sharper and sharper. "What in the world can I say to that man?" Finally he drew a long breath, straightened himself, and determined to make a plunge before his courage waned.

He went over to the man with two leaps and a bound and, waving the razor over his head, cried: "Brother, are you prepared to die?" The poor man was so alarmed he leaped to his feet and ran out the door with the lather on his face, thinking the man was intending to kill him.

Now, we cannot go at it like that. If we want to be winners of souls we must be wise, we must have skill, tact. Oh, yes, it takes skill to be a winner of souls, it takes tact, it takes wisdom. But it takes more than any of these, more than skill and wisdom and tact.

One of the greatest things you need in order to be a soul winner is love. If you want really to be a soul winner for the Lord Jesus Christ you need to have on a robe of love that will cover you from head to foot–the love of the Lord Jesus Christ. You must first of all have given your heart to the Lord Jesus Christ and have put your hand in the hand of the Master. You must have sought His face, not only singing it but meaning, "Draw me nearer, nearer to Thy blessed bleeding heart." Oh, it is when we get close to that bleeding heart, that heart divine, broken for mankind, that some of the love that overflows from the heart divine comes trickling down and fills these hearts of ours, and praise God, ere long, they are running over.

We need to get close to the Lord Jesus Christ. We need such a baptism of love for souls as Jesus had. Then we should see through the eyes of Jesus and feel through the heart of Jesus. You say people would not know it? Yes, they will. Love bears a message all its own. The greatest secret of soul winning is that of having the real love of God and the love of souls upon our hearts.

I know so many precious ministers winning souls for Jesus who have the baptism of love. I know other dear Christian workers who have not or they have effectively concealed it if they have. We may have our training, our theology, and we need it. True, we have training in the Bible; true, we may be just as straight as a die. Our teaching, our doctrine, may have the ring of solid gold. We may stand for the fundamentals of the Gospel, for the inspiration of Scripture, the virgin birth of Jesus Christ, the atonement, the resurrection and our Lord's return; we may preach it right from the shoulder. If we just make our preaching theology, even though our theory is absolutely correct, and have not the love, some way we do not get the results.

You can tell if you have that love when you are winning souls for Jesus. It seems to me sometimes when preaching I have not the love I ought to have. I do want more. I am nothing. I am not setting myself up as an example. Jesus is the example. Yet with that little love that He has given me it seems to me sometimes when I am preaching to sinners my heart is bleeding for them. I am trying to blink back the tears, trying to keep on smiling at them, yet my heart is breaking with longing to see them come to Jesus while I am talking about Him and His goodness, glory, mercy, and love. I feel while I am speaking in the Spirit as though a beautiful shimmering silver net was going out, out, out. Then at a certain time in my sermon, I see the shimmering, silver love net dropping and going around the people, and then at altar call I fairly feel the tugging of nets full to the bursting as strong and willing hands help me pull these souls to land.

If you want to be a soul winner get the love of the Lord Jesus in your heart. Come close to Jesus, seek His face, put your all upon the altar, ask Him to draw you so very close to His heart that His love just fills your heart for a lost and a dying world. And you know, the first fruit of the Spirit is love. It doesn't matter what other gifts we have—speak with tongues, heal the sick, raise the dead, perform every miracle—if we haven't love we are nothing. O Lord, give us a love like Thine. Have you that love, Sister? Have you that love, Brother? If not, let us come and get it. It is the love of Jesus, the Christ.

If you want to be a soul winner for Jesus don't start with a hammer or club. Don't start talking against churches and ministers. Refuse to see anybody or anything but the Lord Jesus Christ. "I know, but so many are against me," you say. Never mind. If God is for us who can be against us?

If we want to be a soul winner we will have to be middle-of-the-roaders, especially when we come into city-wide revival campaigns. Lots of us have our own ideas, theories, particular side lines of doctrine. If you want to win souls in the greatest, widest sense of the word drop everything for a little while, just fix your eyes upon Jesus, the crucified Lamb of God, bleeding, dying, hanging on the tree, saying, "Come unto Me all the ends of the earth and be ye saved."

How I long to stick to the Bible—close to Jesus Christ. One time a man was going to a certain place and was in a great hurry to get there. He was late and the train was about ready to pull out. He got a ticket, saw the first car, got on it. It was packed full of people, and many were hanging on to straps. He looked at the car and said, "This is no place for me." He went through and the last car was empty, not a soul in it. "I am smart to find this out." He congratulated himself and patted himself on his chest, for here he had elbow room and could spread himself out—a private car all to himself. He waited for awhile for the train to go. Waited for twenty minutes, looked at his watch. Ten minutes more. To his amazement the rest of the train had gone and he had a private car all to himself. Indignantly calling to a railroad official he demanded an explanation as to why he was left behind.

"Why," explained the man, "that car was not going with the rest of the train. It had been placed there so that if there were too big an overflow from the other cars they could hook it on at a moment's notice. You thought you were better than the rest, wanted to have elbow room and a private car. You have it now and you can sit in it for three hours and wait for the next train."

So many of us want to have a private car, teach our own little doctrine, nonessentials, feasts, sabbaths, forms. We can have a nice big private car all to ourselves and sit around till the next revival comes. If you want to be with the moving train, keep in the crush. Keep with those who believe in Jesus Christ, the Saviour who died to cleanse us from sin. Lift up this bleeding, dying Lamb of Calvary, this resurrected Lord. Make the cross the theme and the blood the test of fellowship and nothing else. Then, glory to Jesus, we are going to see souls saved, people washed in the blood of Jesus and brought to Him. But let us make souls the great important thing all of the time. If we want to win souls for Jesus I believe we need to be filled with the Holy Spirit to equip us for service and endue us with power from above.

"Mrs. McPherson, do I understand you to mean by that I should not attempt to win souls till I have received this enduement of power?" Not at all. The moment you become a Christian, that moment turn around and help bring the one next to you to the Lord Jesus Christ. Don't wait for anything, become a soul winner right there and then. But oh, how this blessed incoming of the Holy Spirit will strengthen you, guide you, fill you with wisdom and love and holy zeal to lead men and women to Jesus. I believe the filling of the Holy Spirit ought to be intensely practical. It ought to be something to make us more levelheaded, sound, sane, wholesome soul winners for the Lord Jesus Christ than ever in our lives before, not something to put us up on a pedestal where we say, "I thank God I am not as other men! I thank my Lord I am holier than others! I have been filled with the Spirit." No, that is not the idea. When we come to Jesus under the blood, with open hearts praying, "Breathe upon me, Holy Spirit, with Thy love my heart inspire," and are filled with the Holy Spirit, then we are going back down amongst the people, not making ourselves holier than they because we have gone a little further, but we will return to practical soul winning for the Lord Jesus Christ.

Dear little children, it does not matter who you are. You may not have a great education, you may not have the great opportunities but if you are only a farmer's daughter or son, if you are even a coal miner like Evan Roberts, just a baseball player like Billy Sunday, a poor common laborer sweeping the streets, a wife whose babies come at eventide and put their little hands up and pray, "Now I lay me down to sleep," there is an opportunity for you to be a soul winner.

"Mrs. McPherson, you make me feel so sad. I wish that I could be a soul winner, but Sister, I am a mother. I have my children to care for. I haven't time to go out and hold meetings." Of course you haven't. But you can work for Jesus right in your home, right in your church, right in the Sunday School and right among those darling children. Some time ago a minister went to call on a certain mother who was mourning, "Oh, pastor, I feel so discouraged!"

"Why, my dear sister, you have always been so happy. What makes you discouraged now?"

"Because it seems to me as though I have never had to do anything for the Lord. I did want to be a soul winner, pastor. But all my life has been taken up with sewing, washing the dishes, sweeping the floor and tending the family. Now I am old, my hair is white as snow. Soon I'll be laying my head upon my pillow for that last long sleep. Oh pastor, I wish I could have done something for Jesus."

"Wait a minute, my dear sister," replied the kindly old minister. "Where is your oldest son George, now?"

"Why, you know where he is, pastor. He's on the Yunan River in China as a missionary."

"And where is your next son Benny?"

"Why, you know where he is, pastor, he just sailed eight months ago to go to China to be with my eldest son. Why, pastor, you must be forgetting."

"Umhum, and let's see now, where is Sammy today?"

"Sammy went to Africa and is out there in the midst of those people in darkest heathendom teaching them about the Light of the world, that is Jesus."

"Yes, and where is your youngest son, your little boy you have loved so?"

"Why pastor, you know where he is. He is right here at home with me. He said to me the other day, 'Mother, I want to tell you something, I think it will make you happier before you go, mother. I am never going to leave the little old home with the roses climbing over it until the Lord has taken you home. I am going to stay here and look after you. The other three boys have gone, mother, but I think you need me. I have always been your baby, mother. But I thought it might make you happy to know that when you are gone, mother, I am going over to Africa and work with Samuel. I am going over there and stand with him because he says he is alone and needs more help and I am going to help him.' All of my boys are doing well, but I wish I could do something."

"But mother, don't you realize those boys are winning souls every day? They have had a family altar, they have felt the caress of a mother's hand, they have heard you pray, they have seen your tears, and now your children have gone out to do the work of God. Oh mother, don't you realize you are to share their reward? God bless you."

She clasped her dear old wrinkled hands together. On her face was that beautiful look of peace, that peace that passeth understanding, the joy that only a soul winner knows. She thought that she had given nothing, but she had given everything to be a real soul winner. Even as Christ gave His life for us, so we must give our all for Him. You cannot have a selfish heart and be a real successful soul winner. Give your all to Him and He will give His all for you.

Some time ago a minister, whose daughter was called to go to China, felt as though his heart were torn and desolate. He could scarcely bear it. He tried to be brave, but his friend saw his heart bleed. At last the beautiful daughter, his only child that had filled the home with smiles, music and joy, was leaving for China. Next day when the friend went to visit him he found the father smiling and happy. "What has happened?" he asked. "When I was here before you looked so downcast. I almost feared to come today."

"I will tell you," he replied, "when I went down to the big ocean liner this morning to see my daughter set sail for China, a man came along. Both of us stood watching the boat go out. The man stood there with his hands in his pockets whistling. His face lit up with a smile. He must have some one he loved on that boat too. 'Brother,' I asked, 'whom have you on that boat that is going to China?' 'Why don't you know? I have just given $100,000 to send to the missionaries over there. Going to build mission stations, help them spread out their borders, win many souls. Yes, sir, I gave $100,000 and it's all on that boat.' "

The other man said, "I did not have a hundred thousand dollars to give, sir, but I have given my daughter, that little ewe lamb I loved so and cherished close to my heart. She is going to China."

"Oh," said the other man, "I thought I had given something, but sir, I have given nothing. My hundred thousand dollars is not as much as your daughter's little finger. It is you who have given all." Oh, if we want to be soul winners we must be willing to give our all to Jesus, to make a wholehearted surrender, body, soul and spirit.

I remember when Jesus had called me first to go and preach the Gospel, my mother said, "Aimee," (I was just to be married to the evangelist, under whom I had been converted), "Aimee, who is going to buy your things? You know Robert hasn't any salary."

"Mother, I know it."

"Who is going to buy your shoes, your dresses and look after you?"

"I don't know, but I will ask the Lord about it." I prayed before my open Bible, Jesus spake from the pages, "Child, take no thought of what you shall eat, drink or put on. The Lord knows you have need of these things. Consider the lilies, they toil not, neither do they spin and yet Solomon in all his glory was not arrayed like one of these."

I said, "Oh, thank You, Jesus." And from that day to this I have never worried one second about what I had to eat, drink and wear. Many a time we have gotten down to the last nickel, then given that away. For two years I lived in a tent, without a board floor under my feet. Oftentimes I would get up and put on my clothing wet with the dews and rain. But Hallelujah, Jesus always protected and supplied. It is glorious to be a Christian, glorious to be a soul winner. Oh, if I could just take a little bit out of my heart and sow the seed in your hearts, kindle the flame of love and zeal for souls 'til from the altar of every life exultant flames would leap high into the open heaven, how happy I would be.

O Jesus, speak to every heart and burn this text upon every mind. Let us repeat it aloud together: "He that winneth souls is wise."

Sermon

•

THE GREATEST ROBBER IN TOWN

As I have read the daily newspapers I have noticed that almost all of the news lately seems to consist of crimes, murders, bank robberies, holdups, burglaries, and the like. There are many notorious robbers and sometimes people speculate, "Who is the greatest robber in town."

A little child now and then may take pennies off mother's dresser or take cookies out of the cookie jar. He is not the greatest robber in town, though what he does is bad enough.

A pickpocket moves around among crowds looking for purses and pocketbooks. A shoplifter stealthily slips things from store counters into his pockets or bag. A second-story man comes around at one, two or three o'clock in the morning. The burglar is bad enough. The holdup man you meet just around the corner is a bad rascal. But he isn't the greatest robber in the city.

Then there is the embezzler. A man takes widows' and orphans' money and says he is going to invest it right and then invests it wrong. The crooked politician steals money over the water situation, over the oil situation, over the tax situation. He does it on a wholesale scale. But he's not the greatest robber!

Then who is? I will tell you. The answer may surprise! The greatest robber in the world is the Christian who robs God! The professing Christian comes under God's eye and God's rule. When we are God's children we are expected to obey God's rules and laws. Here is a most astounding verse:

"Will a man rob God? Yet you have robbed Me. You say, Wherein have we robbed Thee? In tithes and in offerings."

It does not mean going up and stealing the golden

streets out of Heaven. It does not mean taking the pearly gates off their hinges. It does not mean taking the jasper throne and selling it! It does not mean taking the precious stones from out the great wall that surrounds the Foursquare City. One does not do that. But in tithes and in offerings God says many have robbed Him. Are you a robber of God?

When this was first brought to my heart I went to my knees before God. I said, "Lord, you do not mean that, do you? That was for the Old Testament time, was it not?"

"No, my child," He answered, "it was not under law, because the law did not begin until Moses' day, and the tithes began over a thousand years before that, in Abraham's day and in Jacob's day. Tithing did not begin under the law. It was My plan in perpetuity to carry on and support My work everywhere."

"But, Lord, it is only optional, is it not? I can do as I like about it; it is not arbitrary surely?"

"Yes, child, it is arbitrary. It is a command. Bring all your tithes to the storehouse–"

"Well, Lord, I did not even know about it."

"Nevertheless, my child, you are a robber."

"O Lord, please don't say it!"

"It is true."

"But I did not know about it."

"That is your fault. I have given you My Bible; you have been a Christian now for eight years, but you have not been tithing."

"But I believe in giving everything I can."

"Yes, but most people who say that do not even give a tenth. You have robbed Me."

"I have robbed You, Lord? I have given my testimony."

"But your testimony will not support the church."

"I am helping the missionaries."

"But that does not support the church."

"But, Lord, there is nothing stable in my income."

"That doesn't matter. If you only have ten cents, one penny belongs to Me."

"But, Lord, can't I pay my bills out of it first, then give a tenth?"

"No; ten per cent of all that comes into your hands belongs to the Lord."

"Lord, I have not been doing it."

"I know, and you are a robber."

"Why, Lord, no one ever called me anything like that in my life. I have not robbed anyone. I have never knowingly taken a penny from anyone."

"Yet you have robbed Me, God."

Then and there I said, "Lord, I am going to be a tither. I am going to give my tenth to You."

But now what about you? Are you a robber of God? Or are you doing your duty?

God is an orderly God. He planned the lovely flowers; He put those tiny leaves and petals there, He put that delicate green and pink color together. Hidden in the heart of that flower He put a seed, and He so planned it that when this flower drops and its seed is scattered, that seed shall go down into the earth and shall perpetuate the flowers and bring up thousands upon thousands of other flowers. And then in turn go to seed and bring thousands of others.

He put a seed in the heart of the rose, a bulb beneath the lily. He put the kernel on the corn and the wheat. In the apple He put the seed and packed the fertilizer round about it so that when the apple drops it will bring out a whole apple tree.

In other words, God is a perfect planner. That is, He is not just a dreamer. He did not just make a flower and never plan for it to go on. Everything He makes, He puts the seed within itself—the tree, the flower, that it may go on and on and on.

Dearer to God than a tree, dearer to God than a rose, dearer to God than an apple is His church, the apple of His eye. Does it stand to reason that God would give all these other things seed that they might go on and perpetuate themselves and never plan for the perpetuity of His church? Of course not. He planned for the financing of the church. And I believe passing the collection plate is not God's plan. I wish I never had to take a collection. It is a huge undertaking to keep this great work going. But God's plan is not passing the plate and asking constantly for money.

God's plan is, "Bring all your tithes into the storehouse." If your income this month is $500.00, then $50.00 belongs to the Lord. What you give beyond that would be your free-will offerings.

You say, "The idea! I cannot afford to do it."

You cannot afford not to. The Lord says, "Because you have robbed Me, even this whole nation, therefore a plague has come upon you, therefore the vine casts her fruit and the boll weevil and the caterpillar is upon your land."

People say, "I cannot afford to tithe. We have had a hard year. We have had all this cotton plague and we have had a hard time with our fruit trees."

I wonder if sometimes that is because you are not tithing. God has made a definite promise and it is just wonderful to dare to take God at His word.

"You have robbed Me, even this whole nation."

"Why, wherein have we robbed Thee?"

"In tithes and in offerings." He says, "Therefore the plague is upon you; therefore your vine casts her fruit before her time in the field." And then He says, "Prove Me. Bring all your tithes into the storehouse of the Lord and prove Me now herewith if I will not open the windows of Heaven and pour—" not dribble, but *pour*; not rain, but *pour*; not shower, but *pour*; "—pour you out such a blessing that there shall not be room to contain it."

I think that is the greatest thing I ever read. To think that God loved His church so much He planned to perpetuate it, and if God wants $10.00 He has to give you $90.00 in order to get $10.00. You cannot help making money if you go into partnership with God.

Certainly God will be with us in a program of tithing for He said, "Prove Me now and see if I will not pour you out a blessing such that there shall not be room to contain it." The Lord wants to take an interest in everything about you.

"My husband will not let me give a tenth," someone may excuse herself.

People often find alibis, don't they? But all you are responsible for is what comes into your hands. The Lord is standing by you and He says He will be your business partner. "I will bless you with basket and store," He says, "I will bless you with health."

A prosperous business man in England was visited by the secretary for the British Foreign Missionary Society and asked if he would give a subscription for missions.

"Certainly," answered the business man, and wrote a check for $250.00.

Almost at the same moment he handed the check to the secretary, a cable came to his desk. He tore it open and read it. His face turned white, and he said,

"Sir, one of my ships has just gone down with its precious cargo. This materially alters my financial standing and I must ask you to give me back the check and I will make you a new one."

"Certainly, sir, I am terribly sorry."

The man with trembling hand wrote out a check. When the missions secretary looked at it, to his utter amazement he found the check was for $1,000.00.

"Why, sir," he said, "how is this?"

"My brother, I feel that the telegram was a telegram from Heaven and my Father spoke to me and said, 'Lay not up for yourselves treasures on earth.' I must do this, and as I do it God will make it back to me some way, sometime, somehow."

Will a man rob God? Have you robbed Him in tithes and offerings? Stop robbing God now. Instead bring all your tithes into the storehouse.

Chapter IV PROJECTING THE FOURSQUARE GOSPEL

"All I can do is keep on preaching Jesus. . . . Right now I'm busy preaching the emblems: the cross, the torch, the cup, and the crown!"

Aimee Semple McPherson addressed these words to an overflow audience in Angelus Temple on October 9, 1938. It was her birthday, and she was narrating the story of her life–a message available either on tape or on long-play recording. Near the conclusion, Sister emphatically declared that persecution and opposition need never deter the progress and growth of God's work or God's workmen: "People say this about me and say that about me. I haven't time either to deny it or affirm it. All I can do is keep on preaching Jesus. Some people ask, 'Well, why don't you ever get up and defend yourself?' Maybe I'll get a chance sometime. But right now I'm busy preaching the emblems–the cross of Jesus Christ. I'm busy preaching the torch of the fiery baptism of the Holy Ghost. I'm busy preaching the cup of divine healing and the crown of Christ's second coming."

The Foursquare Gospel certainly lends itself well to exemplification by emblems. Foursquaredom did not invent emblems as expressive of faith, of course. Since the morning of time God Himself has illustrated spiritual truths with visible symbols. The first emblems appeared in Eden. The coats of skin God gave Adam and Eve symbolized the robes of righteousness provided at the cost of the life of the Lamb of God who in the fullness of times would take away the sin of the world. Scripture abounds with types and shadows, symbols and emblems divinely sanctified to signify spiritual truths.

EMBLEMS

Now a variety of emblems tend to project the Foursquare Gospel. Ezekiel's vision of the four faces—man, lion, ox, and eagle—prompted our founder to proclaim the phrase, "the Foursquare gospel," as is explained in chapter one of Part One of this volume. There is hardly need to elucidate further here on that remarkable representation of the ministry of Jesus. The reader would do well, however, to review the discussion there. For many years the Declaration of Faith of the International Church of the Foursquare Gospel carried on its cover an artist's portrayal of Ezekiel's vision as it is used to symbolize our faith.

When we desire to particularize, however, a specific phase of the Foursquare Gospel, the emblems of the cross, the torch, the cup, and the crown prove especially fitting.

Concerning the cross, which memorializes Jesus Christ's one sacrifice for sin forever, Lon Woodrum exclaimed, "They crossed a couple of sticks and started a new world." He did not exaggerate. No event of human history can compare in significance and importance with the crucifixion and its sequel, the resurrection. Since Constantine's time at least, and probably before, the cross has been hailed as the symbol of Christianity itself. But the overwhelming impact of the cross is redemptive. The cross represents the most eloquent emblem possible to proclaim that Jesus Christ is the only Saviour.

Foursquaredom displays the torch to symbolize the ministry of Jesus as the baptizer with the Holy Spirit. The term torch does not appear in the Bible in connection with this baptism, but this experience is associated both in word and in demonstration with flame. John promised that Jesus would baptize believers with the Holy Ghost "and with fire." When Christ commenced this particular ministry on the day of Pentecost, a visible manifestation of fire ensued (cf. Acts 2:3). The Greek text suggests that this phenomenon began with the appearance of one tongue of fire which then divided and lighted on everyone present, transforming believers into torches or firebrands for God.

The emblem for Christ's ministry of healing for the body is the cup. We use the cup as a symbol of divine healing because of the command in James 5:14-15 that the elders be called to anoint with oil and pray the prayer of faith for any sick believers.

The crown symbolizes the Coming King. Three emblems point to the past and present—salvation, the baptism with the Holy Spirit, and divine healing minister to the present needs of men—and rest upon the finished work on earth of the incarnate Christ. One emblem looks to the future. The crown thrills us with sure hope for the future. Jesus Christ will return first for His church and then with His church. Jesus shall reign as King of Kings and Lord of Lords. A golden age is coming! The best is yet to be, not as a result of human efforts and endeavors, but as the result of direct divine take-over of the affairs of earth.

THE FOURSQUARE FLAG

Numerous other symbols dramatically project the Foursquare message. Perhaps the most familiar is our flag. In 1930 Aimee Semple McPherson felt a need for a banner which would depict the fullness of the gospel more adequately than the respected Christian flag. During the first six months of the following year she sewed the first Foursquare Flag. The first photograph of this banner appeared in the July, 1931, *Bridal Call Foursquare.*

The Bible has a great deal to say about flags. Of course, they are called banners in the Scripture. The Psalmist enthused that God provides His people with a flag: "Thou hast given a banner to them that fear thee, that it may be displayed because of the truth. Selah. That thy beloved may be delivered" (Psalm 60:4). Moreover, believers triumphantly may fly the flag of faith: "We will rejoice in thy salvation, and in the name of our God we will set up our banners" (Psalm 20:5). Indeed, one of God's compound names includes the word banner: *Jehovah-nissi* literally means "The Lord is our banner" (Exodus 17:15).

The Foursquare flag may certainly prompt us to proclaim, "The Lord is our banner," for the flag symbolizes for us the ministry of our Lord Jesus Christ.

Sister McPherson studied closely the Old Testament before designing the flag. She wanted every aspect of the banner to have Scriptural precedent. Even the fringe is Biblically significant, for it reminds us of the fringe God commanded the Israelites to wear around the bottom of their garments. The purpose of that fringe was that when the Israelites looked at it, it would help them to remember and do God's commandments (cf. Numbers 15:38-40). The colors in the flag come from the four colors in the breastplate of the high priest of ancient Israel (Exodus 28:16). These colors also were prominent in the hangings of the tabernacle. Red typifies the blood Jesus shed to save sinners. Gold represents the fire of the Holy Spirit. Blue symbolizes the heavenly health ministered to sick bodies by Jesus the divine Healer, while purple signifies the royalty of the Coming King.

The field of the flag displays a four on a square on the Word. The four reminds of the ministries of Jesus as Saviour, Baptizer, Healer, and Coming King, while the square represents that we dare never cut a corner in proclaiming and experiencing this full gospel of Jesus Christ. This faith and experience rest upon the inspired Word of God, while the cross which also appears in the field of the flag spotlights the highlight of the gospel–redemption from sin.

FOURSQUARE SONGS

After designing this banner, Sister McPherson composed the song, "The Foursquare Flag," which outlines

in detail the meaning of the flag and challenges the hearer steadfastly to "stand, 'til o'er sea and o'er land reigns our Saviour and Coming King." That number is only one of an inspiring array of "Foursquare Gospel Battle Songs" which have resounded around the world as this message has penetrated every continent. "Preach the Foursquare Gospel" was the first of these compositions, written as our founder sailed home from Australia in 1922 just prior to the opening of Angelus Temple on January 1 the following year. Each verse of this number hails one of the four cardinal phases of our faith. Best known, perhaps, of the Foursquare marches is "Preach the Word" which lends itself marvelously to instrumental renditions. Worthy of wider presentation than they have enjoyed are "Up the Foursquare Way," "Forward March, O Foursquare Host," and "Forward to the Fray." The reader is referred to the appendix of this volume for the words and music of these compositions.

THE SCRIPTURE MOTTO

In addition to the emblems and flag and battle songs, the movement displays a motto from Scripture which capsulizes our faith. Hebrews 13:8 is required by Foursquare By-Laws to appear in the auditorium of every church of the movement: "Jesus Christ the same yesterday, and today, and forever." This verse trumpets our insistence that there is available to the present-day church every blessing and every ministry enjoyed by the apostolic church in Bible days.

ILLUSTRATING THE MESSAGE

The Foursquare movement of today might do well to study in depth the methods employed by our founder in projecting the Foursquare message. She appropriated almost every occurrence of the number four in the Bible to symbolize our faith. Usually she dramatized her points with illustrated sermons.

Taking as her text John 19:23, where the soldiers divided Jesus' garment into four parts, she likened those four to the garment of salvation (Isaiah 61:10), the clothing of healing (Luke 8:35 where the Gadarene demoniac appeared clothed and in his right mind after encountering Jesus the great physician), the mantle of Holy Spirit power (II Kings 2:9), and the purple robe of resurrection and the second coming (I Thessalonians 4:16-17).

Discussing the four anchors of Acts 27:29, many of our ministers have followed the Founder's lead and likened each one individually to the work of Christ as Saviour, Baptizer, Healer, and Coming King. The four rivers which flowed out of Eden, the four winds of the valley of dry bones, the four corners of the tabernacle's altar, the four cords used by the men who lowered the paralytic through the roof to be healed by Jesus, all lend themselves to similar treatment. Chaplain Howard Rusthoi took the title "Magnificent Obsession" and hailed each of the four phases of our gospel as such. The present writer had a sermon in the Foursquare Magazine entitled "Home Run" which was prompted by the fact that in some Latin American countries the same word which translated "Foursquare" into the local language, *Cuadrangular*, also meant "home run"! Each base of the baseball diamond then was likened to one of the cardinal doctrines. Following this chapter appears Sister McPherson's sermon, "The Lighthouse Foursquare," which likens light rays to the same ministries of Jesus.

With such a variety of methods available to express and explain our faith, certainly no one in a Foursquare church should be unaware of what constitutes this gospel. The Sunday School and Youth Departments from time to time distribute programs which, if used, will keep before our people both our Foursquare heritage and emphasis. God has raised up this movement to publish to the whole world the *good news* that Jesus saves, Jesus **baptizes with the Holy Spirit, Jesus heals, and Jesus will come again. Therefore, let us all who are associated with this movement join together to**

". . . hold the Foursquare banner high;
And beneath its folds we'll live and die!
May it proudly wave, 'til Christ's pow'r to save
Leaps each bounding ocean wave.
Then let our banner be unfurled.
Forward march to all the world,
And forth the Foursquare message pour,
'Til He reigns from shore to shore."

(Aimee Semple McPherson).

Sermon

THE LIGHTHOUSE FOURSQUARE

THE FIRST WORDS GOD spoke that are recorded in His Word, are: "Let there be light." And we read the results, "There was light."

Long had the world lain in spiritual darkness. Long had the dark clouds of unbelief and sin obscured the sky. Men and women had been wandering from God. Gross darkness was over the hearts of the people. God had looked down from His throne above at the moving multitudes, lost in the darkness, and His Spirit brooded over them, even as it had brooded over the darkness-enveloped earth those ages gone. And even as He had said, "Let there be light," and caused the light of the heavens to shine in upon the poor old darkened earth; so again He sent to the world a great Light—even His only begotten Son, Jesus Christ, full of grace and truth, the saviour of men, the redeemer of the lost, the Son of the living God.

When Jesus, grown to manhood, walked and talked with the people, He began to teach them. He lifted up His hands and said:

"I am the light of the world."

Everywhere He moved in those shining garments of white, He brought hope. He came to those in the dark prison cells, and the doors of the prison fell off. He came to those bound by chains, and the shackles fell off. He came to those who were blind, and their eyes were open and they beheld the only begotten of the Father, full of grace and truth. He was truly the Light of the World.

EVERY CITY HE PASSED THROUGH was illumined. Everybody who met Him was the better because the Light had shone in. When Jesus went to Calvary, truly the Light of the World was He. He carried in His hand, unseen by man, a torch, a symbol of light eternal, and when He hung there on the cross 'twixt heaven and earth, it was as a man climbing the spiral steps of the lighthouse tower, leaving crimson steps upon the stairs, carrying a light, as it were that should gleam and glow evermore, lighting poor, sinful, storm-tossed men into the harbor of eternal life.

There He hung upon the cross. How pitiful He looked, unable to save Himself—just the butt of the jests of the multitude, swearing, mocking, cursing Him—yet there He hung. He refused to help Himself. He just gripped the nails the tighter and said: "Father, forgive them, they know not what they do."

He was faithful to the cause for which He had come forth. He was as a man climbing the steps of the lighthouse tower, and because He was willing to climb those steps for our sake, the glow of Salvation gleams forevermore. Away in the top of the lighthouse, by faith I see the light, shining bright and clear, warning from the rocks, warning from danger, and pointing the way back home to the Father, God.

That lighthouse is God's Word; for Jesus is the Word. It is builded on the Rock of Ages and can never be removed. The waves of Satan and his hosts have beaten against it and buffeted it. They have hurled themselves in their vengeful anger upon it; but the rock still stands. Upon that immovable rock stands the lighthouse of God's Word; and in it gleams the light kindled by the death and resurrection of Jesus Christ—the light which leads to salvation and eternal life.

From that great light it is as though four mighty rays shine out.

First, on the left upper side, is the crimson shaft—representing Jesus Christ, the Saviour.

It is shining forth with the invitation: "Come unto me, all ye ends of the earth, and be ye saved." It is calling to the sinner, unbeliever, backslider, going down in the sea of sin, sinking in despair—calling him to turn into the safe harbor, away from the reefs of sin, and into the safety of God's salvation.

THEN THERE IS A SECOND RAY—a ray of heavenly blue. It represents Jesus Christ, the Great Physician. He not only saves from sin, but heals the sick body. I have seen Christ open blind eyes in answer to prayer, unstop deaf ears, make the lame walk. Tumors have melted like snow before the summer's sun when we have looked to God and prayed the prayer of faith. I have seen people rise from their beds, leave their wheelchairs and walk out in praise to Him as that beautiful healing ray fell upon them.

The third ray is the golden beam bespeaking the fire of the Holy Spirit.

Have you been converted? Do you know Jesus Christ as your Saviour? Then from the lighthouse of God's Word comes this message to you—"Receive ye the Holy Ghost. Tarry ye in Jerusalem until ye be endued with power from on high."

There is more for you beyond your born again experience. There is land ahead to be possessed. There is power and glory and blessing and a closer walk with the Lord if you will but follow the pointing finger of that beautiful golden ray from the lighthouse of God's Word.

Then there is a fourth ray—a gorgeous purple ray—and it represents Jesus Christ the Coming King.

THE CLOUDS THAT RECEIVED HIM from earthly sight, shall bring Him back again. We shall hear the shout of His voice on that day when the heavens shall roll back as a scroll and the Lord, who was persecuted and crucified while upon the earth, shall return with power and great glory to rule and to reign.

All about the base of this lighthouse—the Word of God and the Light, which is Jesus Christ—is the sea with its turbulent billows, angry, foaming, storm-tossed. There are ships sailing that ocean. Each life is as a little barque, a little fail craft sailing toward eternity.

God has made our church a lighthouse—a shining light, a city set upon a hill. He has permitted us who are workers to be lighthouse keepers for Him—to stand and trim the lamp and to keep it brightly burning and shining.

We are ships that pass in the night. We may never come into close contact with each other.

As the ships go by into eternal woe or eternal happiness, the church has her lighthouse of Jesus the Saviour, the Baptizer, the Healer and the Coming King, ready to light the way to Jesus for every man, woman and child in the world. Have you seen the Light? Is the Saviour yours?

Oh, let the light of the Gospel stream across your way! Let it show you the peril, the rocks and the reefs—show you that you are bound for despair if you go on without Jesus. Let the Gospel rays point the way to the harbor of His love.

This old world is sailing along with millions who say they do not need Jesus. They laugh at people who dare to believe the good old Book from cover to cover, and believe in the Lighthouse Foursquare and all it stands for.

Brother, Sister, the moment you give your life to Jesus, the moment the Light shines into your heart, you will be ready to go out and bring others to Christ. You immediately realize you are your brother's keeper, and you find that it is your brother whom you are bringing home to the Lord.

A man was drowning sometime ago, and he was sinking for the third time. Someone succeeded in reaching him with a rope. He grasped the rope just as he was sinking for the last time, and though he passed into unconsciousness, he clung to the rope with both hands. When they brought him in to shore, unconscious though he was, he still clung to the rope and they could not loose his fingers. When he regained consciousness they asked him how it happened he clung so tenaciously to the rope.

"It was that or death!" he replied.

If you are lost, it is your own fault. The lifeline is even now circling your shoulders. If you cast it aside and shout that you will not accept it, it will be your own fault if you are lost. Jesus loves you. He is pleading with you to accept the line and let Him bring you safely aboard the ship of Zion. The rope of salvation is within your grasp. Take hold of it. Get under the rays of the Foursquare Lighthouse.

APPENDIX

Foursquare Gospel Battle Songs

Creedal Statements

Declaration of Faith

UP THE FOURSQUARE WAY

PREACH THE WORD

A. S. M. — Aimee Semple McPherson

1. Hold the Foursquare Fortress firm, 'Tis the test-ing day. The en - e-my on
2. Be-hold the Four-square faithful come, Day of Ju-bi - lee. We're marching up the

ev - 'ry hand Presseth hard the fray. Lift the blood-stained banner high. It
blood-bought way, Christ hath set us free. Songs of praise are ring-ing clear, And

must not touch the ground. Preach the Four-square Gospel with a cer-tain sound!
Dark-ness all is past. Dawn is on the hill-side, day is come at last!

On ev-'ry hand,............ Throughout the land............... The
On ev - 'ry hand, Throughout the land,
Un-to the north. .... Un - to the south.................. Sound the
Un - to the north Un - to the south,

en - e - my is stirred. But on we go,.................. De-spite the
But on we go,
Four-square message clear. Un - to the east,............... Un-to the
Un - to the east,

PREACH THE WORD

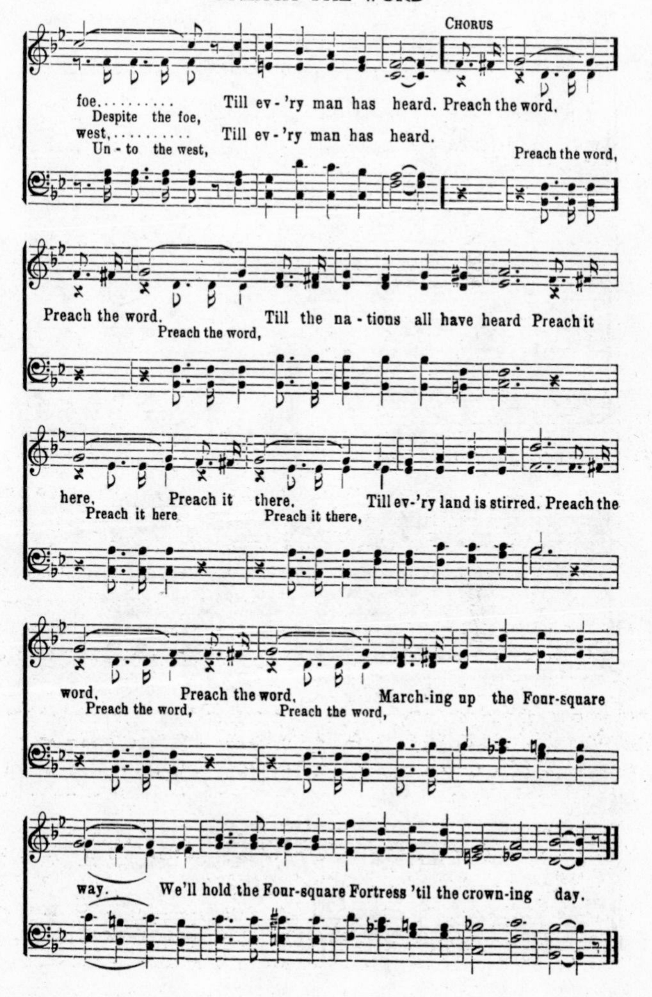

THE FOURSQUARE FLAG

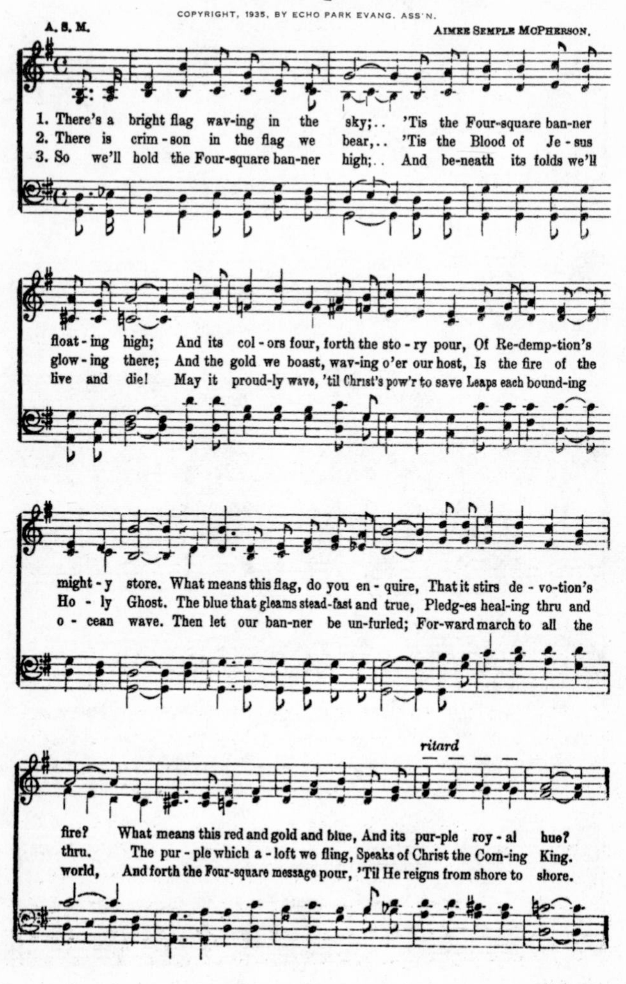

THE FOURSQUARE FLAG

FORWARD MARCH

FORWARD MARCH

PREACH THE FOURSQUARE GOSPEL

PREACH THE FOURSQUARE GOSPEL

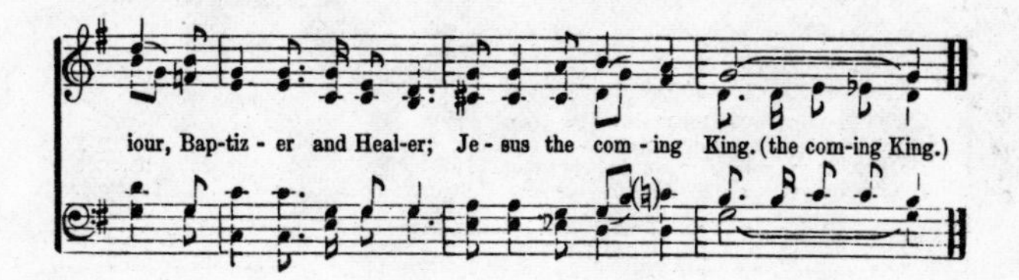

CREEDAL STATEMENTS

We Believe –

1. In the verbal inspiration of the original Scriptures.
2. In the absolute trinity of the eternal Godhead.
3. In the deity of our Lord Jesus Christ.
4. In the personality and deity of the Holy Spirit.
5. In the reality and personality of the devil.
6. In the natural depravity of the human race.
7. In the substitutionary atonement.
8. In the propitiation for sin only by the blood of Christ.
9. In full salvation by grace through faith and not of works.
10. In Divine Healing through the atonement.
11. In the anointing of oil and prayer for the sick.
12. In the personal Baptism of the Holy Ghost as received by the apostles.
13. In the necessity of the new birth.
14. In water baptism by immersion at an age of accountability.
15. In the one and only true church composed of all blood washed believers.
16. In the evangelization of the heathen and the nations of the world.
17. In a middle-of-the-road policy in public worship, between extreme fanaticism and ultra-ritualism.
18. In obedience to civil government.
19. In divorce only on New Testament scriptural grounds.
20. In church government, loyalty and obedience to those in authority over us in the Lord.
21. In tithing as God's financial plan.
22. In restitution for past wrongs whenever possible.
23. In the open table at the Lord's supper.
24. In the free moral will power of man, who can apostatize, backslide, and be lost.

25. In the maintenance of good works and holy living.
26. In the victorious life over sin, self, and bad habits by Bible study and an incessant prayer life.
27. In Christian perfection and holiness, through absolute surrender and consecration.
28. In Christian modesty in the matter of dress, wearing apparel, and jewelry.
29. In the keeping of the Lord's day as a matter of privilege rather than law.
30. As regards recreation–liberty of conscience and a Godly example to the world.
31. In the immortality and conscious existence of the soul.
32. In the resurrection of our literal bodies, the just and the unjust.
33. In a literal heaven and life everlasting for all true believers.
34. In a final day of judgment for the incorrigible wicked.
35. In the everlasting punishment of the impenitent.
36. In the personal, literal, bodily pre-millennial coming of Jesus Christ.
37. In a future, literal, 1,000 years reign of Christ on earth with all His saints.
38. In the judgment seat of Christ where the saints will be finally rewarded for their deeds of commission and omission.
39. In Christian tolerance to all denominations of the Christian faith.
40. "In essentials–unity; in non-essentials–liberty; in all things–charity."

DECLARATION OF FAITH
(Compiled by Aimee Semple McPherson)

I. THE HOLY SCRIPTURES

We believe that the Holy Bible is the Word of the living God; true, [1]immutable, steadfast, unchangeable, as its author, the Lord Jehovah; that it was written by holy men of old as they were moved upon and [2]inspired by the Holy Spirit; that it is a [3]lighted lamp to guide the feet of a lost world from the depths of sin and sorrow to the heights of righteousness and glory; an unclouded mirror that reveals the face of a crucified Saviour; a plumb line to make straight the life of each individual and community; a sharp two-edged sword to convict of sin and evil doing; a strong cord of love and tenderness to draw the penitent to Christ Jesus; a balm of Gilead, [4]inbreathed by the Holy Spirit, that can heal and quicken each drooping heart; the only true ground of Christian fellowship and unity; the [5]loving call of an infinitely loving God; the solemn warning, the distant thunder of the storm of wrath and retribution that shall overtake the unheeding; a sign post that points to Heaven; a danger signal that warns from Hell; [6]the divine, supreme, and eternal tribunal by whose standards all men, nations, creeds, and motives shall be tried.

Scripture References Where Taught

[1]Heaven and earth shall pass away, but my words shall not pass away (Matthew 24:35). For ever, O Lord, thy word is settled in heaven (Psalm 119:89).

[2]All scripture is given by inspiration of God, and is profitable for doctrine, for reproof, for correction, for instruction in righteousness: That the man of God may be perfect, throughly [thoroughly] furnished unto all good works (II Timothy 3:16-17).

[3]Thy word is a lamp unto my feet, and a light unto my path (Psalm 119:105).
[4]We have also a more sure word of prophecy; whereunto ye do well that ye take heed, as unto a light that shineth in a dark place, until the day dawn, and the day star arise in your hearts; Knowing this first, that no prophecy of the scripture is of any private interpretation. For the prophecy came not in old time by the will of man: but holy men of God spake as they were moved by the Holy Ghost (II Peter 19-21).
[5]Search the scriptures; for in them ye think ye have eternal life: and they are they which testify of me (John 5:39).
[6]Study to shew thyself approved unto God, a workman that needeth not to be ashamed, rightly dividing the word of truth (II Timothy 2:15). . . . Let us walk by the same rule, let us mind the same thing (Philippians 3:16; also I John 4:1; Isaiah 8:20; I Thessalonians 5:21; Acts 17:11, I John 4:6; Jude 3; Ephesians 6:17; Psalm 119:59-60; Philippians 1:9-11).

II. THE ETERNAL GODHEAD

We believe that there is [1]but one true and living God; maker of heaven and earth and all that in them is; the Alpha and Omega, who ever was, and is and shall be time without end, Amen; that He is infinitely holy, mighty, tender, loving and glorious; worthy of all possible love and honor, confidence and obedience, majesty, dominion and might, both now and forever; and that in the unity of the Godhead there are three, equal in every divine perfection executing distinct but harmonious offices in the great work of redemption:

The Father—Whose glory is so exceeding bright that mortal man cannot look [2]upon His face and live, [3]but whose heart was so filled with love and pity for His lost and sin-benighted children that He freely gave His only begotten Son to redeem and reconcile them unto Himself.

The Son—[4]Co-existent and co-eternal with the Father, who, conceived by the Holy Spirit and [5]born of the Virgin Mary took upon Himself the form of man, bore our sins, carried our sorrows, and by the shedding of His precious blood upon the cross of Calvary purchased redemption for all that would believe upon Him: then, bursting the bonds of death and hell rose from the grave and ascended on high leading captivity captive, [6]that as the great Mediator betwixt God and man, He might stand at the right hand of the Father making intercession for those for whom He laid down His life.

The Holy Spirit—The [7]third person of the Godhead, the Spirit of the Father shed abroad, omnipotent, omnipresent, performing an inexpressibly important mission upon earth, convicting of sin, of righteousness and of judgment, [8]drawing sinners to the Saviour, rebuking, pleading, searching, comforting, guiding, quickening, teaching, glorifying, baptizing and enduing with power from on high, them who yield to His tender ministrations, preparing them for the great day of the Lord's appearing.

Scripture References Where Taught

[1]. . . Before me there was no God formed, neither shall there be after me (Isaiah 43:10). . . . Is there a God before me? yea, there is no God; I know not any (Isaiah 44:8).
[2]Thou canst not see my face: for there shall no man see me, and live (Exodus 33:20).
[3]For God so loved the world, that he gave his only begotten Son, that whosoever believeth in him should not perish, but have everlasting life (John 3:16).
[4]In the beginning was the Word, and the Word was with God, and the Word was God. The same was in the beginning with God. All things were made by him; and

without him was not any thing made that was made (John 1:1-3; also Job 38:4-7).
[5]Behold, a virgin shall be with child, and shall bring forth a son, and they shall call his name Emmanuel (Matthew 1:23).
[6]I, even I, am the Lord; and beside me there is no saviour (Isaiah 43:11). For there is one God, and one mediator between God and men, the man Christ Jesus; Who gave himself a ransom for all (I Timothy 2:5-6). For through him we both have access by one Spirit unto the Father (Ephesians 2:18).
[7]For there are three that bear record in heaven, the Father, the Word, and the Holy Ghost: and these three are one (I John 5:7).
[8]But when the Comforter is come, whom I will send unto you from the Father, even the Spirit of truth, which proceedeth from the Father, he shall testify of me (John 15:26; also II Corinthians 13:14; Matthew 28:19; Romans 8:11; John 16:7-14).

III. THE FALL OF MAN

We believe that man was [1]created in the image of God, before whom he walked in holiness and purity, but that by voluntary disobedience and transgression, he fell from the Eden of purity and innocence to the depths of sin and iniquity, and [2]that in consequence of this, all mankind are sinners sold unto Satan, [3]sinners not by constraint but by choice, shapen in iniquity and [4]utterly void by nature of that holiness required by the law of God, positively inclined to evil, [5]guilty and without excuse, justly deserving the condemnation of a just and holy God.

Scripture References Where Taught

[1]God created man in his own image (Genesis 1:27).
[2]Wherefore, as by one man sin entered into the world,

and death by sin; and so death passed upon all men, for that all have sinned (Romans 5:12). By one man's disobedience many were made sinners (Romans 5:19; also John 3:6; Psalm 51:5; Romans 5:15-19; 8:7).
[3]We have turned every one to his own way (Isaiah 53:6; also Genesis 6:12; 3:9-18).
[4]Among whom also we all had our conversation in times past in the lusts of our flesh, fulfilling the desires of the flesh and of the mind; and were by nature the children of wrath, even as others (Ephesians 2:3. See Romans 1:18,32; 2:1-16; Matthew 20:15; Galatians 3:10; Ezekiel 18:19-20).
[5]. . . So that they are without excuse (Romans 1:20). That every mouth may be stopped, and all the world may become guilty before God (Romans 3:19; also Galatians 3:22).

IV. THE PLAN OF REDEMPTION

We believe that [1]while we were yet sinners Christ died for us, the Just for the unjust; [2]freely, and by divine appointment of the Father taking the sinner's place, bearing his sins, receiving his condemnation, dying his death, [3]fully paying his penalty, and signing with His life's blood, the pardon of every one who should believe upon Him; [4]that upon simple faith and acceptance of the atonement purchased on Mount Calvary, [5]the vilest sinner may be cleansed of his iniquities and made whiter than the driven snow.

Scripture References Where Taught

[1]But he was wounded for our transgressions, he was bruised for our iniquities: the chastisement of our peace was upon him; and with his stripes we are healed (Isaiah 53:5).
[2]Who gave himself for us, that he might redeem us from all iniquity, and purify unto himself a peculiar people, zealous of good works (Titus 2:14).

[3]Let the wicked forsake his way, and the unrighteous man his thoughts: and let him return unto the Lord, and he will have mercy upon him; and to our God, for he will abundantly pardon (Isaiah 55:7).
[4]Wherefore he is able also to save them to the uttermost that come unto God by him, seeing he ever liveth to make intercession for them (Hebrews 7:25).
[5]Come now, and let us reason together, saith the Lord: though your sins be as scarlet, they shall be as white as snow; though they be red like crimson, they shall be as wool (Isaiah 1:18).

V. SALVATION THROUGH GRACE

We believe that [1]the salvation of sinners is wholly through grace; [2]that we have no righteousness or [3]goodness of our own [4]wherewith to seek divine favor, and must come, therefore, throwing ourselves upon the [5]unfailing mercy and love of Him who bought us and washed us in His own blood, [6]pleading the merits and the righteousness of Christ the Saviour, standing upon His word and accepting the [7]free gift of His love and pardon.

Scripture References Where Taught

[1]By grace are ye saved (Ephesians 2:8).
[2]. . . There is none righteous, no, not one (Romans 3:10).
[3]All have sinned, and come short of the glory of God (Romans 3:23).
[4]But we are all as an unclean thing, and all our righteousnesses are as filthy rags; and we all do fade as a leaf; and our iniquities, like the wind, have taken us away (Isaiah 64:6).
[5]Verily, verily, I say unto you, He that believeth on me hath everlasting life (John 6:47).
[6]But now in Christ Jesus ye who sometimes were far

off are made nigh by the blood of Christ (Ephesians 2:13).
[7]For the wages of sin is death; but the gift of God is eternal life through Jesus Christ our Lord (Romans 6:23).

VI. REPENTANCE AND ACCEPTANCE

We believe that [1]upon sincere repentance, godly sorrow for sin, and a wholehearted acceptance of the Lord Jesus Christ, they who call upon Him may be [2]justified by faith, through His precious blood and [3]that in place of condemnation they may have [4]the most blessed peace, assurance and favor with God; that with open arms of mercy and pardon the Saviour waits to receive each penitent who will in unfeigned contrition and [5]supplication for mercy, open the door of his heart and accept Him as Lord and King.

Scripture References Where Taught

[1]If we confess our sins, he is faithful and just to forgive us our sins, and to cleanse us from all unrighteousness (I John 1:9).
[2]Therefore being justified by faith, we have peace with God through our Lord Jesus Christ: By whom also we have access by faith into this grace wherein we stand, and rejoice in hope of the glory of God (Romans 5:1-2).
[3]There is therefore now no condemnation to them which are in Christ Jesus, who walk not after the flesh, but after the Spirit (Romans 8:1).
[4]To give knowledge of salvation unto his people by the remission of their sins, Through the tender mercy of our God; whereby the dayspring from on high hath visited us, To give light to them that sit in darkness and in the shadow of death, to guide our feet into the way of peace (Luke 1:77-79).
[5]. . . Him that cometh to me I will in no wise cast out (John 6:37).

VII. THE NEW BIRTH

We believe that the change which takes place in the heart and life at conversion is a very real one; [1]that the sinner is then born again in such a glorious and transforming manner [2]that old things are passed away and all things are become new; insomuch that the things once most desired are now abhorred, [3]Whilst the things once abhorred are now held most sacred and dear; and that now [4]having had imputed to him the righteousness of the Redeemer and having received of the Spirit of Christ, new desires, new aspirations, new interests, and a new perspective of life, time, and eternity, fills the blood-washed heart [5]so that his desire is now to openly confess and serve the Master, seeking ever those things which are above.

Scripture References Where Taught

[1]. . . Except a man be born again, he cannot see the kingdom of God (John 3:3).

[2]Therefore if any man be in Christ, he is a new creature: old things are passed away; behold, all things are become new (II Corinthians 5:17).

[3]If ye were of the world, the world would love his own: but because ye are not of the world, but I have chosen you out of the world, therefore the world hateth you (John 15:19).

Page 14

[4]I am crucified with Christ: nevertheless I live; yet not I, but Christ liveth in me: and the life which I now live in the flesh I live by the faith of the Son of God, who loved me, and gave himself for me (Galatians 2:20). Being justified freely by his grace through the redemption that is in Christ Jesus: Whom God hath set forth to be a propitiation through faith in his blood, to declare his righteousness for the remission of sins that are past, through the forbearance of God (Romans 3:24-25).

[5]Blessed is the man that walketh not in the counsel of the ungodly, nor standeth in the way of sinners, nor

sitteth in the seat of the scornful. But his delight is in the law of the Lord; and in his law doth he meditate day and night (Psalm 1:1-2).

VIII. DAILY CHRISTIAN LIFE

We believe that having been cleansed by the precious blood of Jesus Christ and having received the witness of the Holy Spirit at conversion, [1]it is the will of God that we be sanctified daily and [2]become partakers of His holiness; [3]growing constantly stronger in faith, power, prayer, love and service, first as babies desiring the sincere milk of the Word; [4]then as dear children walking humbly, seeking diligently the hidden life, [5]where self decreases and Christ increases; then as strong men having on the whole armour of God [6]marching forth to new conquests in His name beneath His bloodstained banner, ever living a patient, sober, unselfish, godly life that will be a true reflection of the Christ within.

Scripture References Where Taught

[1]For this is the will of God, even your sanctification (I Thessalonians 4:3). And the very God of peace sanctify you wholly; and I pray God your whole spirit and soul and body be preserved blameless unto the coming of our Lord Jesus Christ (I Thessalonians 5:23).

[2]Having therefore these promises, dearly beloved, let us cleanse ourselves from all filthiness of the flesh and spirit, perfecting holiness in the fear of God (II Corinthians 7:1).

[3]The path of the just is as the shining light, that shineth more and more unto the perfect day (Proverbs 4:18).

[4]Therefore leaving the principles of the doctrine of Christ, let us go on unto perfection (Hebrews 6:1).

[5]For they that are after the flesh do mind the things of the flesh; but they that are after the Spirit the things of the Spirit (Romans 8:5).

[6]An highway shall be there, and a way, and it shall be

called The way of holiness; the unclean shall not pass over it; but it shall be for those: the wayfaring men, though fools, shall not err therein (Isaiah 35:8; also I Peter 2:2).

IX. BAPTISM AND THE LORD'S SUPPER

We believe that water baptism [1]in the name of the Father and of the Son and of the Holy Ghost, according to the command of our Lord, is a blessed outward sign of an inward work; a beautiful and solemn emblem reminding us that even as our Lord died upon the cross of Calvary [2]so we reckon ourselves now dead indeed unto sin, and the old nature nailed to the tree with Him; and that even as He was taken down from the tree and buried, [3]so we are buried with Him by baptism into death: that like as Christ was raised up from the dead by the glory of the Father, even so we should walk in newness of life.

We believe in the [4]commemoration and observing of the Lord's Supper by the sacred use of the broken bread, a precious type of the Bread of Life even Jesus Christ, whose body was broken for us; and by the juice of the vine, a blessed type which should ever remind the participant of the shed blood of the Saviour who is the true Vine of which His children are the branches; that this ordinance is as a glorious rainbow that spans the gulf of the years between Calvary and the coming of the Lord, when in the Father's kingdom, He will partake anew with His children; and that the serving and receiving of this blessed sacrament should be ever preceded by the most solemn heart-searching, [5]self-examination, forgiveness and love toward all men, that none partake unworthily and drink condemnation to his own soul.

Scripture References Where Taught

[1]Go ye therefore, and teach all nations, baptizing them in the name of the Father, and of the Son, and of the

Holy Ghost (Matthew 28:19; also Acts 1:47-48; Galatians 3:27-28).

[2]Therefore we are buried with him by baptism into death: that like as Christ was raised up from the dead by the glory of the Father, even so we also should walk in newness of life (Romans 6:4; also Colossians 2:12; I Peter 3:20-21; Acts 22:16).

[3]Then they that gladly received his word were baptized: and the same day there were added unto them about three thousand souls (Acts 2:41; also Matthew 28:19-20).

[4]For as often as ye eat this bread, and drink this cup, ye do shew the Lord's death till he come (I Corinthians 11:26). But let a man examine himself, and so let him eat of that bread, and drink of that cup (I Corinthians 11:28).

[5]Examine yourselves, whether ye be in the faith; prove your own selves (II Corinthians 13:5).

X. THE BAPTISM OF THE HOLY SPIRIT

We believe that the baptism of [1]the Holy Spirit is the incoming of the promised Comforter in mighty and glorious fullness [2]to endue the believer with power from on high; to glorify and exalt the Lord Jesus; to give inspired utterance in witnessing of Him; to foster the spirit of prayer, holiness, sobriety; to equip the individual and the church for practical, efficient, joyous, Spirit-filled soul winning in the fields of life; and that this being still the dispensation of the Holy Spirit, the believer may have every reason to expect His incoming to be after the same [3]manner as that in which He came upon [4]Jew and Gentile alike in Bible days, and [5]as recorded in the Word, that it may be truly said of us as of the house of Cornelius: the Holy Ghost fell on them as on us at the beginning.

Scripture References Where Taught

[1]I will pray the Father, and he shall give you another Comforter, that he may abide with you for ever; Even

the Spirit of truth; whom the world cannot receive, because it seeth him not, neither knoweth him: but ye know him; for he dwelleth with you, and shall be in you (John 14:16-17).

[2]For John truly baptized with water; but ye shall be baptized with the Holy Ghost. . . . But ye shall receive the power, after that the Holy Ghost is come upon you: and ye shall be witnesses unto me both in Jerusalem, and in all Judaea, and in Samaria, and unto the uttermost part of the earth (Acts 1:5, 8).

[3]And they were all filled with the Holy Ghost, and began to speak with other tongues, as the Spirit gave them utterance (Acts 2:4).

[4]Then laid they their hands on them, and they received the Holy Ghost (Acts 8:17).

[5]While Peter yet spake these words, the Holy Ghost fell on all them which heard the word. And they of the circumcision which believed were astonished, as many as came with Peter, because that on the Gentiles also was poured out the gift of the Holy Ghost. For they heard them speak with tongues, and magnify God (Acts 10:44-46).

[6]And when Paul had laid his hands upon them, the Holy Ghost came on them; and they spake with tongues, and prophesied (Acts 19:6). Know ye not that ye are the temple of God, and that the Spirit of God dwelleth in you? (I Corinthians 3:16).

XI. THE SPIRIT-FILLED LIFE

We believe that while the Holy Spirit is as a mighty rushing wind and as tongues of living flame that can shake and set ablaze whole communities for God, He is also as a gentle dove, [1]easily grieved and wounded by impiety, coldness, idle conversation, boastfulness, a judging or criticizing spirit and [2]by thoughts and actions dishonoring to the Lord Jesus; that it is therefore, the will of God that we [3]live and walk in the Spirit, moment by moment, under the precious blood of the Lamb; [4]treading softly as with unshod feet in the presence of the King; being patient, [5]loving, truthful, sincere, prayerful, unmurmuring, instant in season, out of season, serving the Lord.

Scripture References Where Taught

[1]And grieve not the holy Spirit of God, whereby ye are sealed unto the day of redemption. Let all bitterness, and wrath, and anger, and clamour, and evil speaking, be put away from you, with all malice: And be ye kind one to another, tenderhearted, forgiving one another, even as God for Christ's sake hath forgiven you (Ephesians 4:30-32). Praying always with all prayer and supplication in the Spirit, and watching thereunto with all perseverance and supplication for all saints (Ephesians 6:18).

[2]I beseech you therefore, brethren, by the mercies of God, that ye present your bodies a living sacrifice, holy, acceptable unto God, which is your reasonable service. And be not conformed to this world: but be ye transformed by the renewing of your mind, that ye may prove what is that good, and acceptable, and perfect, will of God (Romans 12:1-2).

[3]He that saith he abideth in him ought himself also so to walk, even as he walked (I John 2:6).

[4]Walk in the Spirit, and ye shall not fulfil the lust of the flesh. . . . If we live in the Spirit, let us also walk in the Spirit (Galatians 5:16, 25).

[5]If any man defile the temple of God, him shall God destroy; for the temple of God is holy, which temple ye are (I Corinthians 3:17).

XII. THE GIFTS AND FRUITS OF THE SPIRIT

We believe that the Holy Spirit has the following [1]gifts to bestow upon the believing church of the Lord Jesus Christ: [2]wisdom, knowledge, faith, healing, miracles, prophecy, discernment, tongues, interpretation; that, according to the degree of grace and faith possessed by the recipient, these gifts are divided to every man severally, as He, the Holy Spirit, will; that they are to be most earnestly desired and coveted, [3]in the order and proportion wherein they prove most edifying and beneficial to the church; and [4]that the fruit of the Spirit: love, joy, peace, long-suffering, gentleness, goodness, faith, meekness, temperance, should be put forth, [5]cultivated, and diligently guarded as the resultant adornment, the constant, eloquent, and irrefutable evidence of a Spirit-filled life.

Scripture References Where Taught

[1]Now concerning spiritual gifts, brethren, I would not have you ignorant. . . . But covet earnestly the best gifts (I Corinthians 12:1, 31). But all these worketh that one and the selfsame Spirit, dividing to every man severally as he will (I Corinthians 12:11).

[2]Even so ye, forasmuch as ye are zealous of spiritual gifts, seek that ye may excel to the edifying of the church (I Corinthians 14:12). For the gifts and calling of God are without repentance (Romans 11:29).

[3]Having then gifts differing according to the grace that is given to us, whether prophecy, let us prophesy according to the proportion of faith; Or ministry, let us wait on our ministering: or he that teacheth, on teaching; Or he that exhorteth, on exhortation: he that giveth, let him do it with simplicity; he that ruleth, with diligence; he that sheweth mercy, with cheerfulness (Romans 12:6-8).

[4]Herein is my Father glorified, that ye bear much fruit; so shall ye be my disciples (John 15:8).

[5]And now also the axe is laid unto the root of the trees: every tree therefore which bringeth not forth good fruit is hewn down, and cast into the fire (Luke 3:9).

XIII. MODERATION

We believe that [1]the moderation of the believer should be known of all men; that his experience and daily walk should never lead him [2]into extremes, fanaticisms, [3]unseemly manifestations, backbitings, murmurings; but that his sober, thoughtful, balanced, [4]mellow, forgiving, and zealous Christian experience should be one of steadfast uprightness, equilibrium, humility, self-sacrifice and Christ-likeness.

Scripture References Where Taught

[1]Let your moderation be known unto all men. The Lord is at hand (Philippians 4:5).
[2]That we henceforth be no more children, tossed to and fro, and carried about with every wind of doctrine. . . . But speaking the truth in love, may grow up into him in all things, which is the head, even Christ (Ephesians 4:14-15).
[3][Charity. . .h doth not behave itself unseemly (I Corinthians 13:5).
[4]Put on therefore, as the elect of God, holy and beloved, bowels of mercies, kindness, humbleness of mind, meekness, longsuffering; Forbearing one another, and forgiving one another, if any man have a quarrel against any: even as Christ forgave you, so also do ye (Colossians 3:12-13).

XIV. DIVINE HEALING

We believe that divine healing is the power of the Lord Jesus Christ [1]to heal the sick and the afflicted in answer to believing prayer; that He who is the same [2]yesterday, today and forever has never changed but is [3]still an all-sufficient help in the time of trouble, able to meet the needs of, and quicken into newness of life the body, as well as the soul and spirit in answer to the [4]faith of them who ever [5]pray with submission to His divine and sovereign will.

Scripture References Where Taught

[1]Himself took our infirmities, and bare our sicknesses (Matthew 8:17).
[2]For whether is easier, to say, Thy sins be forgiven thee; or to say, Arise, and walk? (Matthew 9:5).
[3]And these signs shall follow them that believe; In my name shall they cast out devils; they shall speak with new tongues; They shall take up serpents; and if they drink any deadly thing, it shall not hurt them; they shall lay hands on the sick, and they shall recover (Mark 16:17-18).
[4]And now, Lord, behold their threatenings: and grant unto thy servants, that with all boldness they may speak thy word, By stretching forth thine hand to heal; and that signs and wonders may be done by the name of thy holy child Jesus (Acts 4:29-30).
[5]Is any sick among you: let him call for the elders of the church; and let them pray over him anointing him with oil in the name of the Lord: And the prayer of faith shall save the sick, and the Lord shall raise him up; and if he have committed sins, they shall be forgiven him. Confess your faults one to another, and pray one for another, that ye may be healed (James 5:14-16).

XV. THE SECOND COMING OF CHRIST

We believe that the second coming of Christ is personal and imminent; that He will descend from Heaven [1]in the clouds of glory with the voice of the archangel and with the trump of God; and that at this hour, which no man knoweth beforehand, the dead in Christ shall rise, then the [2]redeemed that are alive and remain shall be caught up together with them in the clouds, to meet the Lord in the air, and that so shall they ever be with the Lord; that also seeing that a thousand years is as a day with the Lord, and [3]that no man knoweth the hour of His appearance, which we believe to be near at hand, each day should be lived as though He were [4]expected to appear at even, yet that in obedience to His explicit command, "Occupy till I come," [5]the work of spreading the gospel, the sending forth of missionaries, and the general duties for the upbuilding of the church [6]should be carried on as diligently, and thoroughly, as though neither ours nor the next generation should live in the flesh to see that glorious day.

Scripture Reference Where Taught

[1]For the Lord himself shall descend from heaven with a shout, with the voice of the archangel, and with the trump of God: and the dead in Christ shall rise first: Then we which are alive and remain shall be caught up together with them in the clouds, to meet the Lord in the air: and so shall we ever be with the Lord (I Thessalonians 4:16-17).

[2]. . . Denying ungodliness and worldly lusts, we should live soberly, righteously, and godly, in this present world; Looking for that blessed hope, and the glorious appearing of the great God and our Saviour Jesus Christ (Titus 2:12-13).

[3]But of that day and hour knoweth no man, no, not the angels of heaven, but my Father only. . . . Watch therefore: for ye know not what hour your Lord doth come. Therefore be ye also ready: for in such an hour as ye think not the Son of man cometh (Matthew 24:36, 42, 44).

[4]So Christ was once offered to bear the sins of many; and unto them that look for him shall he appear the second time without sin unto salvation (Hebrews 9:28).

[5]. . . Occupy till I come (Luke 19:13).

[6]Let your loins be girded about, and your lights burning; And ye yourselves like unto men that wait for their lord . . . that when he cometh and knocketh, they may open unto him immediately. Blessed are those servants, whom

the lord when he cometh shall find watching: verily I say unto you, that he shall gird himself, and make them to sit down to meat, and will come forth and serve them (Luke 12:35-37).

XVI. CHURCH RELATIONSHIP

We believe that having accepted the Lord Jesus Christ as personal Saviour and King, and having thus been born into the family and invisible body or church of the Lord, it is the sacred duty of the believer, whenever this lieth within his power, [1]to identify himself with, and [2]labor most earnestly for the upbuilding of God's kingdom with the [3]visible church of Christ upon earth; and that such visible church is a congregation of believers, who have associated themselves together in Christian fellowship and in the [4]unity of the Spirit, observing the ordinances of Christ, worshipping Him in the beauty of holiness, [5]speaking to each other in psalms, and hymns and spiritual songs, reading and proclaiming His Word, laboring for the salvation of souls, giving of their temporal means to carry on His work, edifying, encouraging, establishing one another in the most holy faith, and working harmoniously together as dear children who are many members but one body of which Christ is the head.

Scripture Reference Where Taught

[1]I will praise the Lord with my whole heart, in the assembly of the upright, and in the congregation (Psalm 111:1).

[2]Let us consider one another to provoke unto love and to good works: Not forsaking the assembling of ourselves together, as the manner of some is; but exhorting one another: and so much the more, as ye see the day approaching (Hebrews 10:24-25).

[3]. . . And the Lord added to the church daily such as should be saved (Acts 2:47). And so were the churches

established in the faith, and increased in number daily (Acts 16:5).

[4]So we, being many, are one body in Christ, and every one members one of another (Romans 12:5; also see Romans 12:6-8).

[5]Then they that feared the Lord spake often one to another: and the Lord hearkened, and heard it, and a book of remembrance was written before him for them that feared the Lord, and that thought upon his name. And they shall be mine, saith the Lord of hosts, in that day when I make up my jewels; and I will spare them, as a man spareth his own son that serveth him (Malachi 3:16-17).

XVII. CIVIL GOVERNMENT

We believe that civil government is of [1]divine appointment, for the interests and good order of human society; and that governors and rulers should be prayed for, obeyed, and upheld at all times except only in [2]things opposed to the will of our Lord Jesus Christ, who is the [3]ruler of the conscience of His people, [4]the King of Kings, and the Lord of Lords.

Scripture References Where Taught

[1]. . . The powers that be are ordained of God. For rulers are not a terror to good works, but to the evil (Romans 13:1, 3; also Deuteronomy 16:18; II Samuel 23:3; Exodus 18:21-23; Jeremiah 30:21).

[2]. . . We ought to obey God rather than men (Acts 5:29). And fear not them which kill the body, but are not able to kill the soul (Matthew 10:28; also Daniel 3:15-18, 6:7-10; Acts 4:18-20).

[3]. . . One is your Master, even Christ (Matthew 23:10).

[4]And he hath on his vesture and on his thigh a name written, KING OF KINGS, AND LORD OF LORDS (Revelation 19:16; also Psalm 72:11; Romans 14:9-13).

XVIII. THE FINAL JUDGMENT

We believe that the dead both small and great shall be raised up and stand with the living before the [1]judgment seat of God; and that when a solemn and awful separation shall take place wherein the [2]wicked shall be adjudged to everlasting punishment and the righteous to life eternal; and that this judgment will fix forever the final state of men in heaven or in hell on principles of righteousness as set forth in His holy Word.

Scripture References Where Taught

[1]For we must all appear before the judgment seat of Christ; that every one may receive the things done in his body, according to that he hath done, whether it be good or bad (II Corinthians 5:10).
[2]The Son of man shall send forth his angels, and they shall gather out of his kingdom all things that offend, and them which do iniquity; And shall cast them into a furnace of fire: there shall be wailing and gnashing of teeth. Then shall the righteous shine forth as the sun in the kingdom of their Father. Who hath ears to hear, let him hear (Matthew 13:41-43).

XIX. HEAVEN

We believe that Heaven is the [1]indescribably glorious habitation of the living God; and that thither the Lord has [2]gone to prepare a place for His children; that unto this foursquare city, whose builder and maker is God, the earnest believers who have washed their robes in the blood of the Lamb and have overcome by the word of their testimony will be carried; that the Lord Jesus Christ will present them to the Father without spot or wrinkle; and that there in unutterable joy they will ever behold His wonderful face, in an everlasting kingdom whereunto comes no [3]darkness nor light, neither sorrow, [4]tears, pain, nor [5]death, and wherein hosts of attending angels sweep their harps, sing the praises of our King, and bowing down before the throne, cry: "Holy, holy, holy."

Scripture References Where Taught

[1]. . . Eye hath not seen, nor ear heard, neither have entered into the heart of man, the things which God hath prepared for them that love him (I Corinthians 2:9).
[2]In my Father's house are many mansions: if it were not so, I would have told you. I go to prepare a place for you (John 14:2).
[3]And there shall be no night there; and they need no candle, neither light of the sun; for the Lord God giveth them light: and they shall reign for ever and ever (Revelation 22:5).
[4]And God shall wipe away all tears from their eyes; and there shall be no more death, neither sorrow, nor crying, neither shall there be any more pain: for the former things are passed away (Revelation 21:4).
[5]Therefore are they before the throne of God, and serve him day and night in his temple: and he that sitteth on the throne shall dwell among them. They shall hunger no more, neither thirst any more; neither shall the sun light on them, nor any heat. For the Lamb which is in the midst of the throne shall feed them, and shall lead them unto living fountains of waters (Revelation 7:15-17).

XX. HELL

We believe that hell is a place of outer darkness and deepest sorrow, where the worm dieth not and the fire is not quenched; a place prepared for the devil and his angels where there shall be weeping and [1]wailing and gnashing of teeth, a place of grief and eternal regret on the part of them who have rejected the mercy, love and tenderness of the crucified Saviour, choosing death rather than life; and that there into a [2]lake that burns with fire and brimstone shall be cast the [3]unbelieving, the abominable, the murderers, sorcerers, idolaters, all liars, and they who [4]have rejected and spurned the love and sacrifice of a bleeding Redeemer—passing the cross to their doom, [5]in spite of every entreaty and warning of the Holy Spirit.

Scripture References Where Taught

[1]The Son of man shall send forth his angels, and they shall gather out of his kingdom all things that offend, and them which do iniquity; And shall cast them into a furnace of fire: there shall be wailing and gnashing of teeth (Matthew 13:41-42).

[2]And the devil that deceived them was cast into the lake of fire and brimstone, where the beast and the false prophet are, and shall be tormented day and night for ever and ever. And whosoever was not found written in the book of life was cast into the lake of fire (Revelation 20:10, 15).

[3]The same shall drink of the wine of the wrath of God, which is poured out without mixture into the cup of his indignation; and he shall be tormented with fire and brimstone in the presence of the holy angels, and in the presence of the Lamb: And the smoke of their torment ascendeth up for ever and ever (Revelation 14:10-11).

[4]Then he shall say unto them . . . Depart from me, ye cursed, into everlasting fire, prepared for the devil and his angels (Matthew 25:41). And if thy hand offend thee, cut it off: it is better for thee to enter into life maimed, than having two hands to go into hell, into the fire that never shall be quenched: Where their worm dieth not, and the fire is not quenched (Mark 9:43-44).

[5]. . . As I live, saith the Lord God, I have no pleasure in the death of the wicked; but that the wicked turn from his way and live: turn ye, turn ye from your evil ways; for why will ye die, O house of Israel? (Ezekiel 33:11).

XXI. EVANGELISM

We believe that seeing then that all these things shall be dissolved, and that the end of all things is at hand, the redeemed children of the Lord Jehovah [1]should rise and shine forth as a light that cannot be hid, a city set upon a hill, [2]speeding forth the gospel to the ends of the earth, girding the globe with the message of salvation, declaring with burning zeal and earnestness the whole council of God; that when the Lord of Glory shall appear, they shall be found standing, with their loins girded about with truth, their activities and ministry laden down with the wealth of jewels they have won and guarded for Him, the precious [3]souls, whom, by their faithful testimony they have been instrumental in leading from [4]darkness into light; that soul winning is [5]the one big business of the church upon earth; and that therefore every weight and hindrance which would tend to quench the flame or hamper the efficiency of [6]worldwide evangelism should be cut off and cast away as unworthy of the church, [7]detrimental to the most sacred cause of Christ and contrary to [8]the great commission by our Lord.

Scripture References Where Taught

[1]I charge thee therefore before God, and the Lord Jesus Christ, who shall judge the quick and the dead at his appearing and his kingdom; Preach the word; be instant in season, out of season; reprove, rebuke, exhort with all longsuffering and doctrine (II Timothy 4:1-2).

[2]Redeeming the time, because the days are evil (Ephesians 5:16).

[3]. . . He that winneth souls is wise (Proverbs 11:30).

[4]Let him know, that he which converteth the sinner from the error of his way shall save a soul from death, and shall hide a multitude of sins (James 5:20).

[5]Son of man, I have made thee a watchman unto the house of Israel: therefore hear the word at my mouth,

and give them warning from me. When I say unto the wicked, Thou shalt surely die; and thou givest him not warning, nor speakest to warn the wicked from his wicked way, to save his life; the same wicked man shall die in his iniquity; but his blood will I require at thine hand (Ezekiel 3:17-18).

[6]. . . Lift up your eyes, and look on the fields; for they are white already to harvest. And he that reapeth receiveth wages, and gathereth fruit unto life eternal: that both he that soweth and he that reapeth may rejoice together. And herein is that saying true, One soweth, and another reapeth (John 4:35-57).

[7]Pray ye therefore the Lord of the harvest, that he will send forth labourers into his harvest (Matthew 9:38).

[8]. . . Go ye into all the world, and preach the gospel to every creature (Mark 16:15).

XXII. TITHING AND OFFERING

We believe that the method ordained of God to sustain His ministry and the spread of the gospel after His command is "Tithing" and is generally accepted throughout all Foursquare Churches, not only as God's method to take care of the material and financial needs of His church, but to raise the spiritual morale of His people to the extent that God must bless them. We are commanded in Malachi 3:10 to "Bring ye all the tithes into the storehouse, that there may be meat in mine house, and prove me now herewith, saith the Lord of hosts, if I will not open you the windows of heaven, and pour you out a blessing, that there shall not be room enough to receive it."

In the matter of "giving" and "free-will offerings," they are ordered of the Lord and practiced in all Foursquare Churches as part of God's plan for the church's material needs and the spirituality of His people. We are admonished in Luke 6:38, "Give, and it shall be given unto you; good measure, pressed down, and shaken together, and running over, shall men give into your bosom. For with the same measure that ye mete withal it shall be measured to you again."

Being "joint heirs" with Him we know that giving unto His kingdom which is also ours is an enjoyable thing, it being more blessed to give than to receive, for we are commanded in II Corinthians 9:7, "Every man according as he purposeth in his heart, so let him give; not grudgingly, or of a necessity: for God loveth a cheerful giver."

* * * *

Members

Applicants for membership shall be first examined as to their faith, prayed with and encouraged by the Pastor or person or persons designated by said Pastor. Such applicant must show evidence of having genuine born-again experience, and living a Christ-like life, a deep love for the winning of souls and the furthering of the cause of Foursquare Gospel evangelism throughout the earth, and must declare his loyalty to, and willingness to assist in the support of this association, both with his substance, as well as his undivided effort. Each such applicant shall express his recognition of the fact that "a house divided against itself cannot stand," and his adherence to the policy of this association, that there shall be no disloyalty, insubordination, whispering, criticizing, or backbiting of this association, or its leaders, and that if at any time any member feels that he is no longer loyal or in unqualified sympathy or one-accord with this association, he shall ask for a letter of dismissal, and quietly withdraw from membership, and that if he should fail so to do, the authorities of the association reserve the right to tender such member such letter of dismissal; that the love of souls and the passion for soul winning must be the great undergirder and supreme end toward which all efforts lead, and that sidelines, nonessential issues and hairsplitting of doctrines which tend to break the unity and detract from the great white-heated flame of soul winning must be checked wherever found, and that Christ must be made the central Figure and be lifted up till all men will see, love and be drawn near unto Him.